POSTCARD HISTORY SERIES

Around Blue Hill and Ellsworth

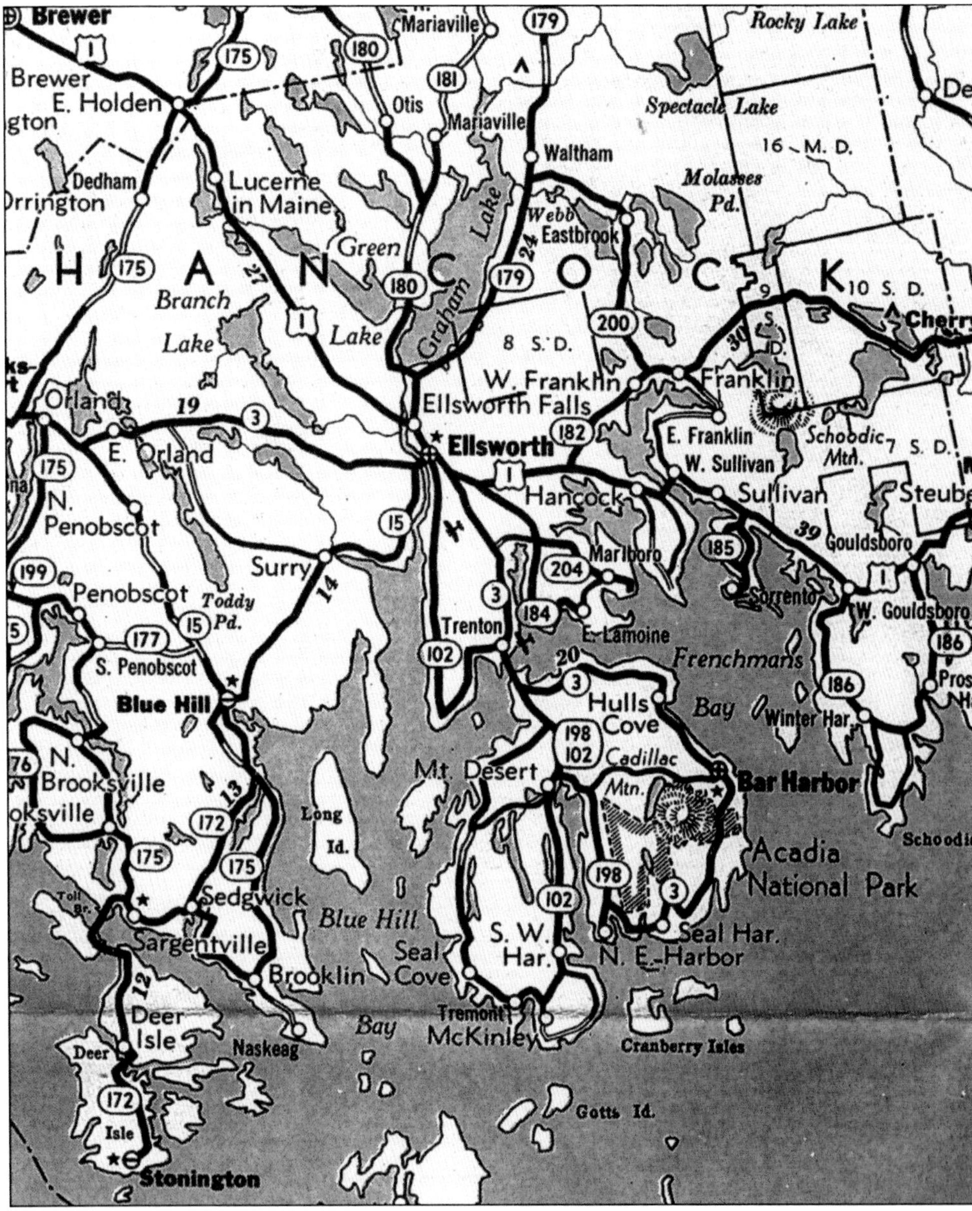

With the city of Ellsworth as its shire town, Hancock County is dotted with dozens of scenic and historic towns spread out in all directions. This 1939 highway map shows the region nicknamed the "gateway to Down East Maine" because it is the junction points of Routes 1, 1A, 3, and other highways. The county has lakes, ponds, rivers, streams, and an Atlantic coastline that intrigues artists and photographers. (Richard R. Shaw.)

On the front cover: A 1908 view of the Blue Hill Fair reveals the delicious blend of agriculture and entertainment that still attracts visitors every Labor Day weekend. (Blue Hill Public Library.)

On the back cover: Ellsworth's First Congregational Church and city hall, pictured in a *c.* 1940 postcard, were built a century apart but complement each other very well. (Richard R. Shaw.)

POSTCARD HISTORY SERIES

Around Blue Hill and Ellsworth

Richard R. Shaw

ARCADIA PUBLISHING

ISBN 978-0-7385-5718-2

Published by Arcadia Publishing
Charleston SC, Chicago IL, Portsmouth NH, San Francisco CA

Printed in the United States of America

Library of Congress Catalog Card Number: 2007941108

For all general information contact Arcadia Publishing at:
Telephone 843-853-2070
Fax 843-853-0044
E-mail sales@arcadiapublishing.com
For customer service and orders:
Toll-Free 1-888-313-2665

Visit us on the Internet at www.arcadiapublishing.com

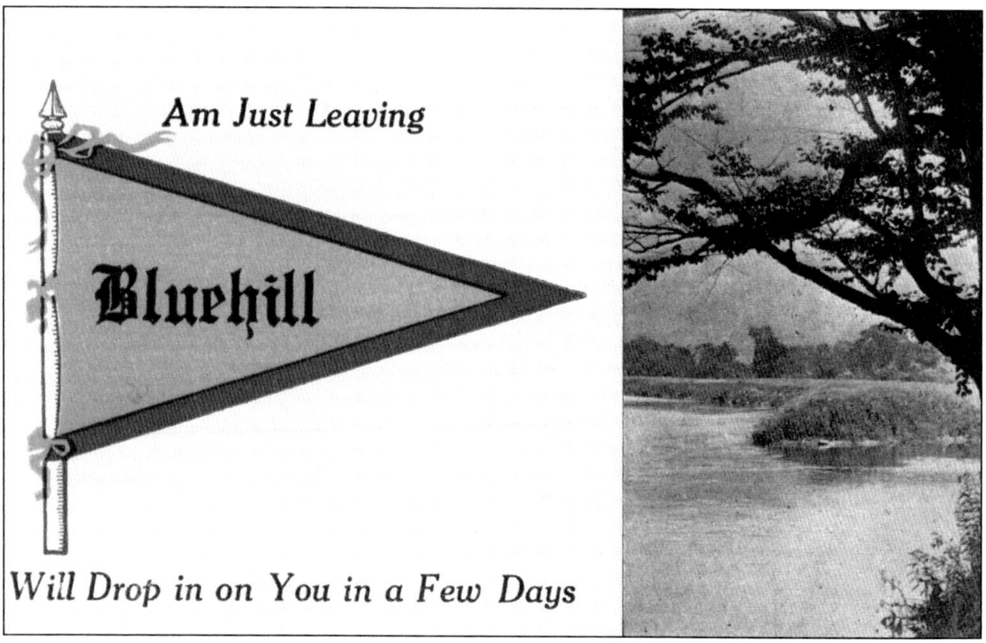

Pennant postcards were inexpensive souvenirs that began appearing throughout Maine in the early 20th century. This one sold for a penny in shops around Blue Hill. It was produced before someone thought the town's name looked better broken into two words. Village scenes have been captured in postcard views for more than 100 years. Some noteworthy examples are featured in this book. (Richard R. Shaw.)

Contents

Acknowledgments

"Do you have any old postcards in your collection?" I have lost count of how many times I asked that question in the past year. Starting in January 2007, I began sifting over vintage postcards that showed the city of Ellsworth, the town of Blue Hill, and nearly a dozen other coastal communities in Maine's Hancock County. At the end of my quest to libraries and other institutions, I had tracked down close to a thousand postcards, showing everything from lobster fishermen to springtime floods. So with great humility, I wish to thank the following for helping with my project. I could not have done it without your encouragement and, most importantly, your trust.

Earle G. Shettleworth Jr., executive director of the Maine Historic Preservation Commission, allowed me full use of his postcard collection. His staff even scanned (and rescanned) scores of postcards.

Rich Boulet, Charley Martin-Berry, and Brook Minner, of the Blue Hill Public Library, loaned many fine old postcards from the library's collection. The images of Parker Point cottages, town churches, and steamboats greatly improved the quality of this book.

Barbara McDade, Sue Wennrich, Bill Cook, and Elizabeth Stevens, of the Bangor Public Library, turned over the impressive James B. Vickery postcard collection. I like to think that my late friend and colleague Jim Vickery would be proud of their cooperation and of this finished book.

Author Sanford Phippen shared memories of Hancock Point, Sturgis Haskins discussed Sorrento, and Virgil Bisset talked affectionately about Blue Hill, the town where he grew up. And a word of thanks to Carl C. Osgood, of Surry, who helped with my 1995 Arcadia book on this region; to Ellsworth's Herbert T. Silsby II; and, in memoriam, the late Ellsworth historians Hale Joy and Deale B. Salisbury.

A key to credit images is as follows: Bangor Public Library, BPL; Blue Hill Public Library, BHPL; Maine Historic Preservation Commission, MHPC; and the author's private collection, RRS.

INTRODUCTION

I like to think this book represents a labor of love. Although I have always lived in neighboring Penobscot County, I have great affection for my neighbors in Hancock County. Ever since I was young, my family and I took Sunday drives down "to the coast" to feast at the Lobster House in Trenton or the Brookside Restaurant in Ellsworth. There was more than salt in the air. There was a down-home feel that stays with me to this day.

I also love postcard collecting. For more than 30 years, I have been snatching up unusual cards at flea markets and antique shops. A little more and a little more has built a modest collection over the years. And now, voila! Some of those images have found a home in this book. The views on page 75 showing Ellsworth's Main Street before and after the great fire of 1933 are mine. So are the ones of the old Surry Playhouse (page 49), and a steamboat tied up at Surry's Contention Cove (page 22).

When Arcadia Publishing invited me to compile a book in its Postcard History Series, I jumped at the chance to combine my affection for Down East people and places with my affinity for old picture postcards. Over the past year, I have designed the book, traveled to nearly a dozen towns and one city, Ellsworth, and met some knowledgeable people along the way.

As with my 1995 Images of America book on this region, *Around Ellsworth and Blue Hill*, I decided again to break the chapters into topics. Schools, churches, natural disasters, village landmarks, seaside scenes, and people all make worthy postcard subjects. It seems every town had a postcard photographer. Blue Hill was especially blessed by several, including one named S. G. Hinckley.

So I had my work cut out for me. I could put my name on a volume containing more than 200 fine old images taken by others. I imagine myself as the guardian of someone else's photography. Unfortunately many postcard photographers' names have been lost to time; otherwise I would mention them all. The best I can do is try and date the cards and do them justice by pointing out a puppy in a yard, a child at a school, or some curious detail in the architecture of a country church.

What a learning experience this has been. Thanks to a wealth of historical material now available on the Internet, as well as wonderful libraries in Bangor, Ellsworth, Blue Hill, Brooklin, Hancock Point, among others, I could imagine the way the Blue Hill–Ellsworth region evolved since first being settled in the 1760s. Many communities, like Marlboro, Brooklin, and Sedgwick, once were part of larger towns. Isn't it just like Maine people to have their own town centers and eventually to declare their independence?

These pictures tell a story of hard-working farmers, fishermen, and the people "from away"—the summer "rusticators" and others—who, while resented at first, transformed Down East into the region that we know today. Many of their cottages at Parker Point in Blue Hill and Hancock Point are shown in this book.

There are trains, boats, and early automobiles in this book. Transportation has always been vital to Hancock County to get visitors from there to here. It helps build the economy, and adds character as well.

If you get a bittersweet taste in your mouth while perusing this book, you are not alone. Many of the faces and landmarks here are not with us anymore. But thanks to old postcards, we can revisit many of them. Hello again to Ellsworth's Hancock House (page 29), and the "Singing Bridge" that once spanned the Taunton River in Hancock-Sullivan (page 17).

But some things never change. The vintage views of the popular Blue Hill Fair, reproduced on the front cover and on pages 43 and 45, could have been taken last Labor Day. The same goes for the students pictured on page 40. Standing in front of an old Brooklin school, they look as serious as today's pupils on photograph day. The only difference is they are wearing high leather shoes, not Reeboks, and the girls' dresses extend all the way to the ground.

So my wish today is that you enjoy this book, both the pictures and the words. I hope it entices you to visit the Blue Hill–Ellsworth region, and maybe to take up postcard collecting. But do me a favor? Leave a few postcards for me. I may want to compile another book someday.

—Richard R. Shaw
Bangor, Maine
February 2008

One

Water, Water, Everywhere

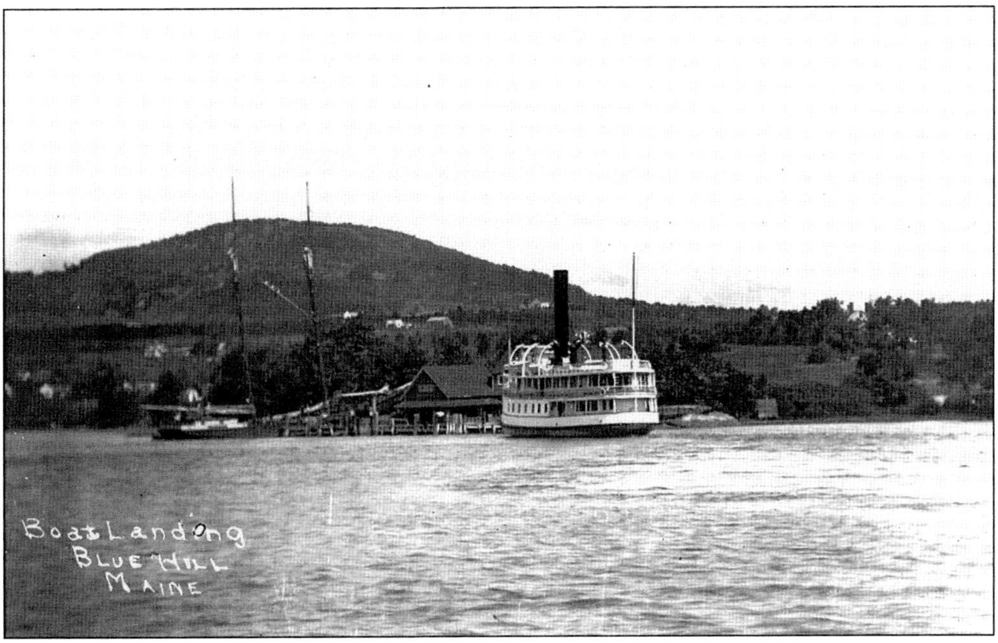

"Where the mountains meet the sea" is the motto of the coastal community of Camden. Blue Hill's slogan may be "Where the mountain meets the sea," as shown in this *c.* 1910 view of a steamer docked at the Parker Point Wharf. Passengers on the Blue Hill Line were ferried across Penobscot Bay from Rockland. Boats made regular stops at Dark Harbor, Eggemoggin, South Brooksville, Brooklin, South Blue Hill, Surry, and Ellsworth. (BHPL.)

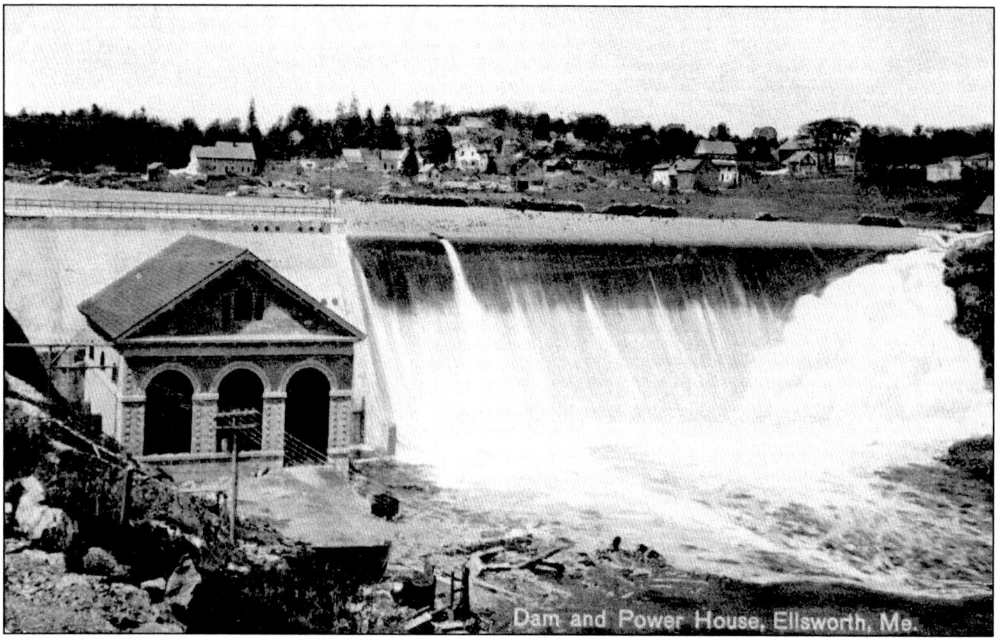

The Ellsworth Dam and Power House supply power for the Ellsworth area and all of Mount Desert Island. They were built in a remarkable 11 months by the Bar Harbor and Union River Power Company, which began producing power on January 1, 1908. The river falls 60 feet over the dam, which today is operated by Bangor Hydro-Electric Company. Leonard Lake, named for chief engineer James L. Leonard, was formed by the dam's construction. (RRS.)

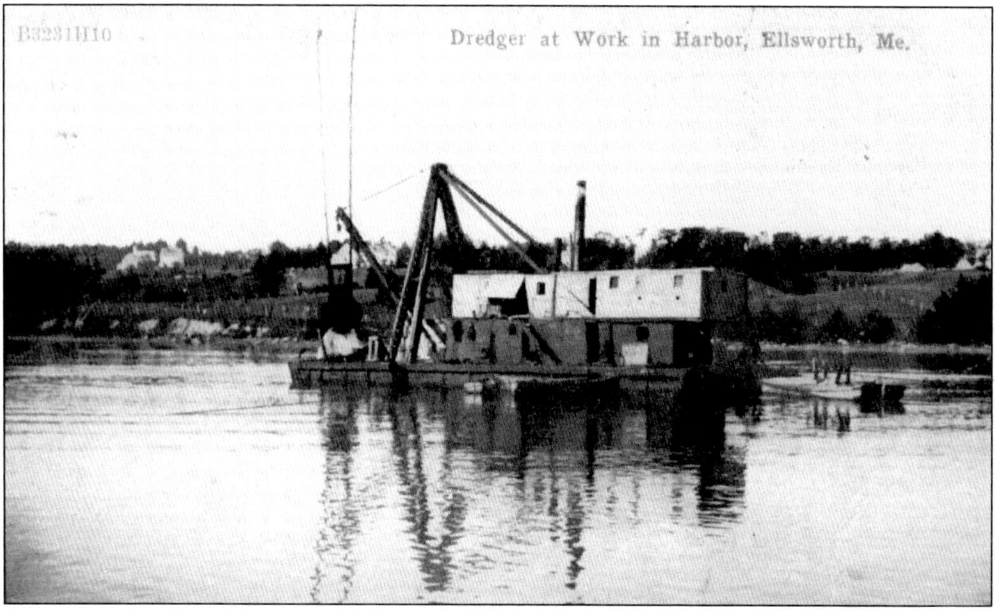

Dredging equipment has been brought in over the last century and before to deepen the Union River. This unusual view, dating to 1911, shows a strange array of mechanical equipment loaded onto a long barge. It was taken just below the village of Ellsworth. Deepening the harbor allowed commercial vessels coming in from the ocean to get closer to the town center. River dredging continued as late as 2007. (RRS.)

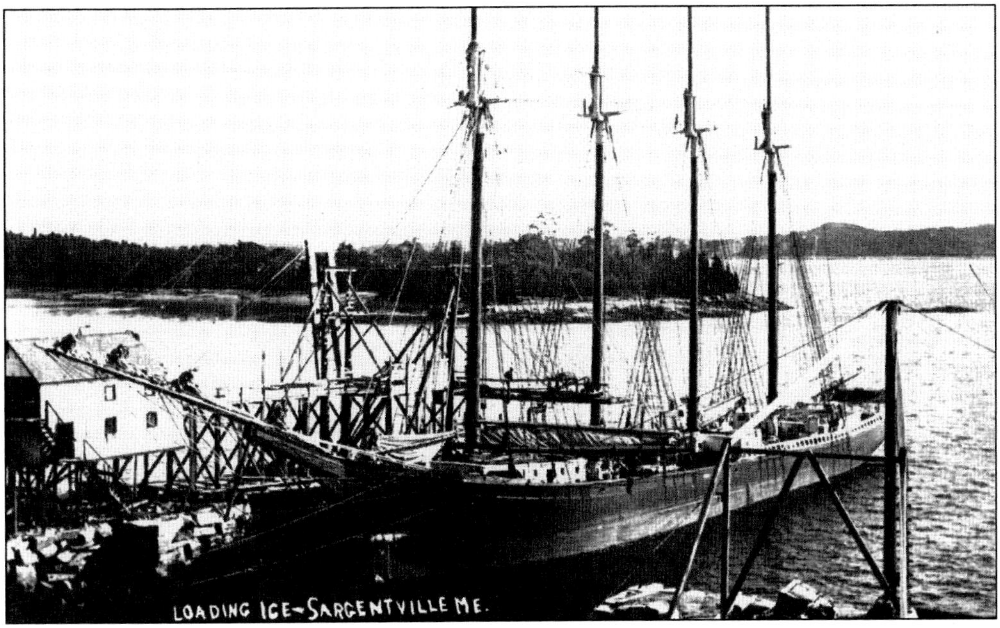

Coastal schooners were the workhorses of the Maine coast in the 19th and early 20th centuries. This four-masted "coaster" is shown loading ice in Sargentville, located south of Blue Hill, around 1915. Before the days of refrigeration, pure Maine ice was in great demand throughout North and South America. The ice was packed in sawdust, which made it last for months. (MHPC.)

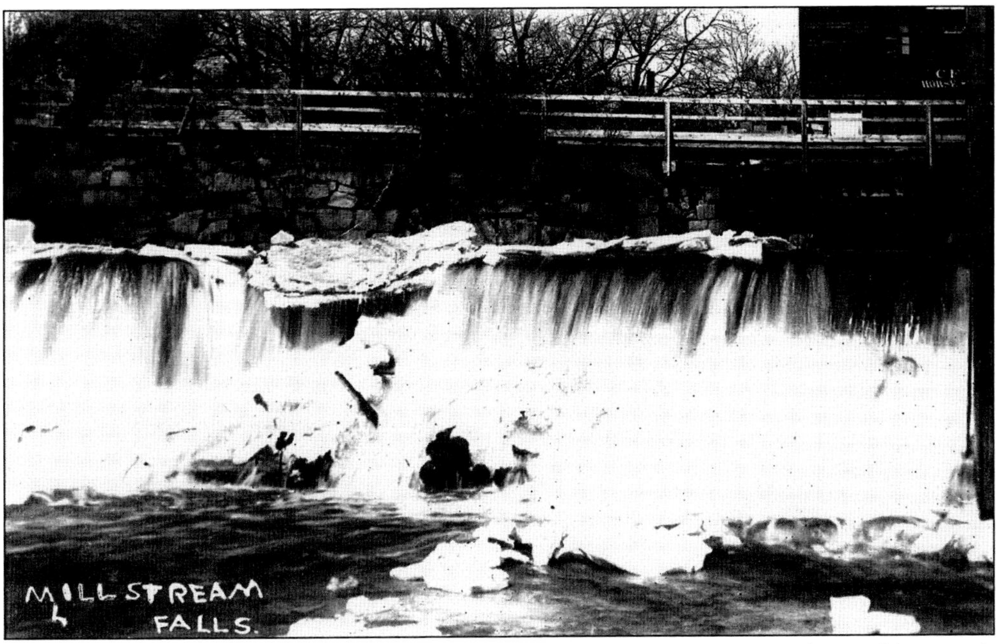

Mill Stream Falls in Blue Hill was a favorite subject for postcard photographers. This scene is postmarked May 13, 1912, and shows what appears to be a springtime view of the falls with chunks of ice below. A long wooden bridge in the background helps to frame the photograph. One assumes the photographer found dry ground from which to capture such a dramatic scene. (BHPL.)

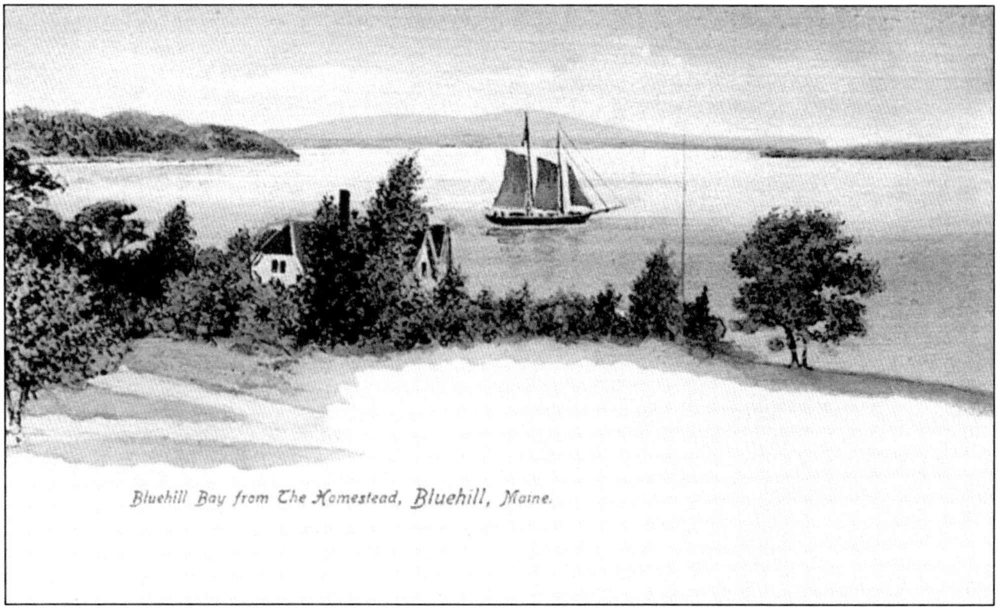

A solitary sailboat is silhouetted against Blue Hill Bay. Distant mountains form a picturesque backdrop in this early scene, taken from a rambling Parker Point house called the Homestead. Author and educator Esther E. Wood wrote, "Blue Hill–built craft took lumber, masts and shingles to Atlantic coastal cities. Other cargo included farm products, fish, clams, porgy oil, and kiln wood." (BPL.)

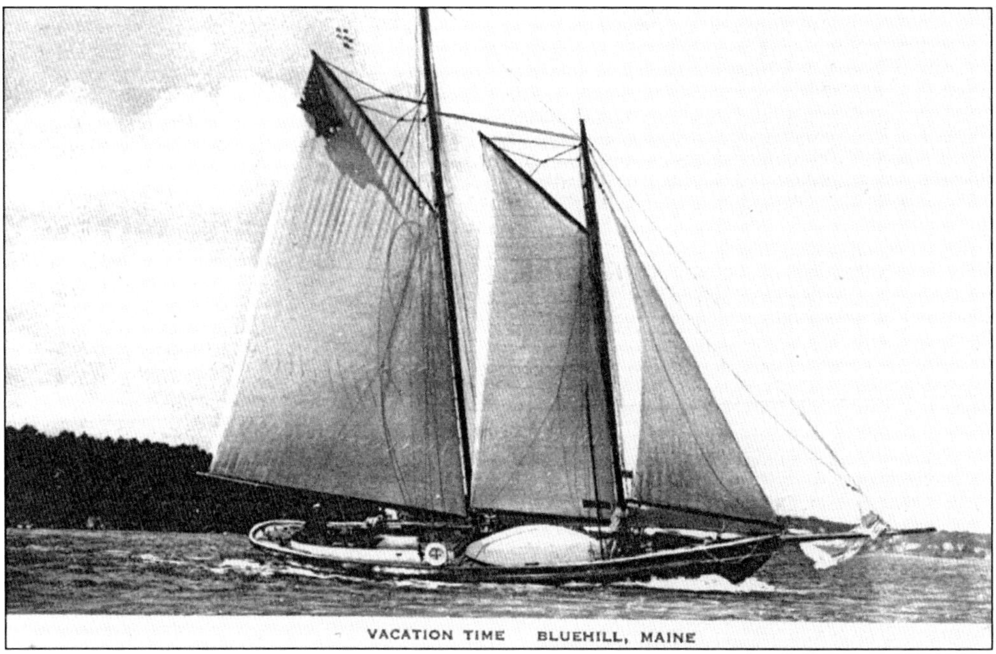

Summertime sees an array of pleasure craft in Blue Hill Bay. The boats come in all designs, and the sails in every color. These craft are of special interest to the 600 students who study boat building at the WoodenBoat School in Brooklin. In 2008, the school entered its 28th season offering courses designed around the arts of boat building, seamanship, and related crafts. (BHPL.)

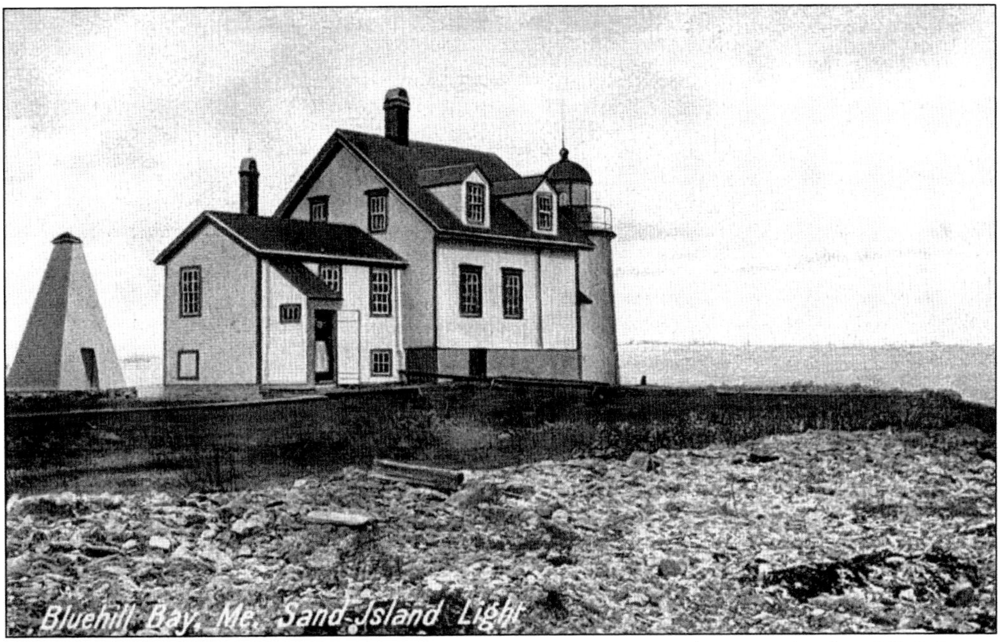

Blue Hill Bay Light stands like a sentinel at the bay's entrance. The tiny island and lighthouse are privately owned and not open to the public. Established by the Blue Hill Light Station on Green (or Sand) Island in 1857, families stopped manning the lighthouse in 1935, and it has been automated ever since. Six light keepers tended the fourth-order Fresnel lighthouse between 1877 and the 1920s. (BPL.)

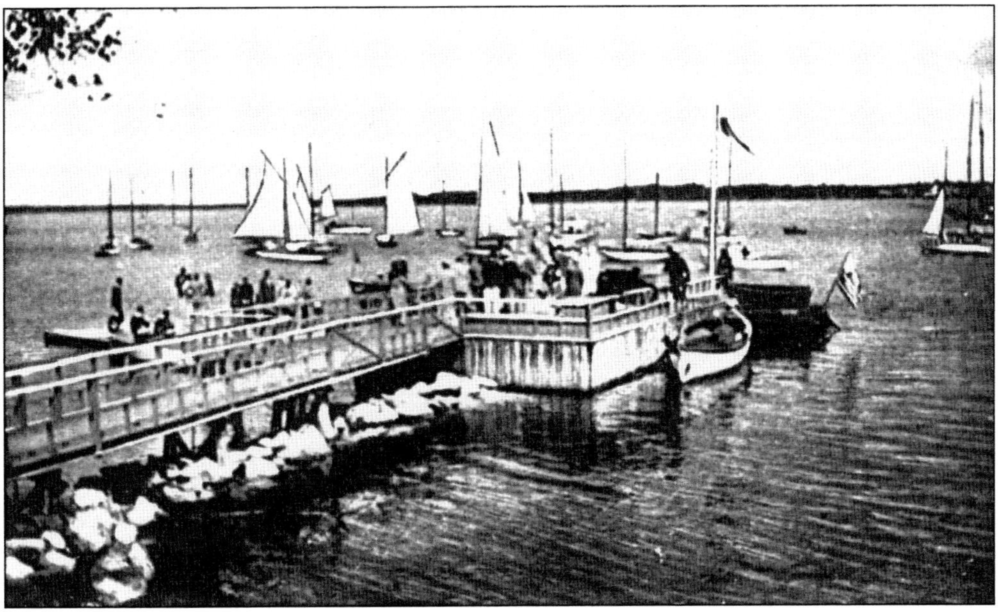
The Kollegewidgwok Yacht Club, shown here in East Blue Hill around 1938, was founded in 1924 by Seth Milliken for his children and their friends. The club still puts "teaching children to sail" high on its agenda. In 2003, the Junior Program was spun off into its own nonprofit, the Kollegewidgwok Sailing and Education Association (KSEA), with a mandate to teach sailing to as many children of the Blue Hill Peninsula as possible (see page 48). (RRS.)

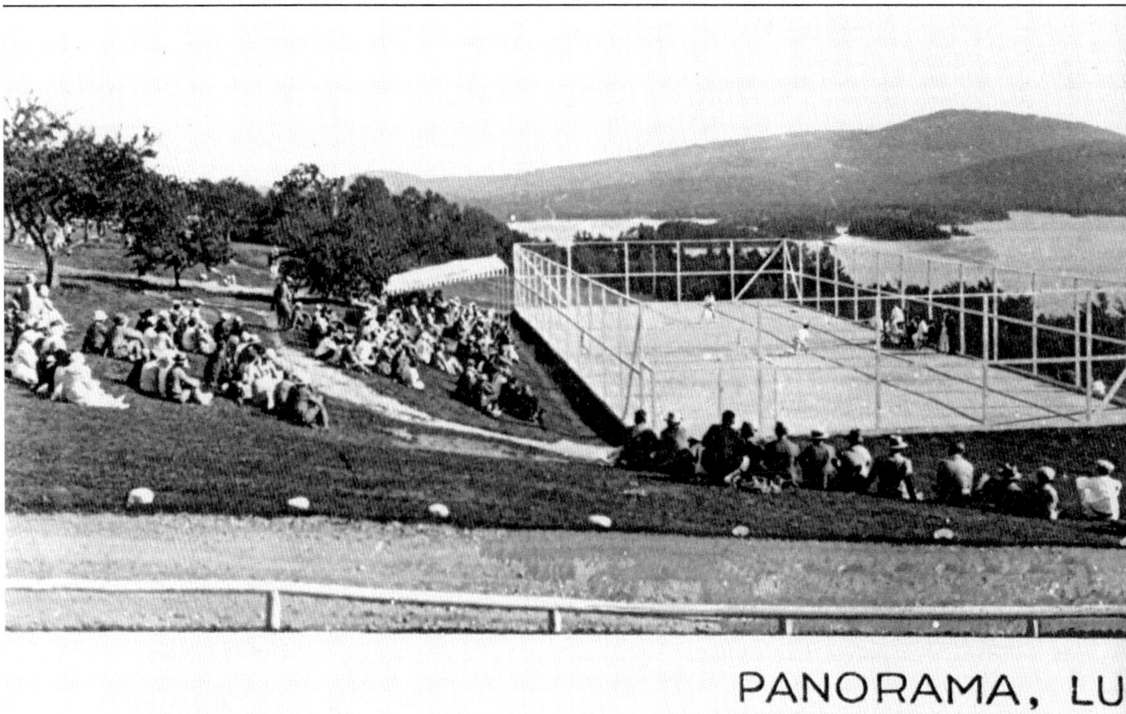

With Phillips Lake as its backdrop, this Lucerne-in-Maine panorama from the 1930s was a favorite collectible for visitors to the resort. Legend has it that the alpine resort was planned by

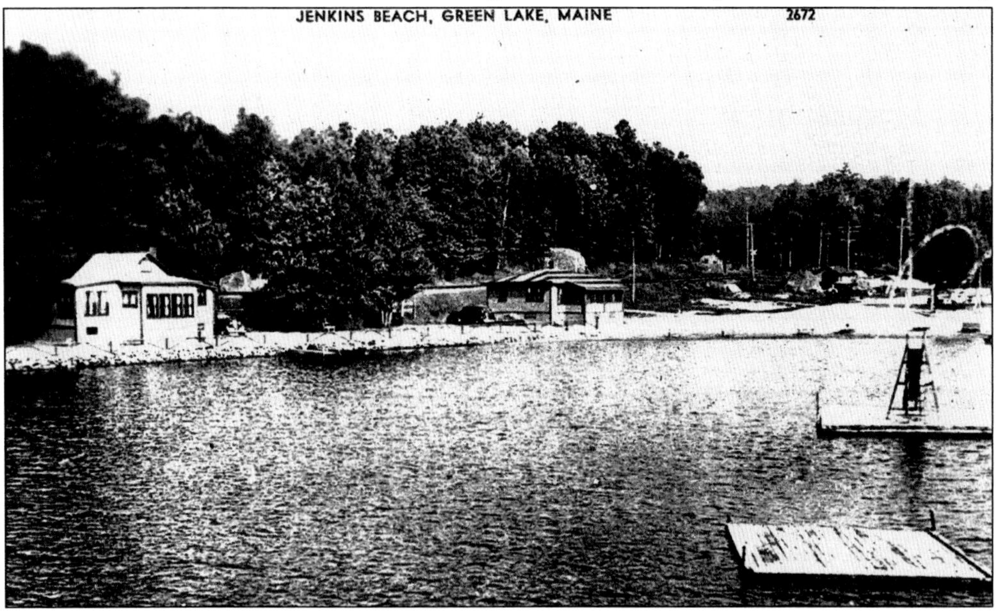

On steamy summer days, Jenkins Beach can be thronged with swimmers. Located at Green Lake, the beach's allure is lots of sand and sparkling water. It is also an easy drive on Route 1A from Bangor and Ellsworth. Into the early 20th century, day visitors arrived at Jenkins and Nicolin beaches by Maine Central Railroad coach, an era that Thomas Testa of the Downeast Scenic Railroad plans to revive with 11-mile excursion trains. (RRS.)

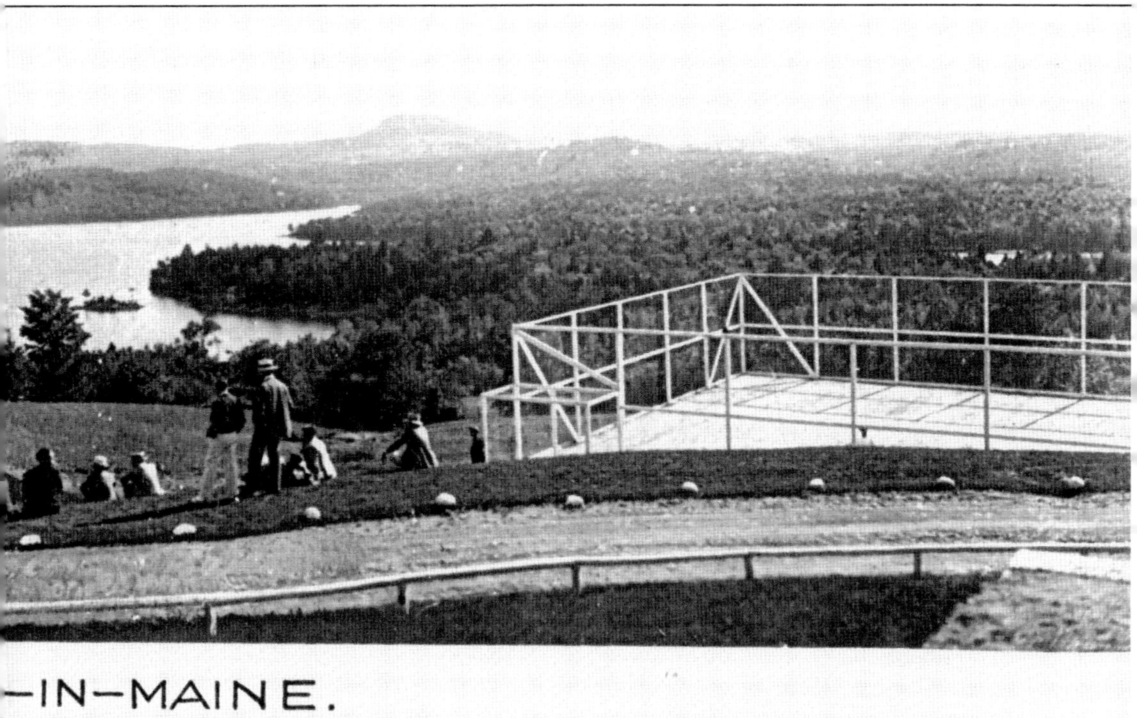

the head of a lumbering company who could not bear to see the natural beauty of the hills and lakeshore spoiled by gaudy development. (RRS.)

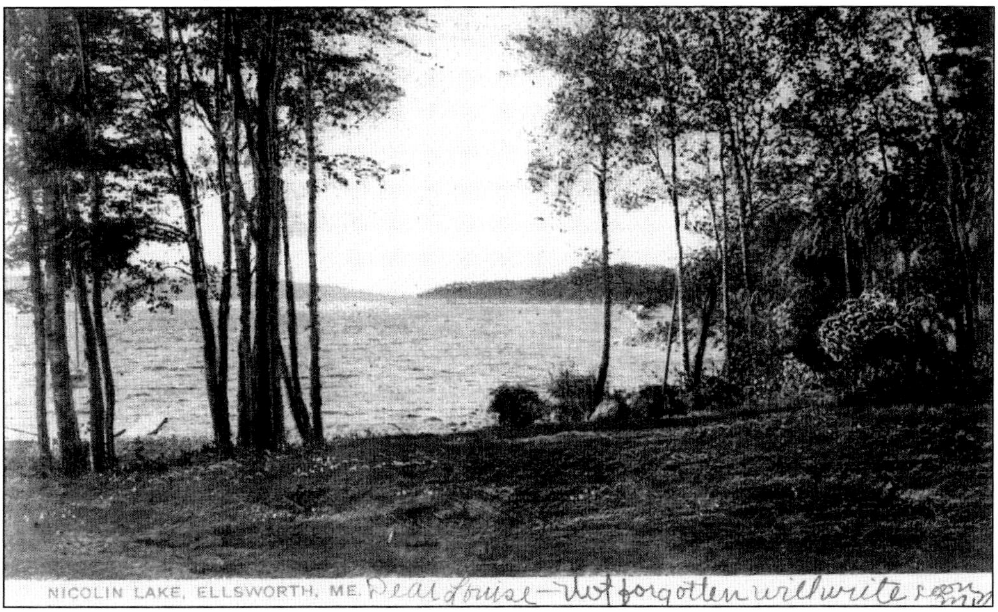

One of the quirks of collecting postcards is spotting mistakes in scene identification. There is no Nicolin Lake on the north side of Ellsworth. Nicolin Beach is located on the west side of Green Lake. For years, a campground there has drawn visitors from Canada and the eastern United States. Year-round homes have sprouted up on the Nicolin Road, which branches off of Route 1A at the former J. N. Hurd and Son store (see page 72). (RRS.)

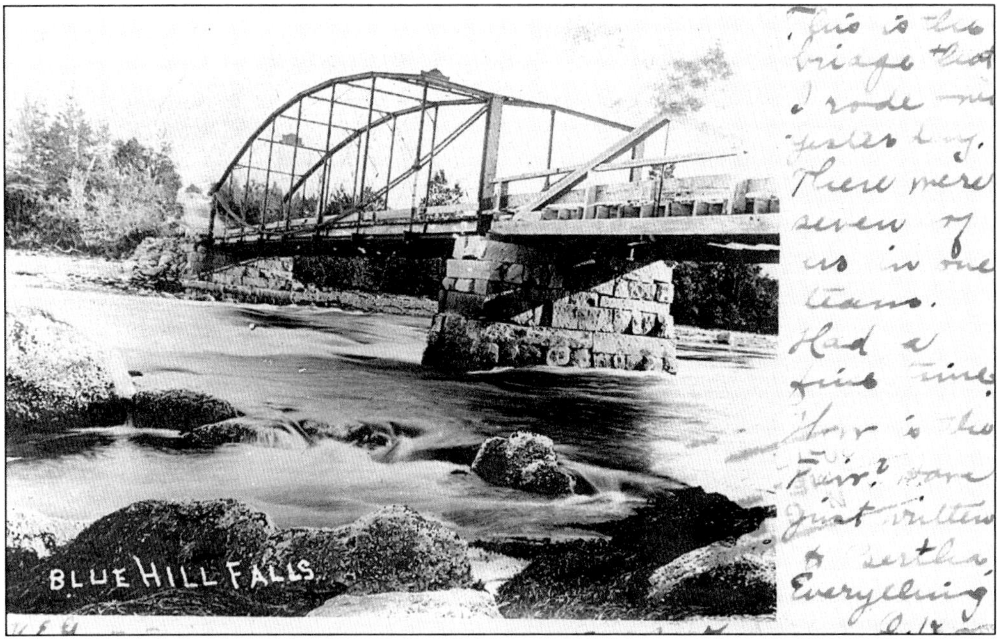

"This is the bridge that I rode on yesterday," reads the message on this rare old postcard. "There were seven of us in one team [of horses]. Had a fine time." Routes 172 and 175 pass through this spot at Blue Hill Falls, on the way to Brooklin and Naskeag Point. (BPL.)

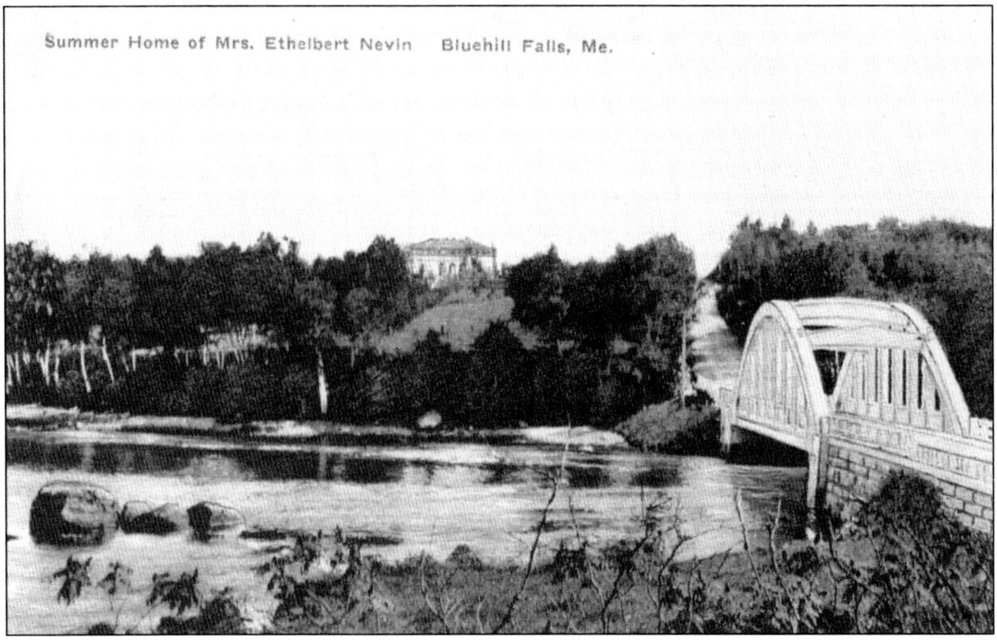

A later view shows the concrete replacement bridge of the 1920s. Mill Island is nearby, along with the summer home of Ann Paul Nevin, wife of Ethelbert Nevin, visible on the hill in the distance. Kayakers return to this site every year to experience the rush of the tidal falls, which backs up into a salt pond to the right of this view. The late artist Francis Hamabe, who had a studio on Mill Island, created a silkscreen print titled *Kayaks at the Blue Hill Falls.* (BPL.)

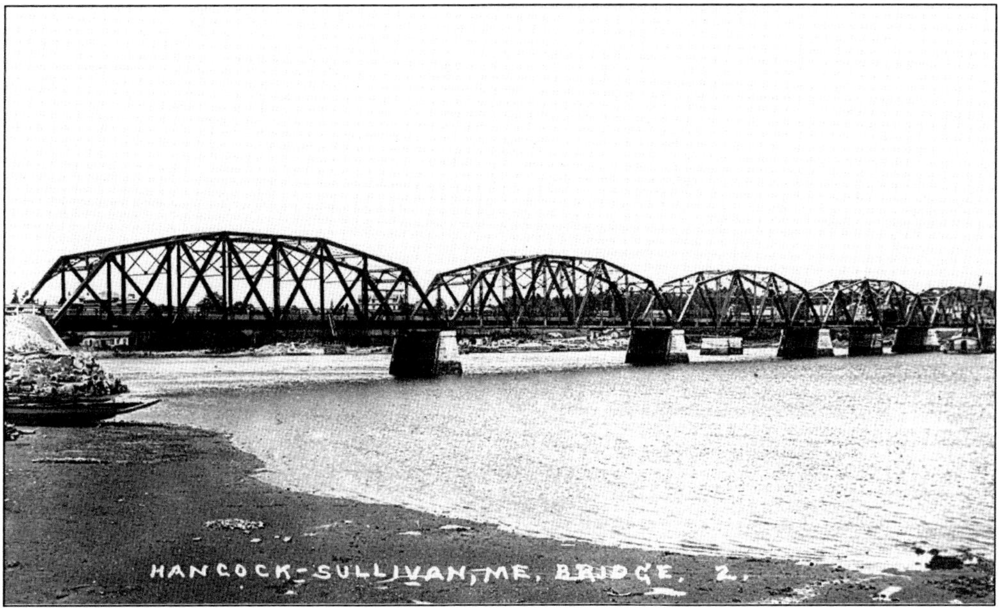

Until 2000, when a new bridge replaced it, Route 1 travelers drove over the Hancock-Sullivan Bridge. Engineers braved the whirlpools of the Taunton River to build the pilings of the five-span steel bridge in 1923. Fans of the structure took to calling it the "Singing Bridge" in later years, in a failed effort to save it from demolition. Historian Sanford Phippen recalled reading an early description of the bridge as being "built to break the worm's teeth." (RRS.)

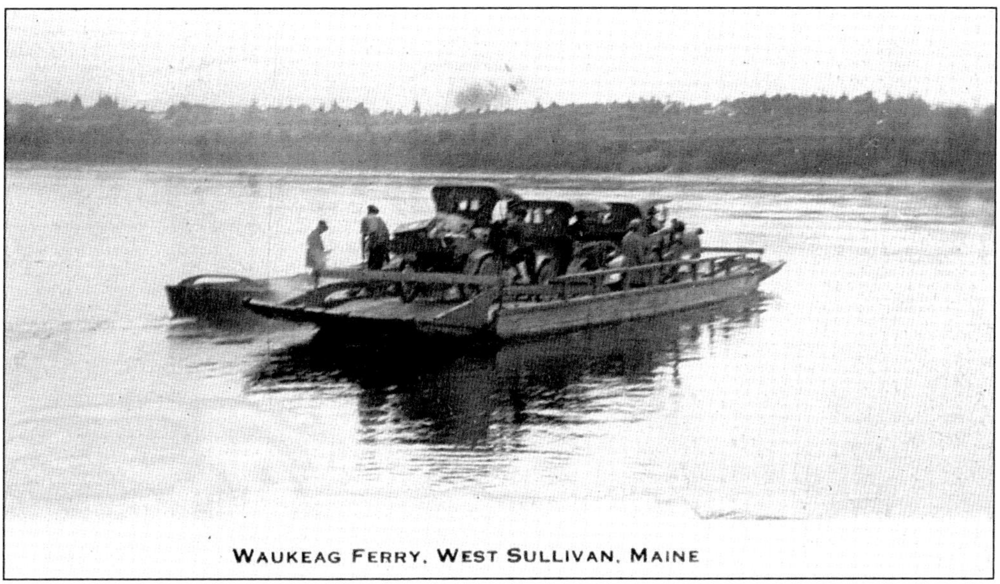

Before a bridge connected Hancock to Sullivan on Route 1, travelers took the Waukeag Ferry. Paying customers would blow a horn on the beach at West Sullivan to summon the ferry tender. One day, a peddler named Jake Altman and his horse and wagon fell off the ferry and landed in the Taunton River. He survived to tell and retell the story to anyone who would listen. (BPL.)

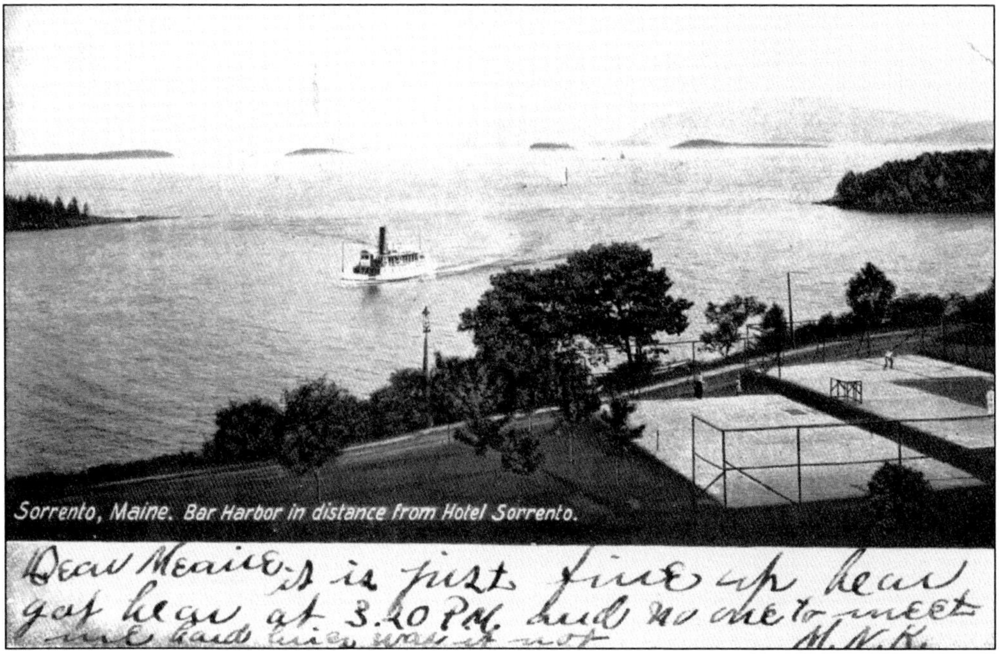

On July 8, 1900, the *New York Times* reported, "Charming Sorrento on the Bay, likened by its residents to the Old World Sorrento, is rapidly assuming its summer life. Every boat brings some increase of warm weather population, seeking welcome relief from the stifling heat of cities in the cool breezes from Frenchman's Bay." This view was taken from the Hotel Sorrento in the Hancock County village shortly before it burned in 1906. (RRS.)

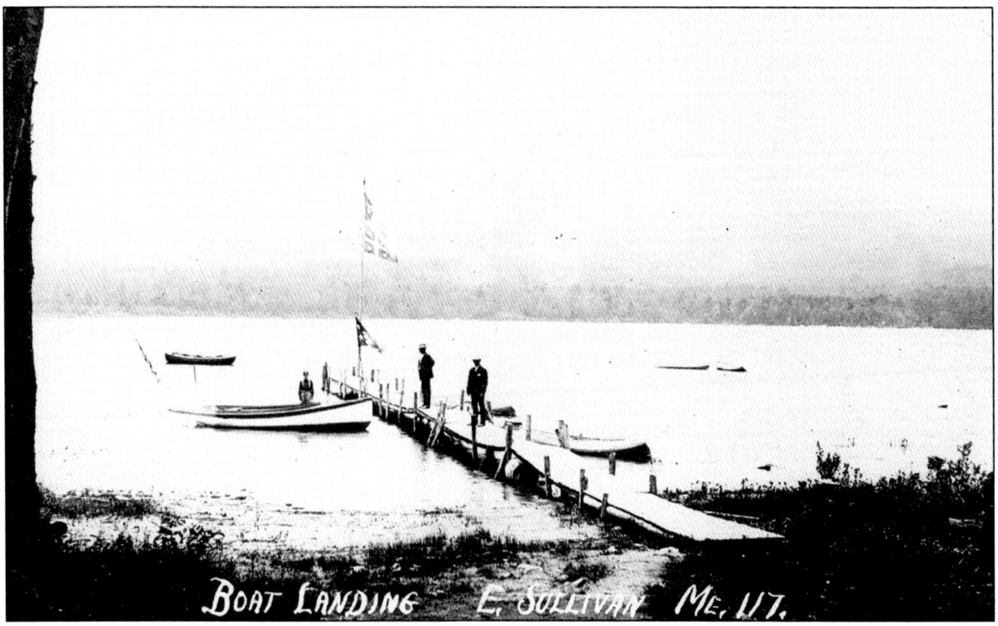

The boat landing in East Sullivan was a busy place on a summer day. It was located off of Route 1, on Long Cove. Situated near Sumner Memorial High School, the site is now a much frequented picnic area. This view probably dates to the 1920s and is noteworthy because of the colorful boat flags, the long wooden wharf, and the men in suits, hats, and ties. (RRS.)

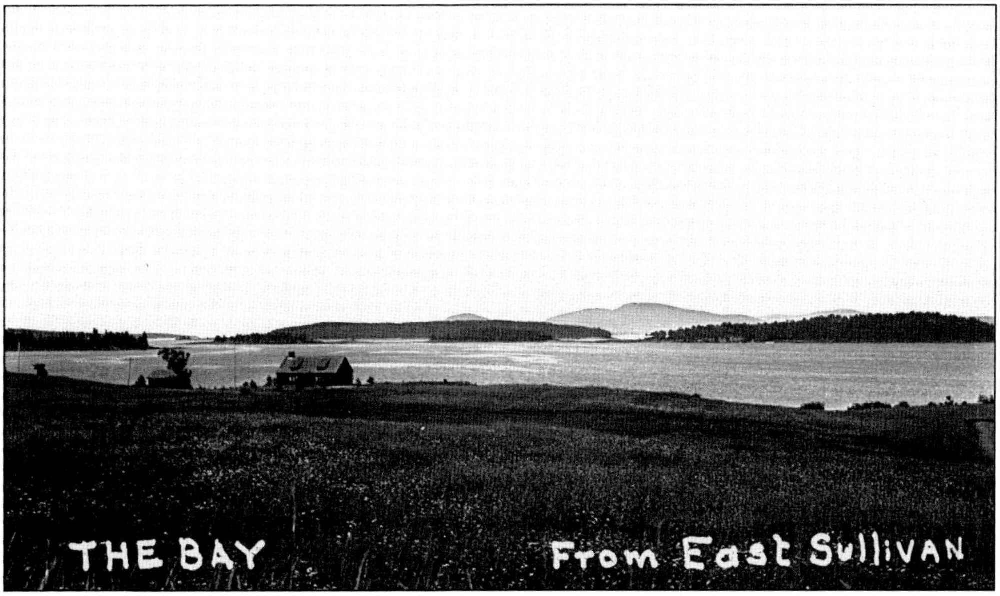

Another view taken from East Sullivan in the 1920s shows a sunny meadow filled with wildflowers and a breathtaking shot of the bay and Mount Cadillac in the distance. The old farmhouse is still standing, making this a popular photograph stop for tourists traveling east on Route 1. Several other openings along the coast in Sullivan also afford photograph opportunities. (RRS.)

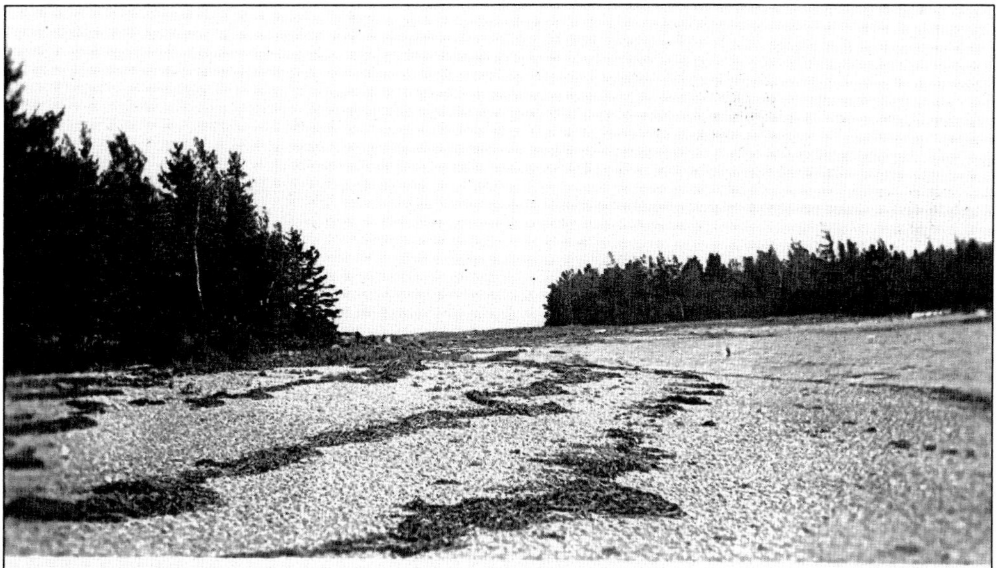

The tide was out when this early view was taken of the "natural gateway" at Lamoine Beach. The "gateway" moniker must have derived from Lamoine's central location in Frenchman's Bay, and this shot is looking toward the ocean beyond the opening in the trees. Lamoine Beach was the site of a large sardine cannery in the early 20th century, and an impressive hotel named Shore Acres. (RRS.)

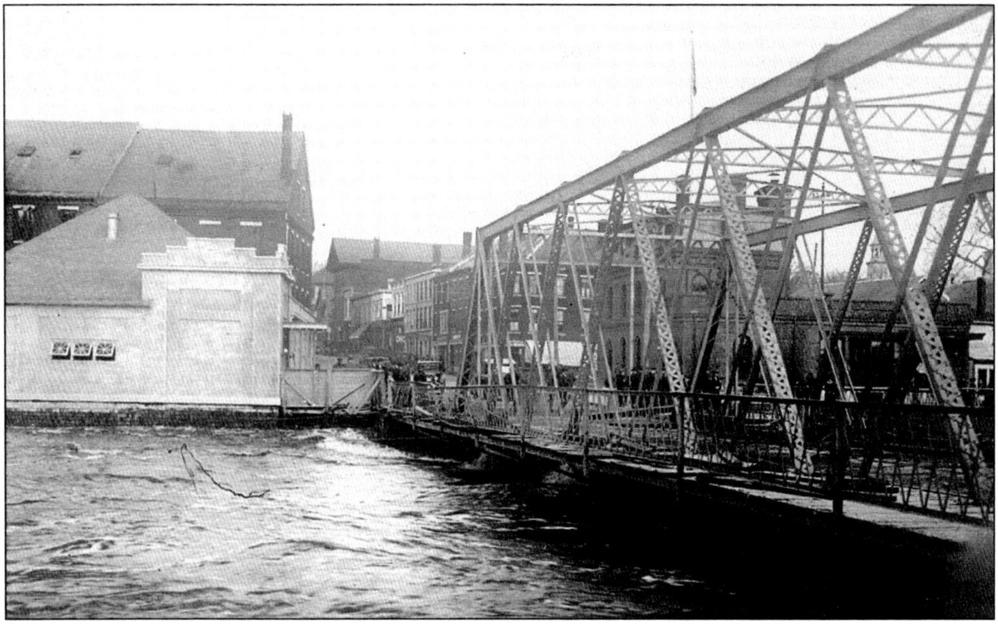

The raging waters of the Union River took out the Main Street Bridge in the spring flood of May 1923. The freshet started with 4.60 inches that fell in a 24-hour period. When a storage dam on the river was breached, much of downtown Ellsworth was submerged. This view shows the floodwaters and buildings along the east side of the river. The Dirigo Theater and a steam laundry were two of the casualties. (BPL.)

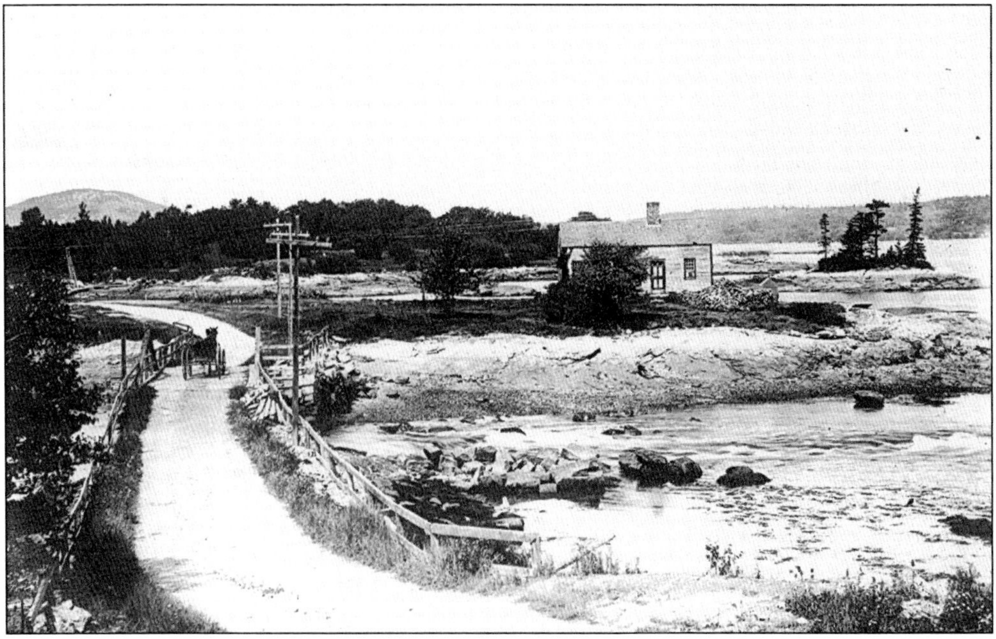

A very rare and early view of the bridge at Blue Hill Falls shows a simple wooden house at the right, and the outline of Blue Hill Mountain in the distance. Postcard photographers often staged a wagon or people along roadways to punctuate the scene. Note the early utility poles, a sign of progress that came to the tiny seaside village. (BHPL.)

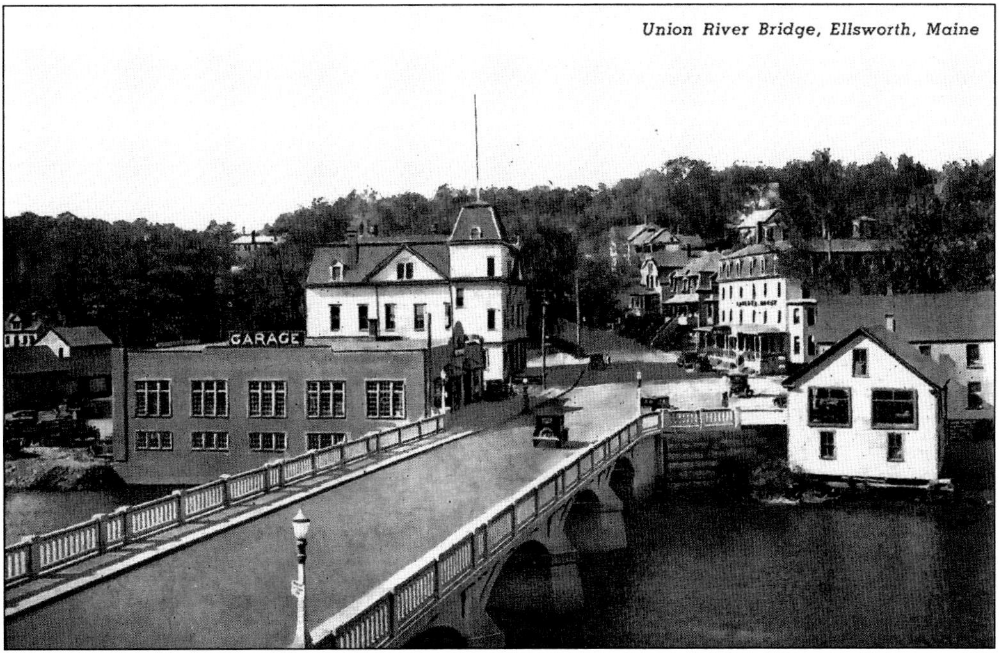

Following the destruction of the old steel Main Street Bridge in the 1923 flood, a new concrete span was dedicated on July 4, 1924. Historian Deale B. Salisbury writes that this bridge is still being used but was repaired and altered in appearance at the end of the 20th century. This is actually the fourth bridge to cross the Union River at this point, the first having been built in 1793. (RRS.)

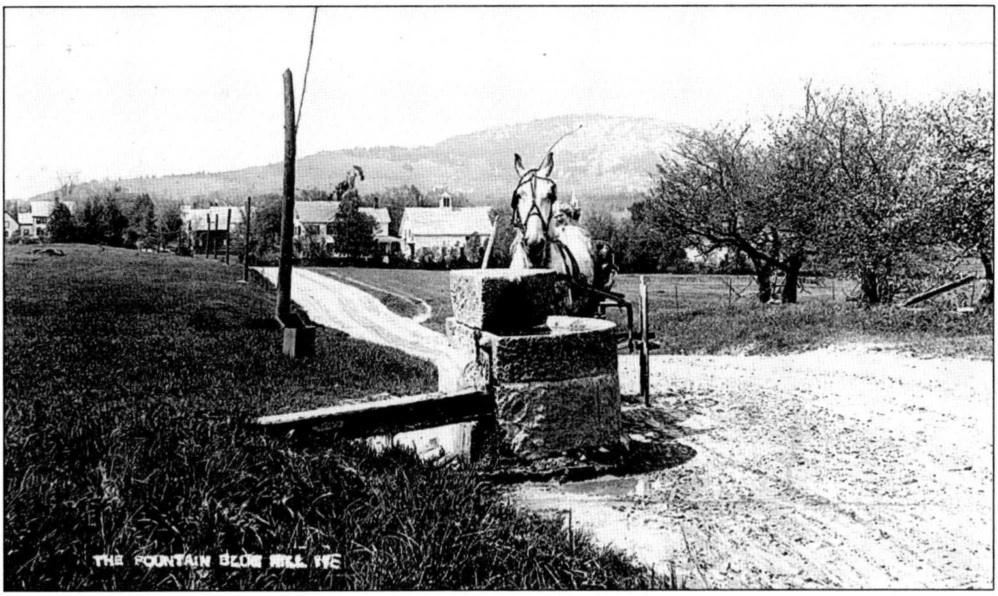

Every village had a watering trough into the early 20th century, when this Blue Hill view was taken. Towns would budget an appropriate amount into the annual budget to maintain the stone troughs from which horses and other animals could drink. The trough at Hancock Corner was moved to Hancock Point some years ago and now is a relic from another era on the village green. (BHPL.)

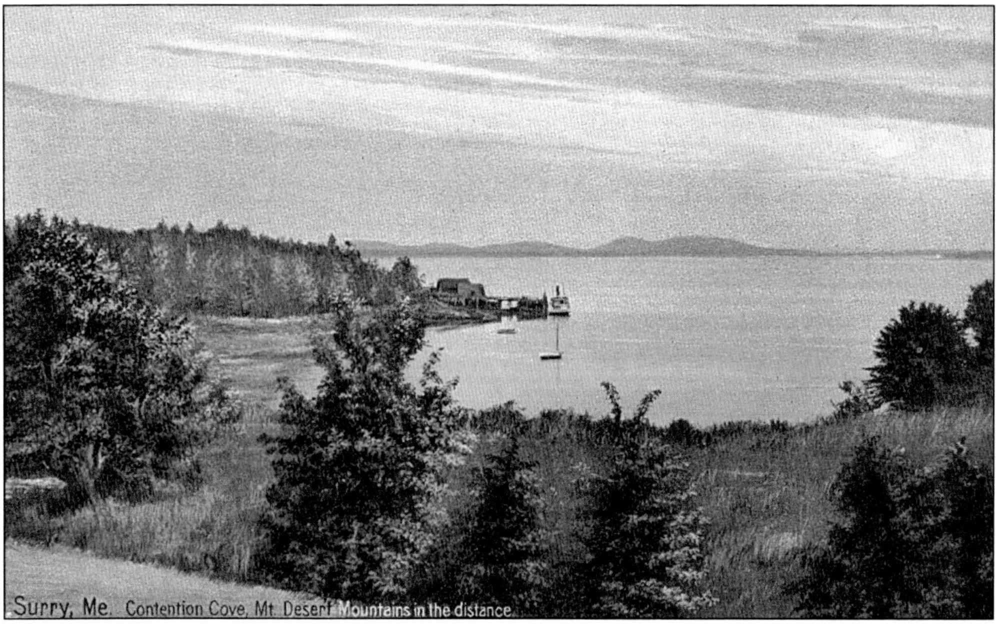

When steamboat service came to Surry in 1881, the town was connected to the outside world. A wharf at Contention Cove, visible in the center of this postcard, was a bustling place as locals and tourists traveled over to Mount Desert Island and other places, as they never had before. Cadillac Mountain and other mountains on the island rise like apparitions across Frenchman's Bay in the background. (RRS.)

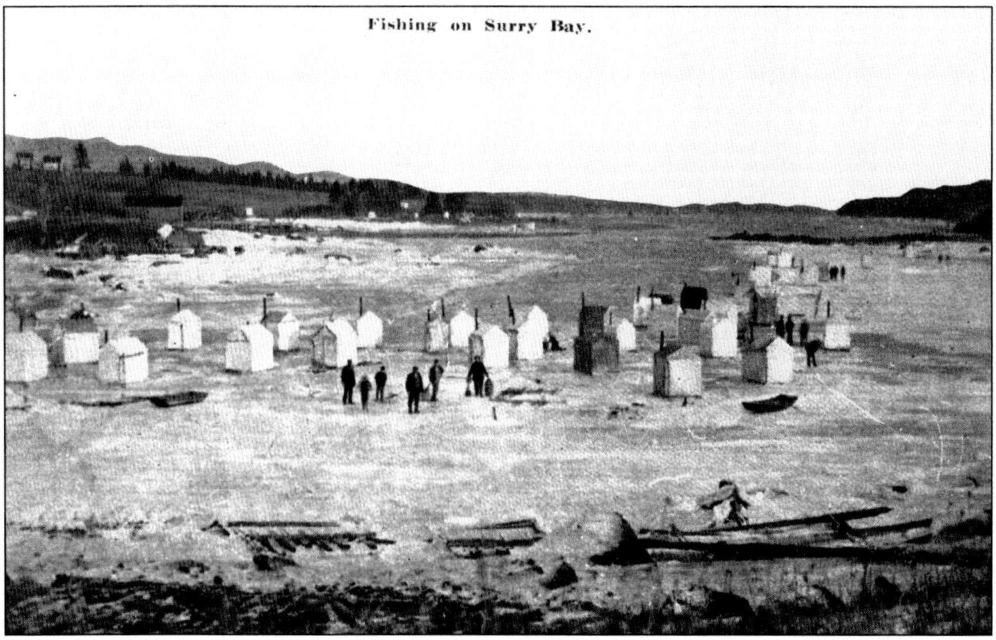

Fishing on Surry Bay was a favorite winter pastime by the 1920s. Tentlike icehouses with chimneys sprouted up, and people hovered over holes in the ice to await a tug on the string. Smelts were caught here close to shore. Apparently the saltwater did not freeze at that location. In the springtime, fishermen caught and smoked alewives that ran up Patten Stream to spawn. (BPL.)

Two

Eat, Sleep, and Be Merry

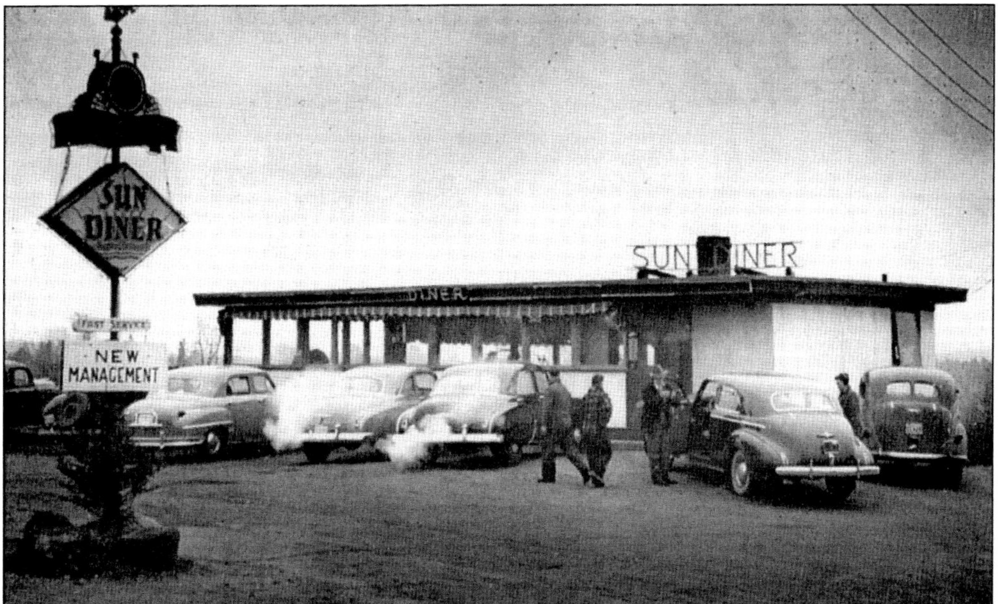

The hamburgers were juicy and cheap at the Sun Diner on High Street in Ellsworth. Seen here in the 1950s, the diner catered to locals, tourists, and teenagers out on a date. The fancy sign notes that the place is under new management and that it features fast service. If one wanted carhop service, one had to drive down the road to Jasper's. The Sun Diner later operated under the name of Dick's Diner and for a time was managed by Bertram C. Whalen. (RRS.)

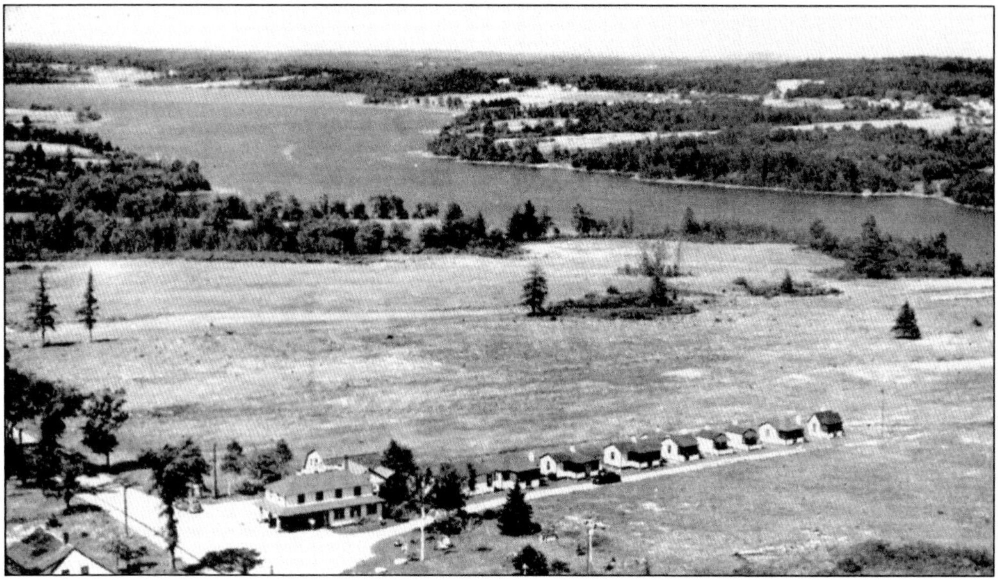

The Green Moth may sound like a science fiction character, not a popular tourist court. But the odd name and the large wooden moth displayed in a wooden cage did not deter tourists on Route 3 (the Ellsworth–Bar Harbor Road) who stayed in the "modern" cabins, shopped at the general store, and dined in the restaurant. Edward K. Sutton operated the Trenton landmark, seen here around 1948. (RRS.)

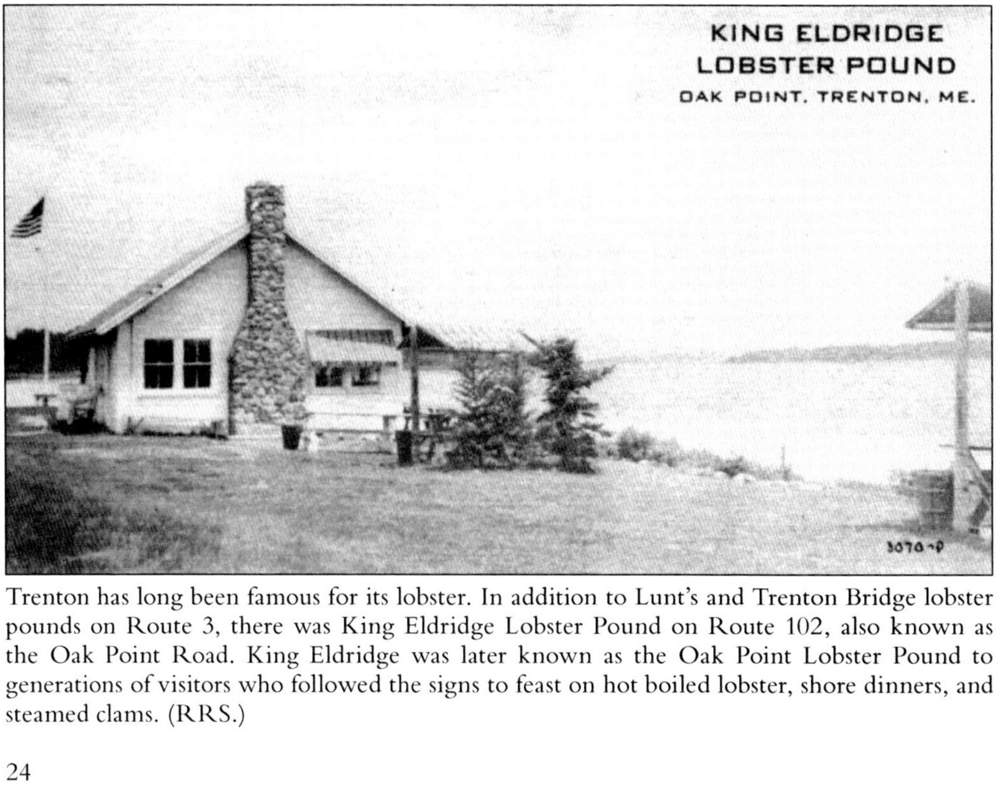

Trenton has long been famous for its lobster. In addition to Lunt's and Trenton Bridge lobster pounds on Route 3, there was King Eldridge Lobster Pound on Route 102, also known as the Oak Point Road. King Eldridge was later known as the Oak Point Lobster Pound to generations of visitors who followed the signs to feast on hot boiled lobster, shore dinners, and steamed clams. (RRS.)

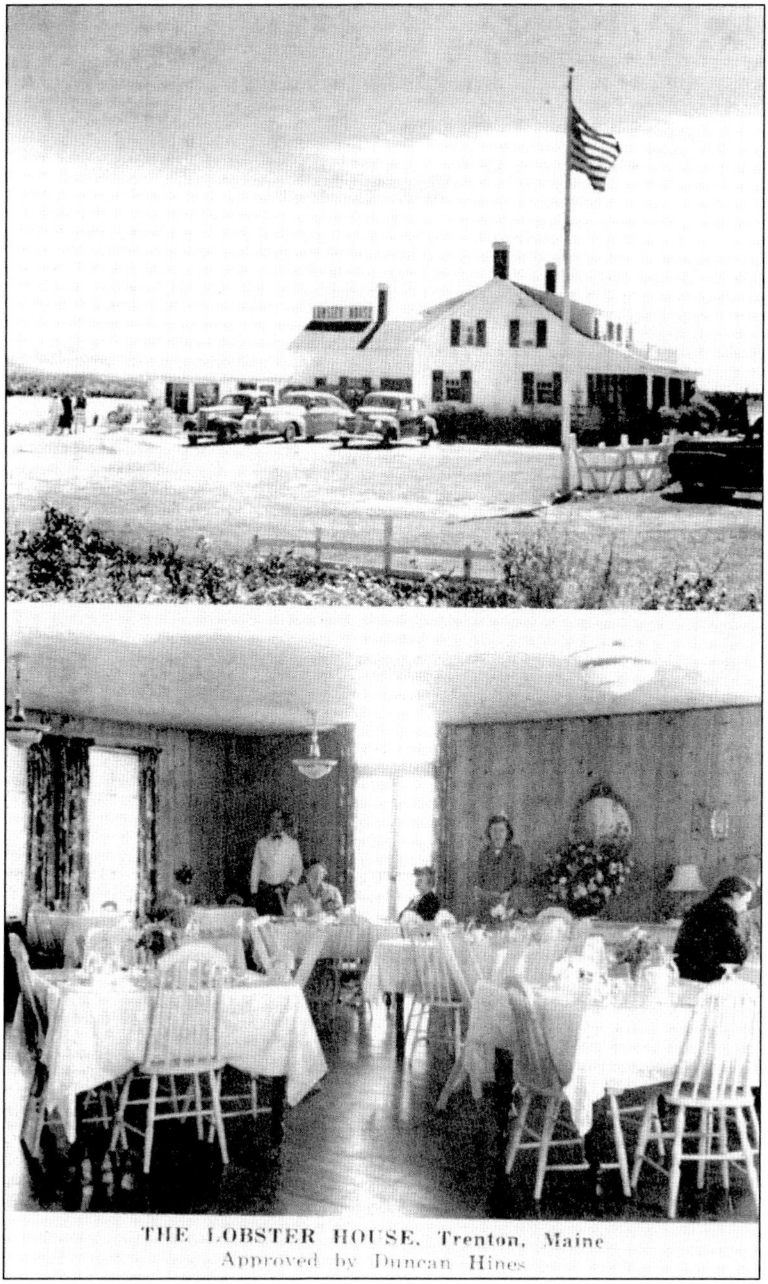

The granddaddy of all the Trenton seafood restaurants was the Lobster House. Located on Route 3, just before crossing the Thompson Island Bridge onto Mount Desert Island, the Lobster House had a pleasant ambiance and served excellent lobster, shrimp, scallops, and clams, as well as fried chicken and steaks. The seasonal eatery attracted returning tourists each year, as well as patrons from Ellsworth, Bangor, and beyond, who celebrated birthdays, weddings, and anniversaries there. Being approved by Duncan Hines apparently was a distinction worth boasting about. Note the crisp white-linen tablecloths, wooden chairs, and floral bouquet. Today seasonal dining is far more casual at most restaurants. A little gift shop sold souvenirs behind the main building. (RRS.)

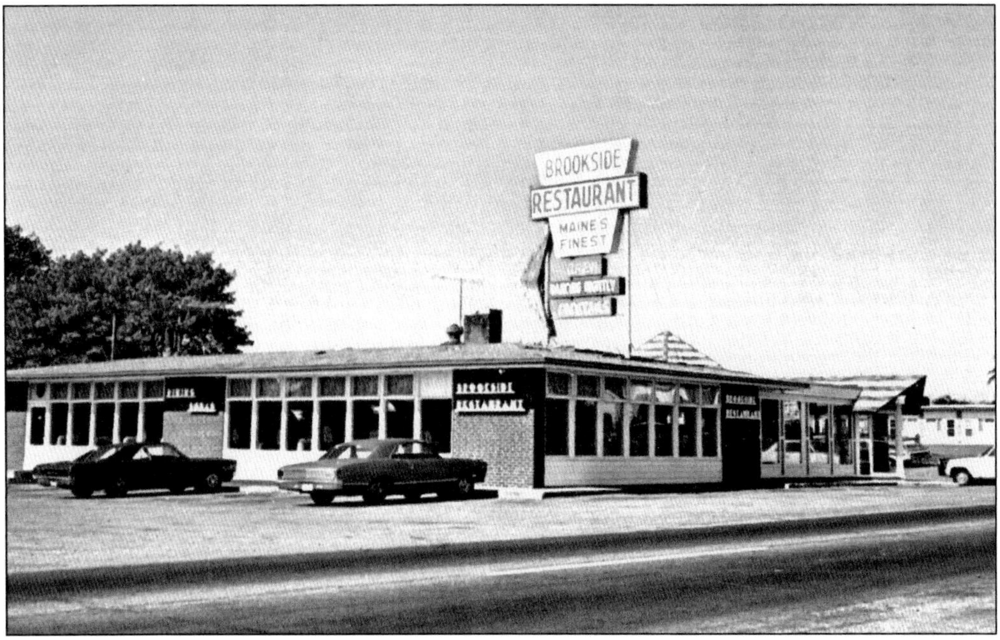

The only reminder of the Brookside Restaurant, once located on Routes 1 and 3 (High Street), was the Brookside Motel, which operated for many years next door. Seen here in the 1960s, the popular restaurant boldly billed itself as "Maine's finest." It served cocktails, seafoods, steaks, and chops, and there was dancing nightly with live entertainment. The seating capacity was 200. (RRS.)

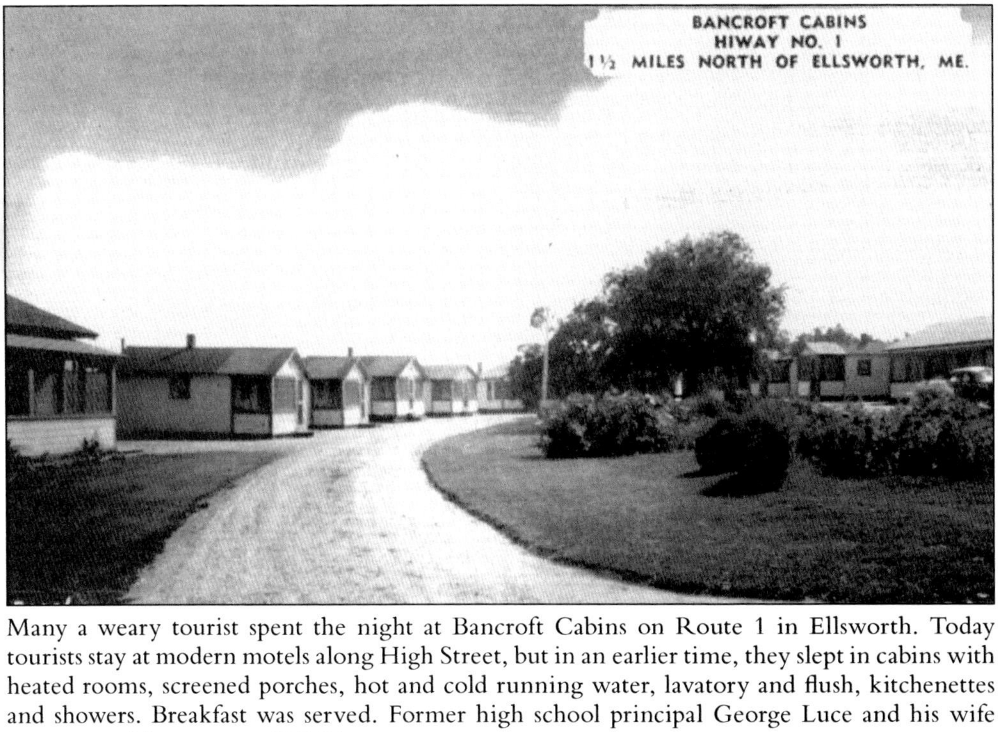

Many a weary tourist spent the night at Bancroft Cabins on Route 1 in Ellsworth. Today tourists stay at modern motels along High Street, but in an earlier time, they slept in cabins with heated rooms, screened porches, hot and cold running water, lavatory and flush, kitchenettes and showers. Breakfast was served. Former high school principal George Luce and his wife were two of the owners. (RRS.)

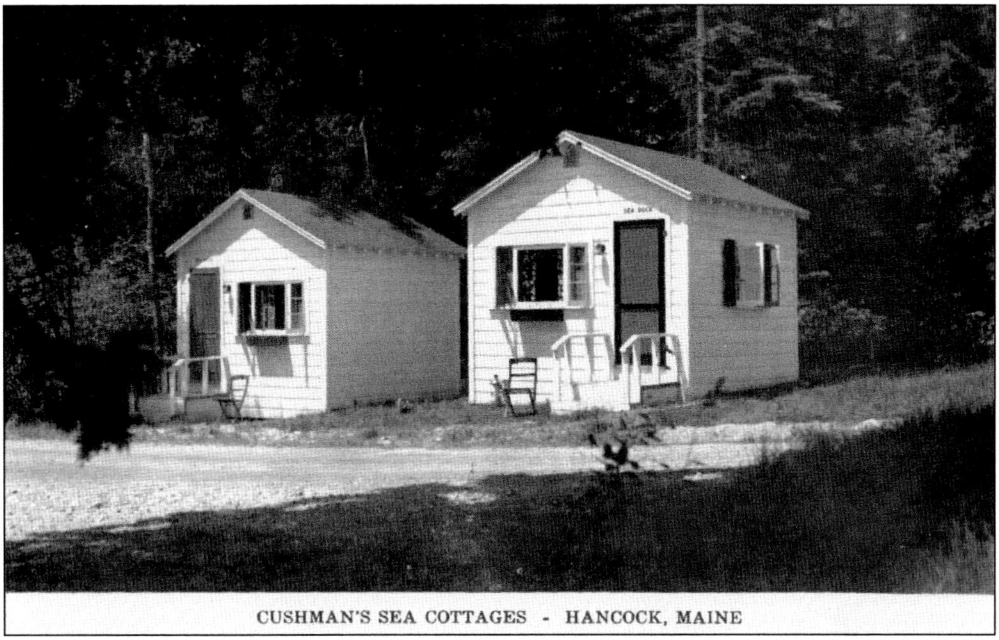

Dan Cushman's Sea Cottages at Mount Desert Ferry near Hancock Point boasted scenic views of Frenchman's Bay and Acadia National Park. Each of the tidy cabins had a name over the front door. The one on the cabin at the right was Sea Rock. Travelers typically were headed Down East, toward Machias, Calais, and New Brunswick, Canada. (RRS.)

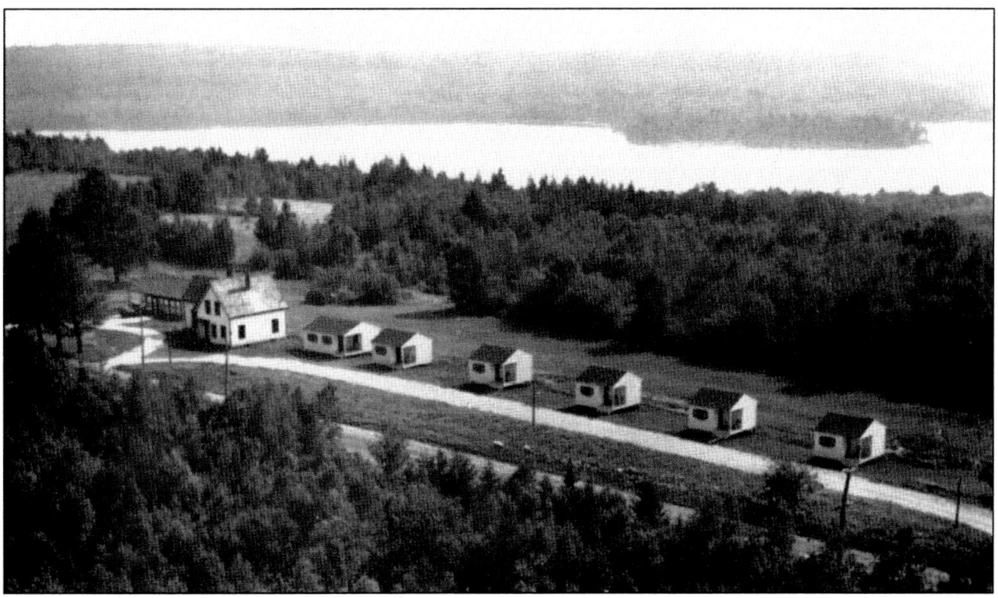

Nan's de Luxe Cabins also catered to travelers going to Bar Harbor and points east (Washington County). The cabins were located six miles west of Ellsworth, at Routes 1A and 3. In addition to motels, some cabins have survived the onslaught of time. Apparently a select group of tourists still prefer the coziness and privacy of cabins along Route 3 in Trenton, Hulls Cove, and Bar Harbor. (RRS.)

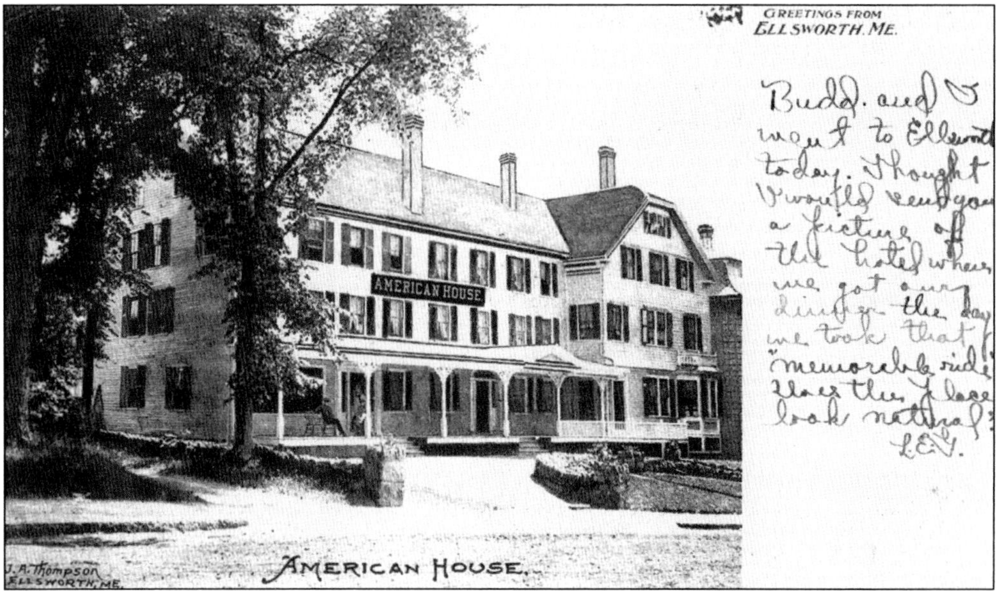

U.S. presidents such as Ulysses S. Grant, Theodore Roosevelt, and William Howard Taft all dined at the American House. The rambling wooden hotel was built in 1836, as Ellsworth was gaining strength as a lumbering capital of eastern Maine. Located on Main Street, where the post office now sits, the hotel was dismantled during World War I, and according to local lore, its timbers were used to construct local buildings. (BPL.)

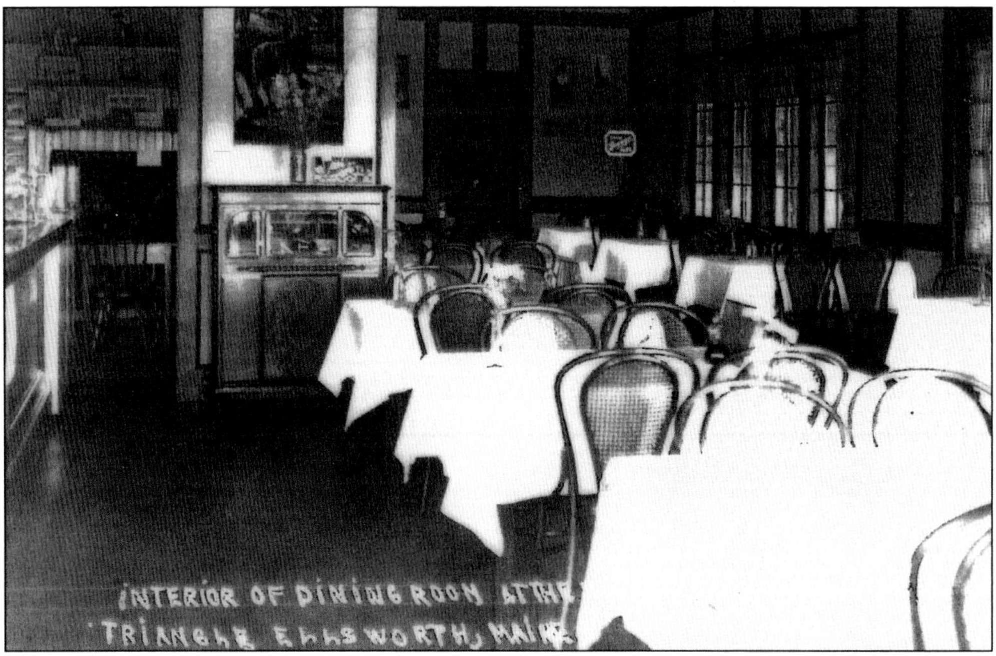

The dining room at the Triangle in Ellsworth in the 1920s was made homey with wicker-backed chairs, linen tablecloths, and fresh-cut gladiolas. A large painting of a buck hung on the wall. Another favorite lunch stop was the Willows Inn on Route 1A in North Ellsworth (see page 72). Over time, the Triangle, which forms the junction of busy Routes 1 and 3, became a morass of filling stations and fast food restaurants. (RRS.)

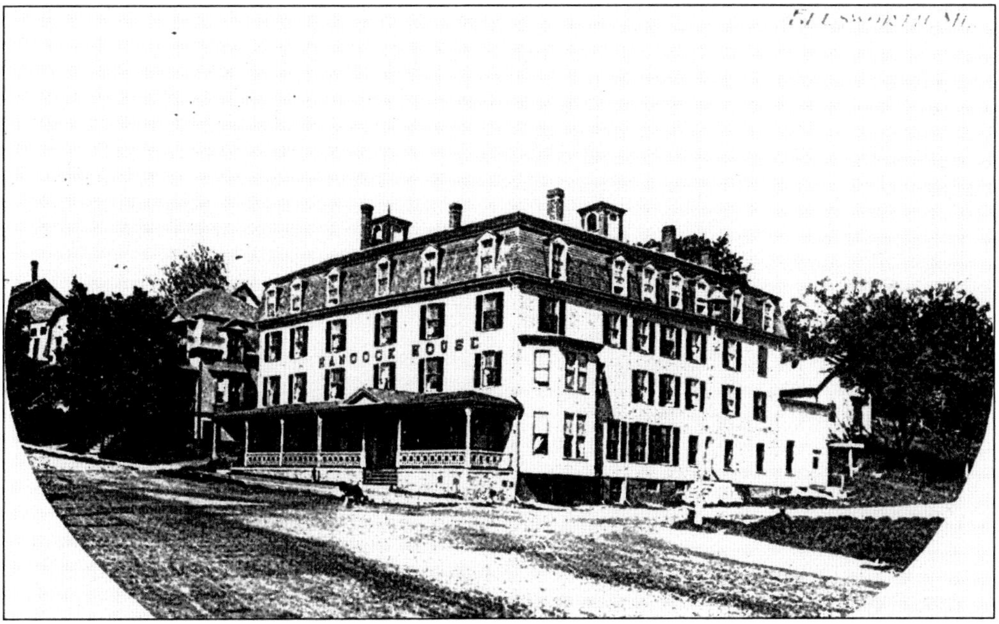

Ellsworth's Hancock House stood at West Main and Grant Streets and accommodated thousands of guests during many decades. The traveling public as well as local residents enjoyed holiday meals there. "Old-fashioned hospitality prevails in dining room and cocktail lounge," reads a 1913 advertisement, "Delightful rooms with bath." The Hancock House was razed in the late 1950s, and a Ford dealership was built in its place. (RRS.)

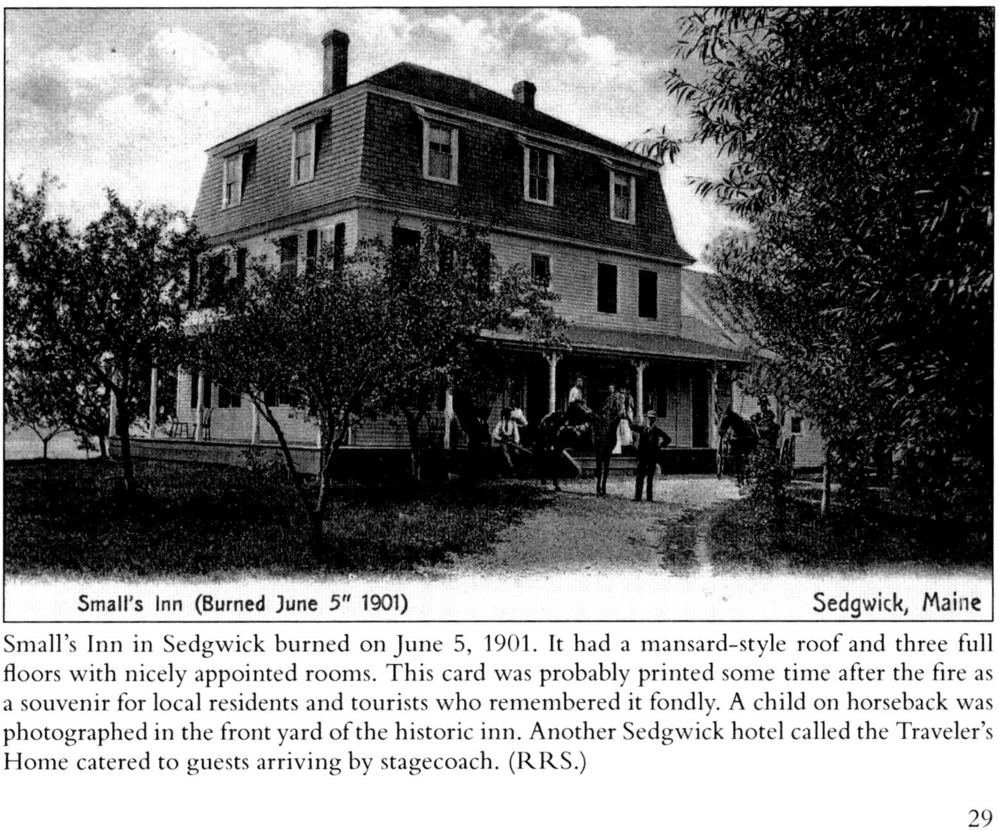

Small's Inn in Sedgwick burned on June 5, 1901. It had a mansard-style roof and three full floors with nicely appointed rooms. This card was probably printed some time after the fire as a souvenir for local residents and tourists who remembered it fondly. A child on horseback was photographed in the front yard of the historic inn. Another Sedgwick hotel called the Traveler's Home catered to guests arriving by stagecoach. (RRS.)

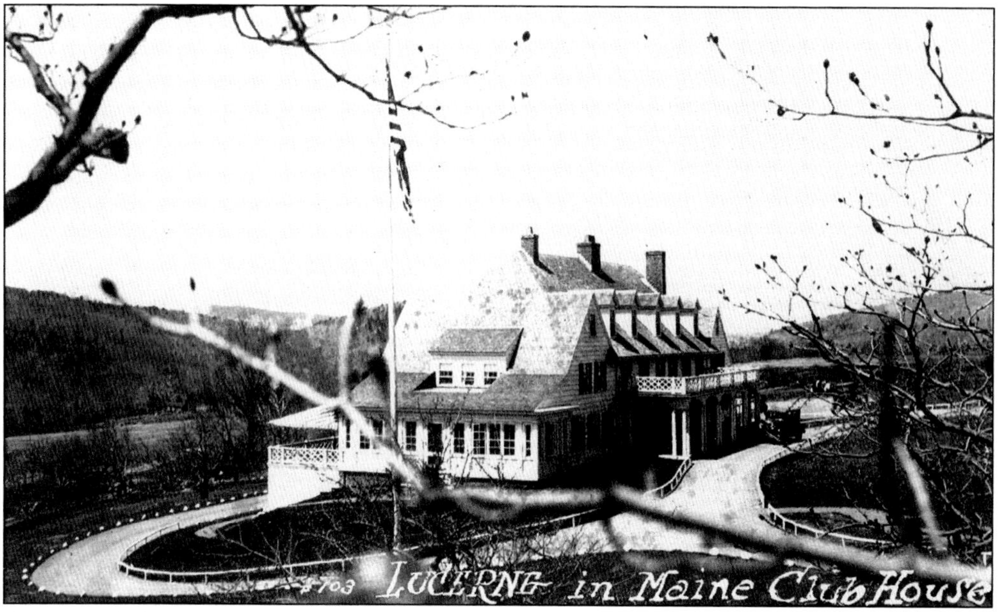

For nearly 200 years, the Lucerne Inn has been a landmark on Route 1A in Dedham. Overlooking Phillips Lake, it began as the Lake House in the early 1800s and in 1814 became the only stop for travelers seeking food and drink halfway between Ellsworth and Bangor. Eventually the highway hostelry became the elegant hotel of today, which has been enlarged. It is listed in the National Register of Historic Places. (RRS.)

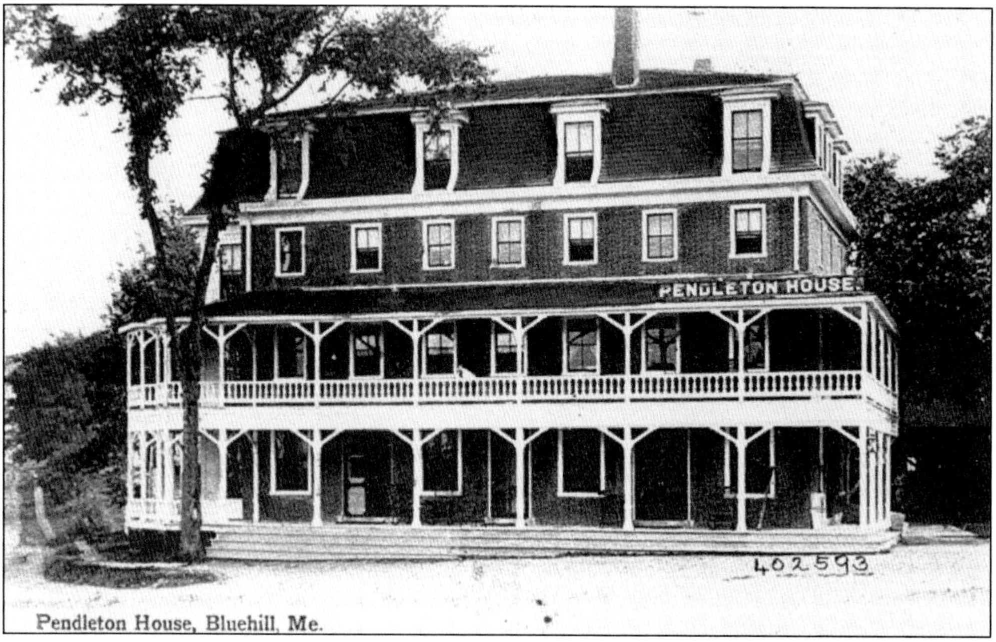

The Pendleton House is one of Blue Hill's most enduring landmarks. Although it has not been operated as a hotel since 1912, the name lives on. Built before 1832 by Jeremiah T. Holt, the building, located near the center of town, was purchased by Nathan P. Pendleton of Boston in 1878 and later was leased by Eugene Leach and his brother. Shops, eateries, and apartments occupy the landmark today. (BPL.)

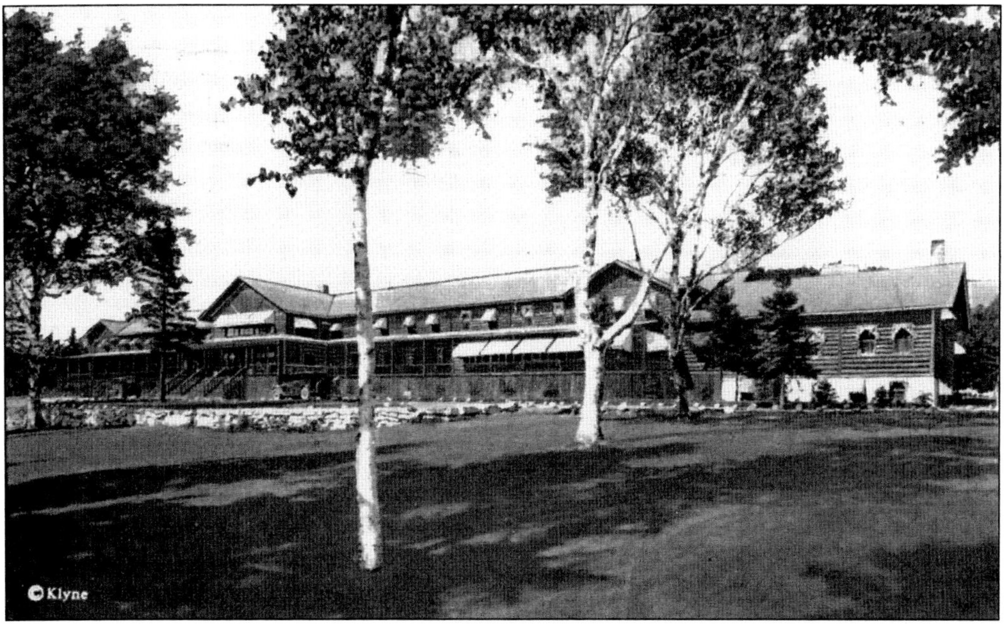

Lucerne-in-Maine's Log Lodge was the centerpiece of an alpine village plotted by developers in the 1920s. Visitors to the long, attractive lodge danced, drank, and dined while enjoying romantic sunsets over Phillips Lake. The Dedham landmark, situated near a golf course, hosted aviator Amelia Earhart in 1934 and other celebrities over the years. It burned to the ground in the late 1950s and was never rebuilt. (RRS.)

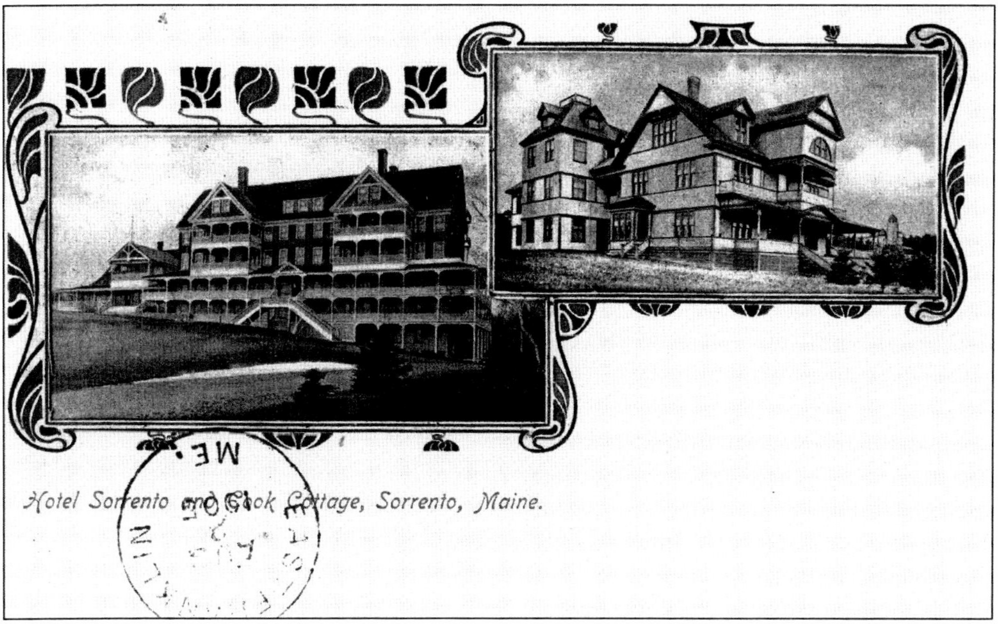

Sorrento is often called Maine's best-kept secret, being a secluded community of year-round and seasonal homes. Located on Route 185, it separated from Sullivan in 1895, after which it continued to gain favor as a summertime resort. Unlike many seasonal communities, it decided not to rebuild its major hotel, the Hotel Sorrento (left), after it burned in 1906. The Cook Cottage was also a landmark. (RRS.)

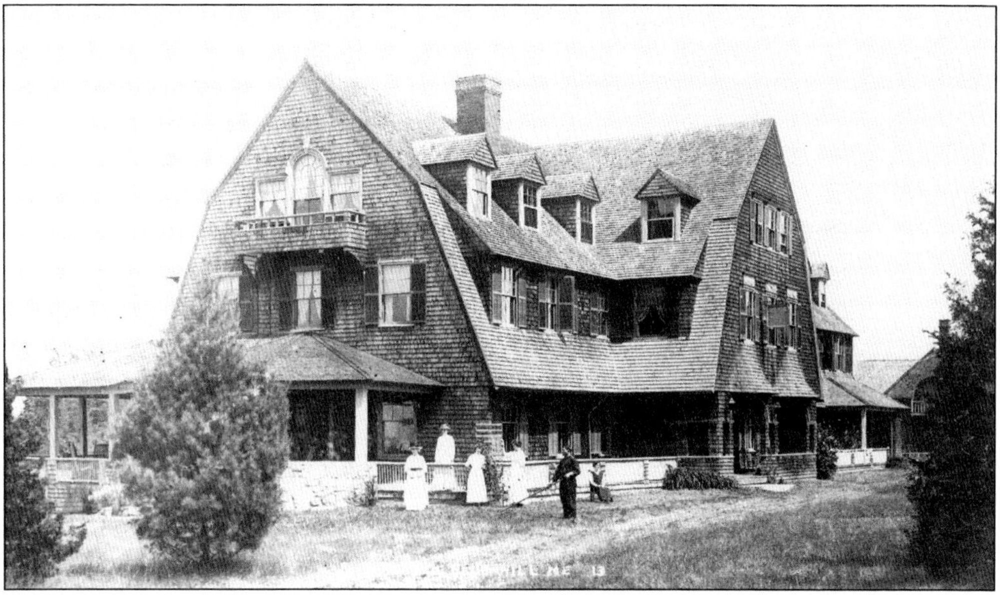

Travelers nearing the crest of Tenney Hill could not miss the Blue Hill Inn. George Stover built the large, shingled inn in 1892, and it enjoyed great success before being destroyed by fire in 1932. Hotel staff arranged optional sailboat excursions down the bay and buckboard rides to Castine and other points in Hancock County. Young townspeople could join the guests Saturday nights when an orchestra played. (MHPC.)

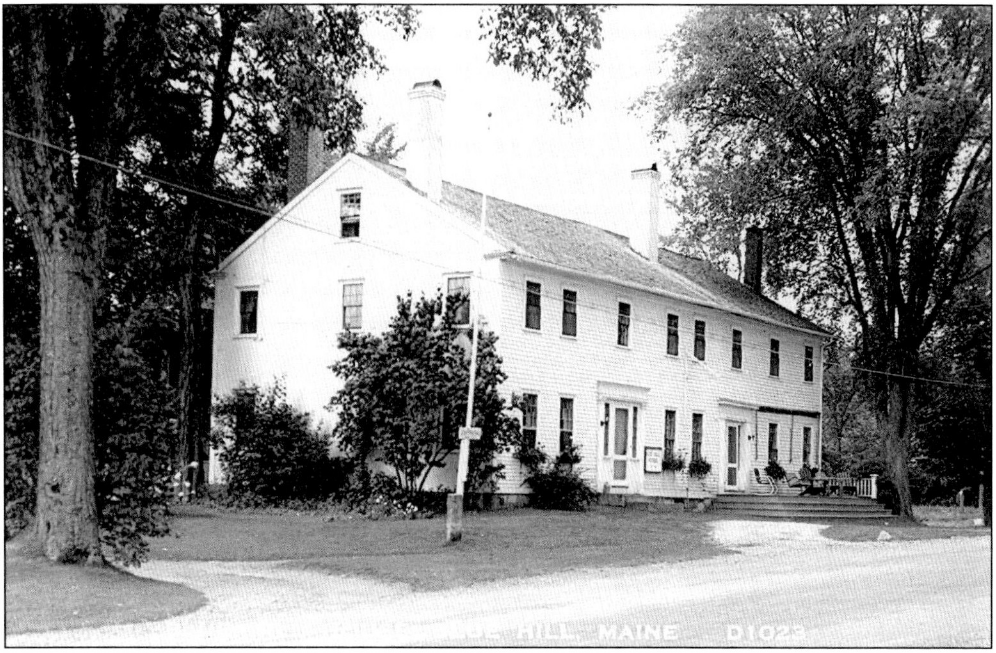

The Blue Hill House, now called the Blue Hill Inn, was built around 1830 as a private residence by local blacksmith Edward Varnum Stevens. He had already converted the federally styled building to an inn when he sold it to Haskell Hinckley, whose wife Fannie operated the place for many years. Today's Blue Hill Inn has 11 guest rooms, a dining room, 2 parlors, and 6 fireplaces. (RRS.)

Three

Dear Old Golden Rule Days

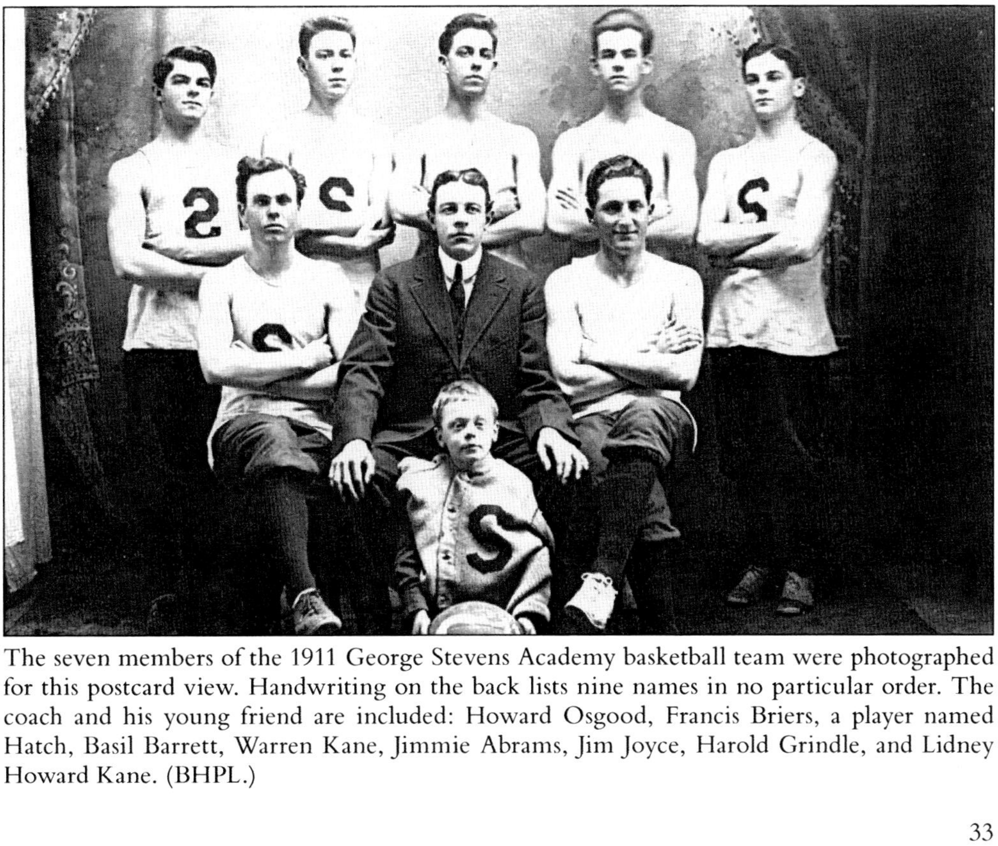

The seven members of the 1911 George Stevens Academy basketball team were photographed for this postcard view. Handwriting on the back lists nine names in no particular order. The coach and his young friend are included: Howard Osgood, Francis Briers, a player named Hatch, Basil Barrett, Warren Kane, Jimmie Abrams, Jim Joyce, Harold Grindle, and Lidney Howard Kane. (BHPL.)

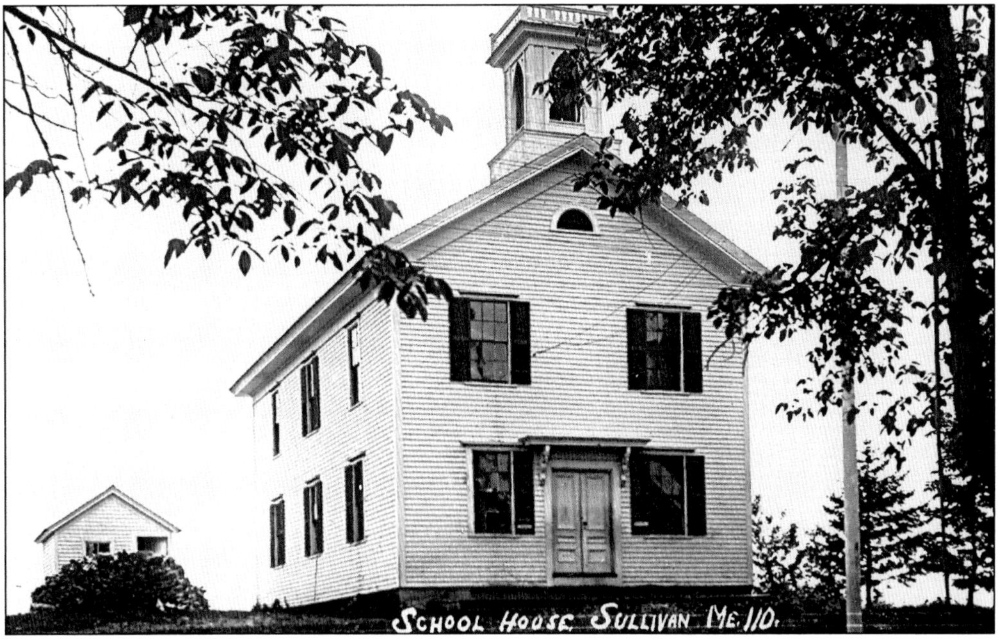

The old Sullivan schoolhouse, around 1920, is a study in functional design. Two full floors with large windows served the coastal students, grades kindergarten through eighth. A bell hung from the churchlike cupola. In 2008, Sullivan was served by two outstanding schools. Mountain View School, located at 542 Bert Gray Road, had 297 students and 26 teachers. Sumner Memorial High School, on Route 1, had 327 students and 32 teachers. (BPL.)

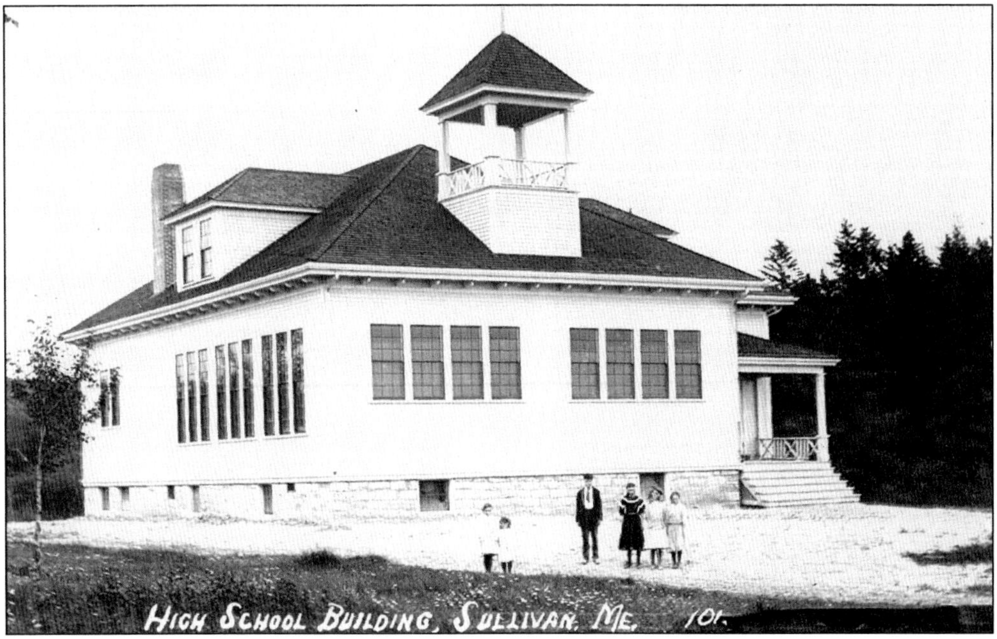

Many Sullivan residents received a solid education in this distinctive wooden building. Located on Route 1 in West Sullivan, it served as the town's high school until 1952, when Sumner Memorial High School opened. After that, the old school was converted to a grammar school. If it looks familiar to present-day residents, it is because it lives on as the Sullivan Town Hall. (BPL.)

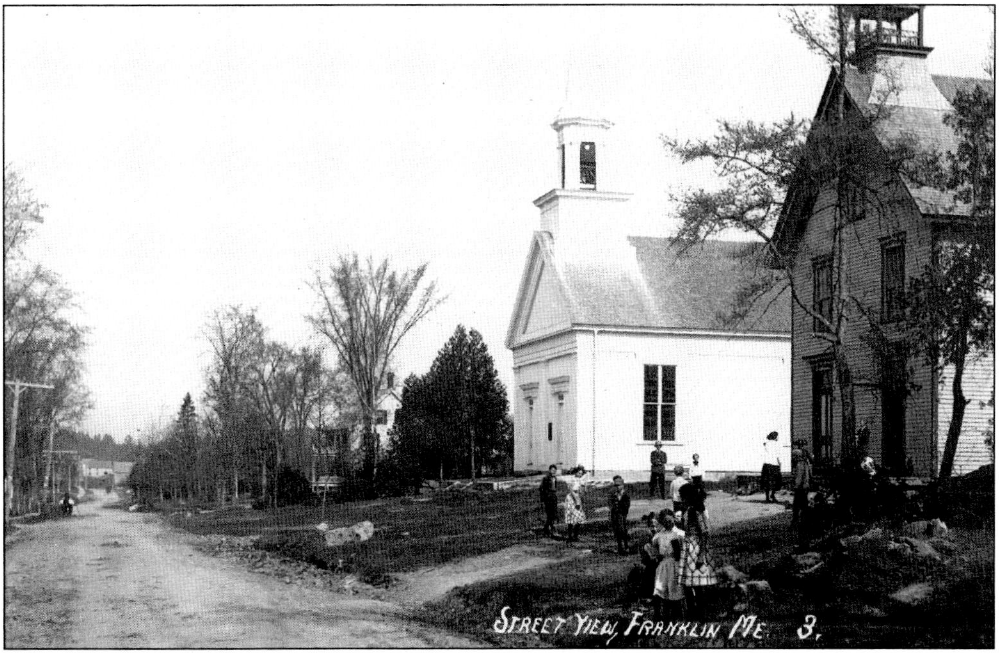

An early street view in Franklin shows children playing in front of the two-story school. Next-door is the Methodist Episcopal Church. Many students left school after grade 8 to work in Franklin's nine lumber mills, two gristmills, tannery, and three granite quarries. And the sea, not far away, beckoned with plenty of work for young men. Franklin has no schools of its own today, and students are bussed to schools in neighboring Sullivan and other towns. (MHPC.)

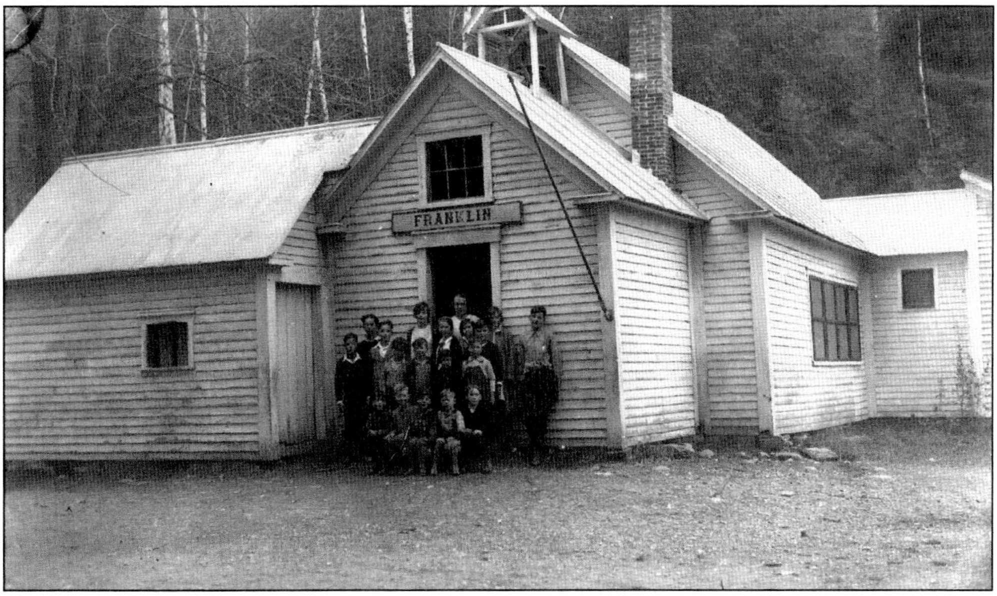

This view of the old Franklin schoolhouse, from around 1915, tells its own story. One bespectacled woman teacher stands watch over her 18 students. Such schools typically were grades kindergarten through eighth. A flagless flagpole protrudes from the front of the tiny school. A bell summoned children to school in the morning and back from recess in forenoon. Note the high chimney, probably connected to a pot-bellied stove. (MHPC.)

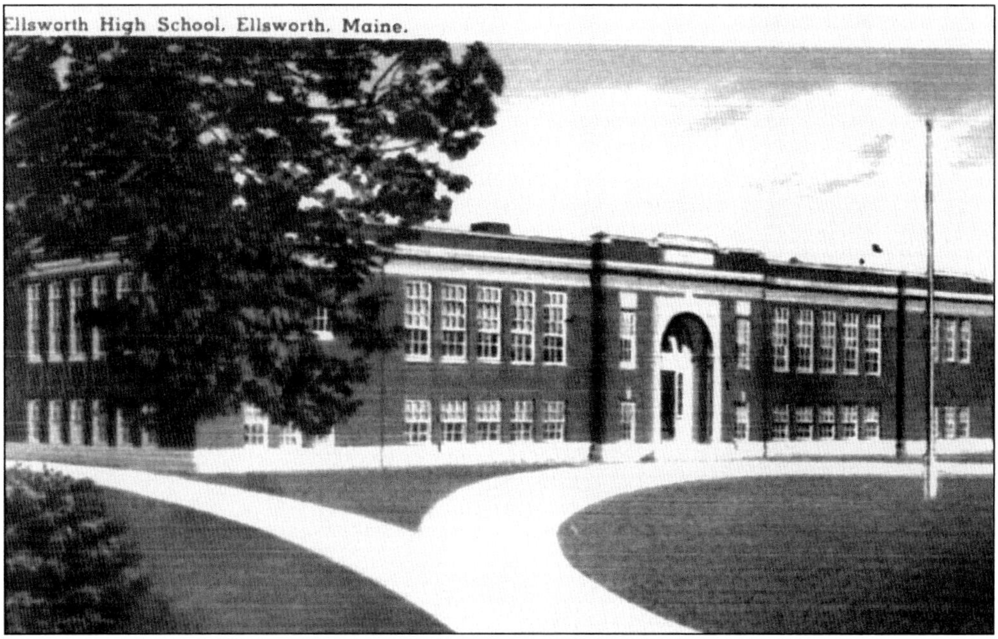

This familiar brick building on State Street served as Ellsworth High School from 1925 to 1951. Over time, the city needed a larger, more modern high school, and on February 10, 1952, the new school overlooking Leonard's Lake was dedicated. This old building was converted to a grammar school and renamed the Bryant E. Moore School after the distinguished Ellsworth High School graduate and West Point general. (RRS.)

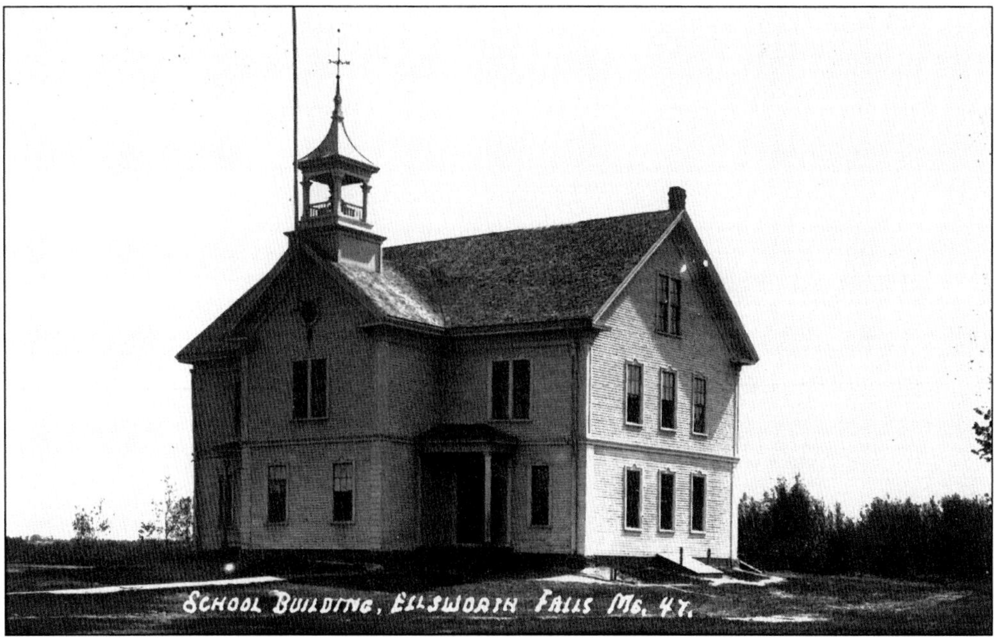

Early Ellsworth schools were spread throughout the area. This two-story building served students' needs in District 17 at Ellsworth Falls. Historian Deale B. Salisbury writes that in the earliest days, children received an education as an activity of the home or church. Teaching stressed two things, Bible study and knowing the laws of the country. (MHPC.)

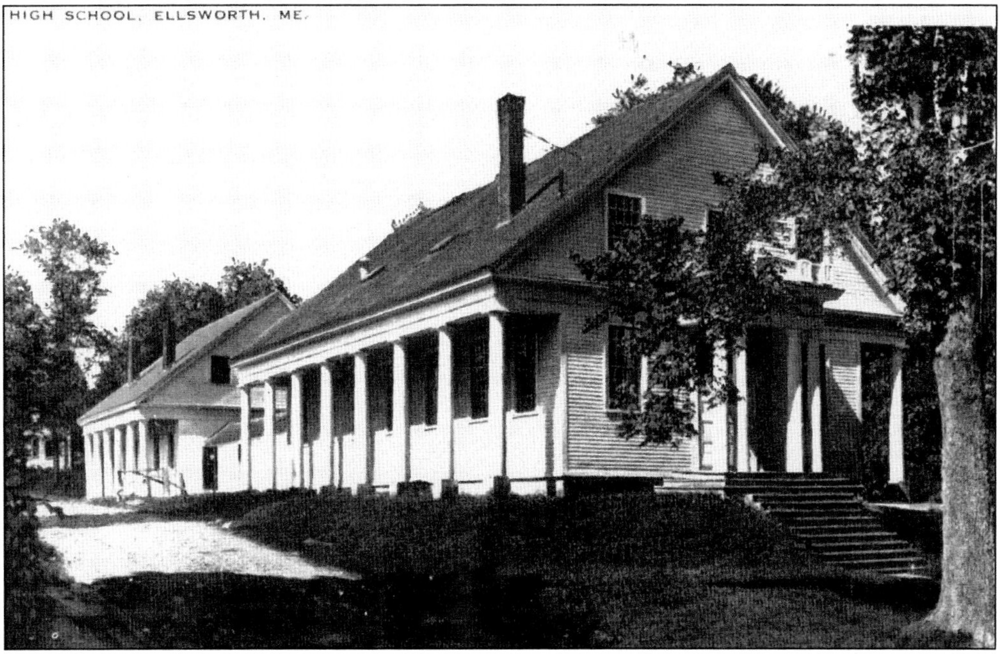

These buildings, which still stand on Bridge Hill, are reminders of Ellsworth's early education. High school students received their education here from 1886 to 1924. Students walked through "Ice House Alley" while passing between the school's two sections. (MHPC.)

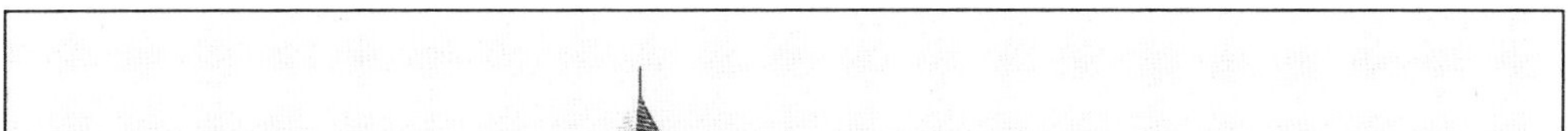

Historian Sanford Phippen well remembers attending the Hancock Corner School. The fifth and sixth grades attended downstairs, seventh and eighth went upstairs. "There was even an outhouse down back," he recalled. It started out as a two-year high school in the 1930s and closed altogether in 1953. Caldwell Diesel and Coastal Moving Company later occupied the building, which still stands just off of Route 1. (RRS.)

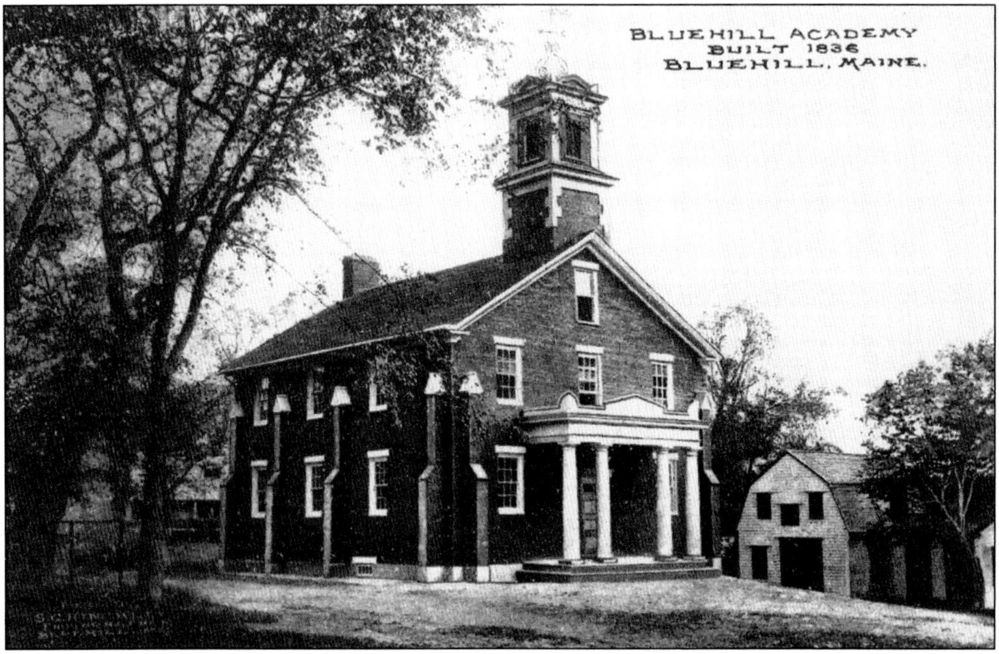

Blue Hill Academy was located in this building from 1833 to 1898, when a new academy building was built on the property of George Stevens. Stevens was a businessman and devout Baptist who bequeathed most of his estate to a board of trustees that incorporated the school in his name. This landmark at 85 Main Street is now the Duffy-Wescott Post of the American Legion. (BHPL.)

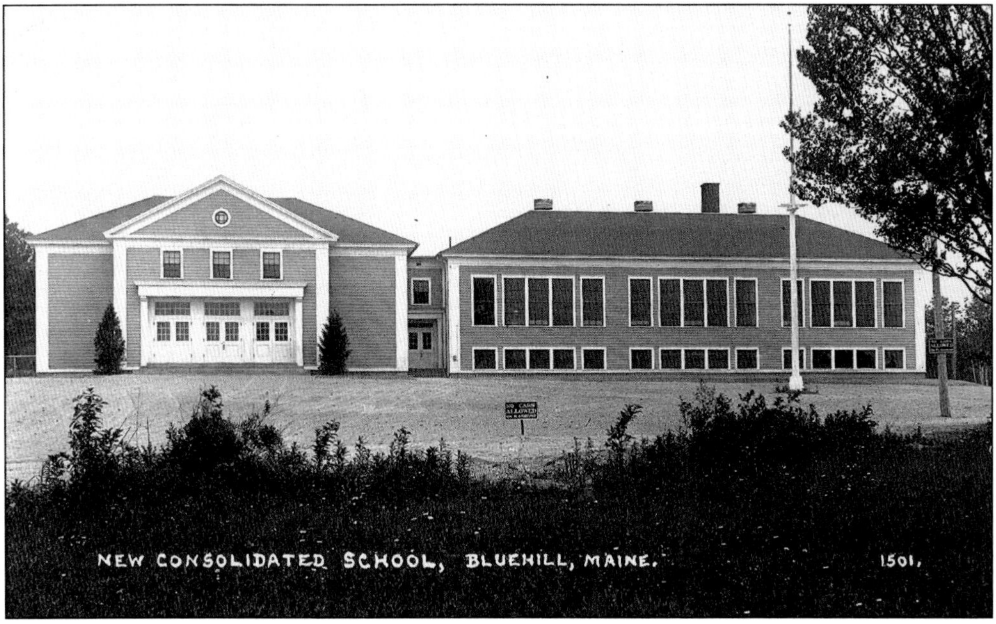

The new consolidated school was a vast improvement over the dark, poorly ventilated classrooms of early Blue Hill. It was bright and well landscaped. And by its opening in the 1940s, the same high standards of education were evident in the quality of its teaching staff. (RRS.)

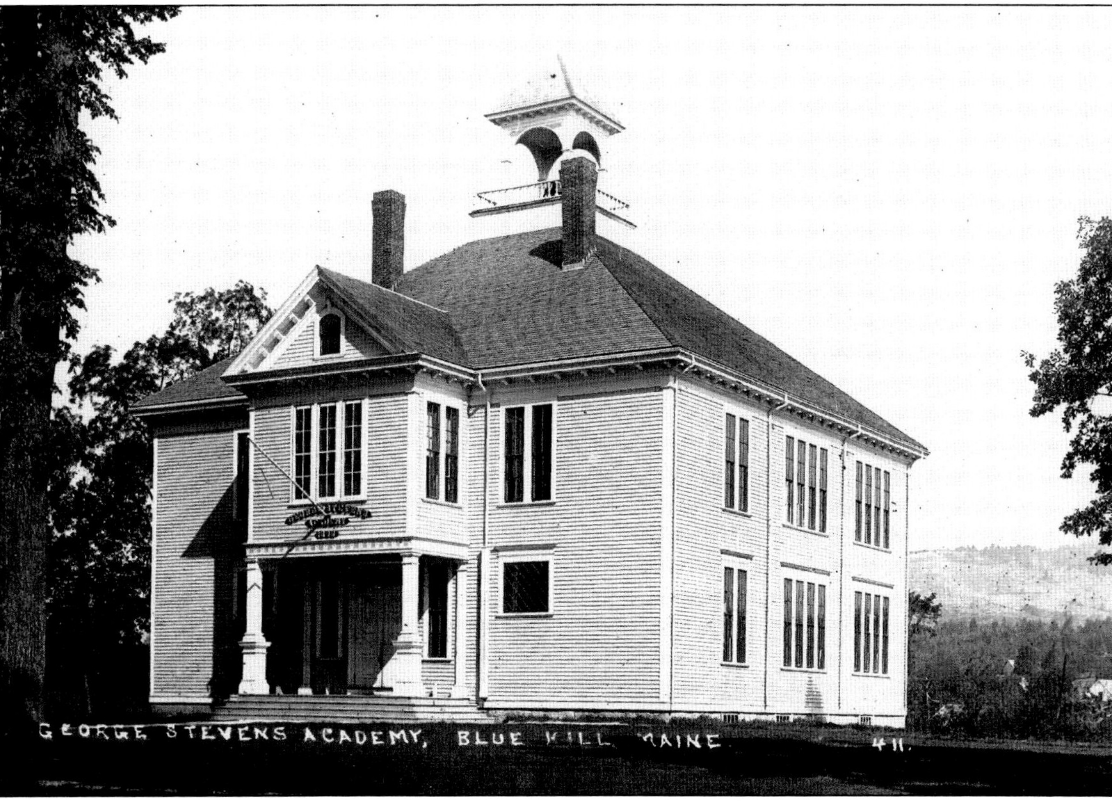

The academy operated from 1803 to 1898, save for the year 1870 when there was a temporary closing. In 1832, the original academy building was sold and moved. A brick building on Main Street replaced the old wooden structure. Blue Hill Academy was helped by the Congregational church and by the Reverend Jonathan Fisher, who became the president of the board of trustees. In 1891, the legislature incorporated the George Stevens Academy. In 1898, the academy opened its doors to students. The old academy cooperated with the new institution. Their boards merged, but it was not until 1943 that the two groups merged and incorporated under the name of Blue Hill-George Stevens Academy. Officially the name of the institution is George Stevens Academy as of 2008, located in expanded quarters at 23 Union Street. (BHPL.)

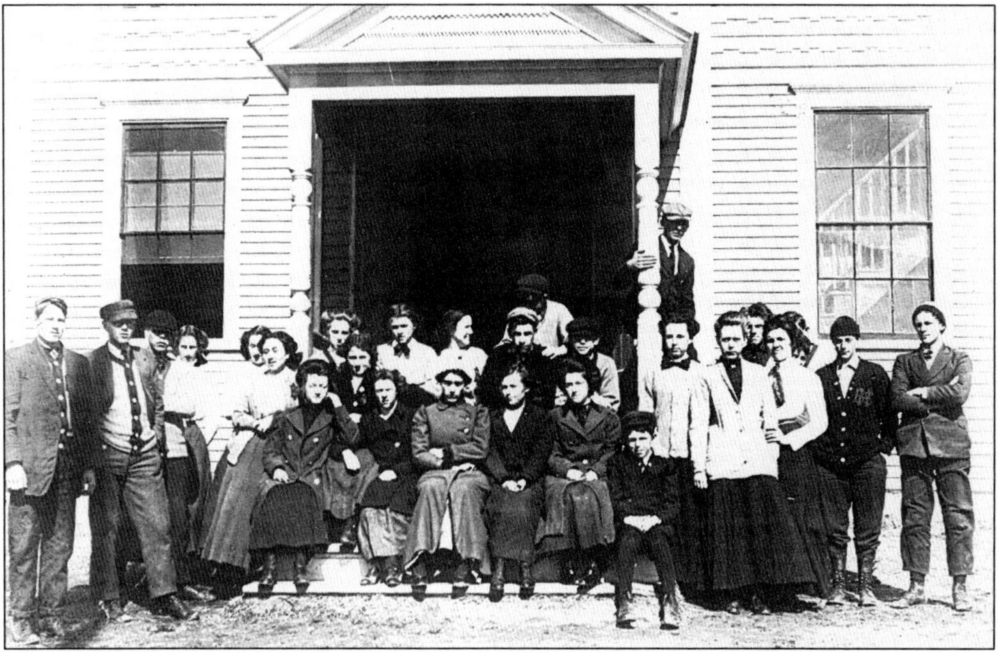

Historian Jane Hooper writes that Brooklin, a small town that covers a large area, had 10 school districts in 1849. By 1876, there were only 344 students and nine school districts. As the town's population and transportation methods changed, the one-room schools were either closed or combined. By 1909, only six schools remained. (RRS.)

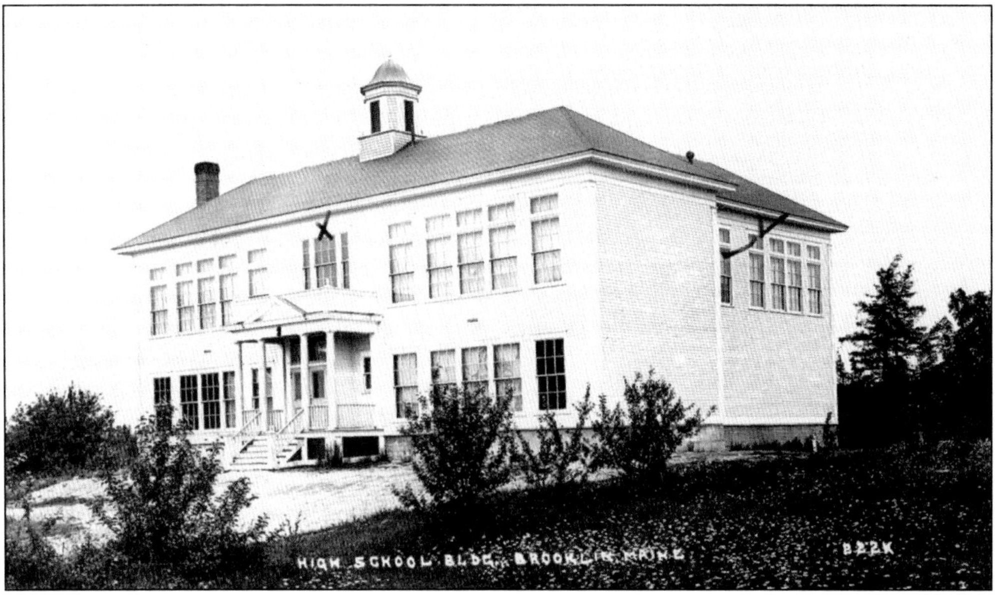

Brooklin's third high school was completed in 1932 on the site of the previous two high schools. Someone marked an *X* over the center upstairs window of the Brooklin High School building. Maybe this was a student who wished to show a friend where his classroom was located. Brooklin has not had a high school since 1969, when this building became a junior high school. Students today attend either George Stevens Academy in Blue Hill or Deer Isle-Stonington High School. (MHPC.)

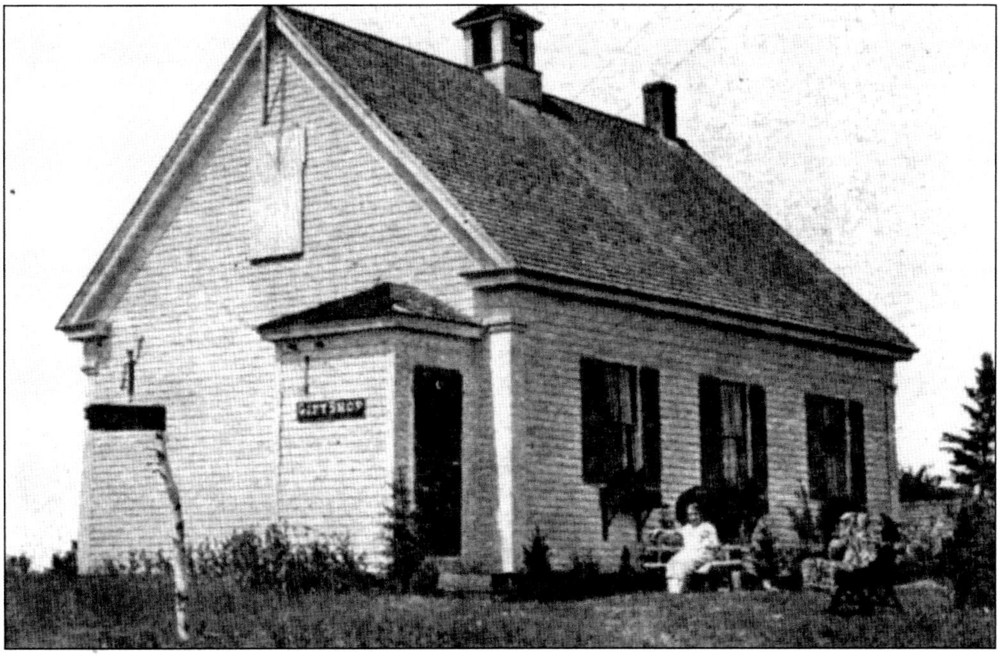

Elementary school No. 5 was located in West Brooklin, across from the Rock Bound Chapel. Students often could not see the blackboard because there was only daylight by which to read. All the windows were on one side and on the back. In 1930, state law specified how lighting should be controlled in a school. After the school closed in the early 1940s, it became the White Schoolhouse Gift Shop. It is now a private residence. (MHPC.)

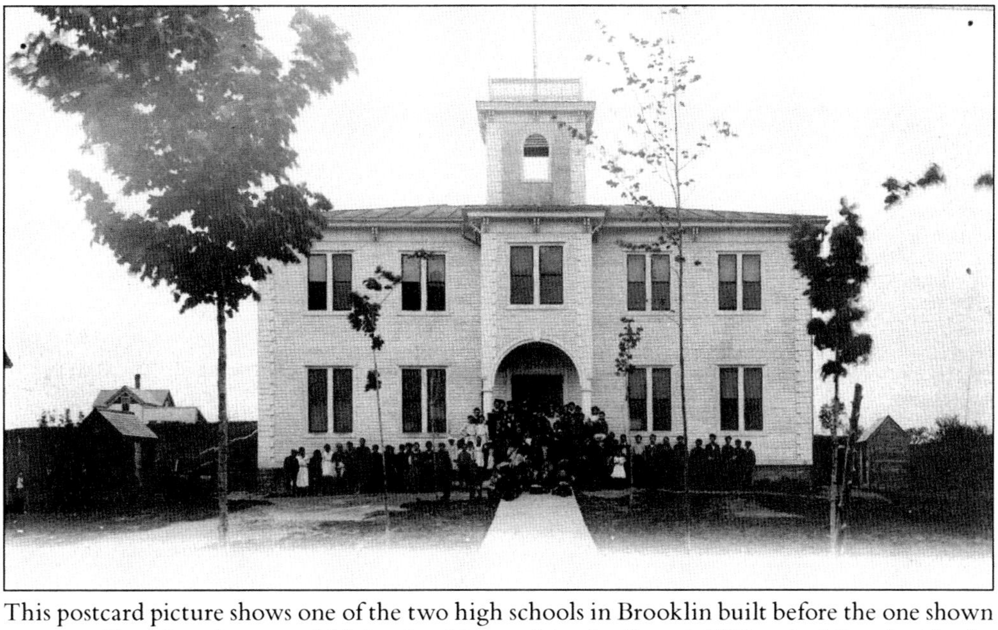

This postcard picture shows one of the two high schools in Brooklin built before the one shown on page 40. After the second high school burned in the fire of 1930, a building beside the Baptist church in Brooklin Center was used as a temporary school. In 1850, school expenditures in the Brooklin town budget were $400; by 1950, school expenses increased to $1,500. In 1850, the average teacher's weekly salary was $2; in 1949, it was $44. (MHPC.)

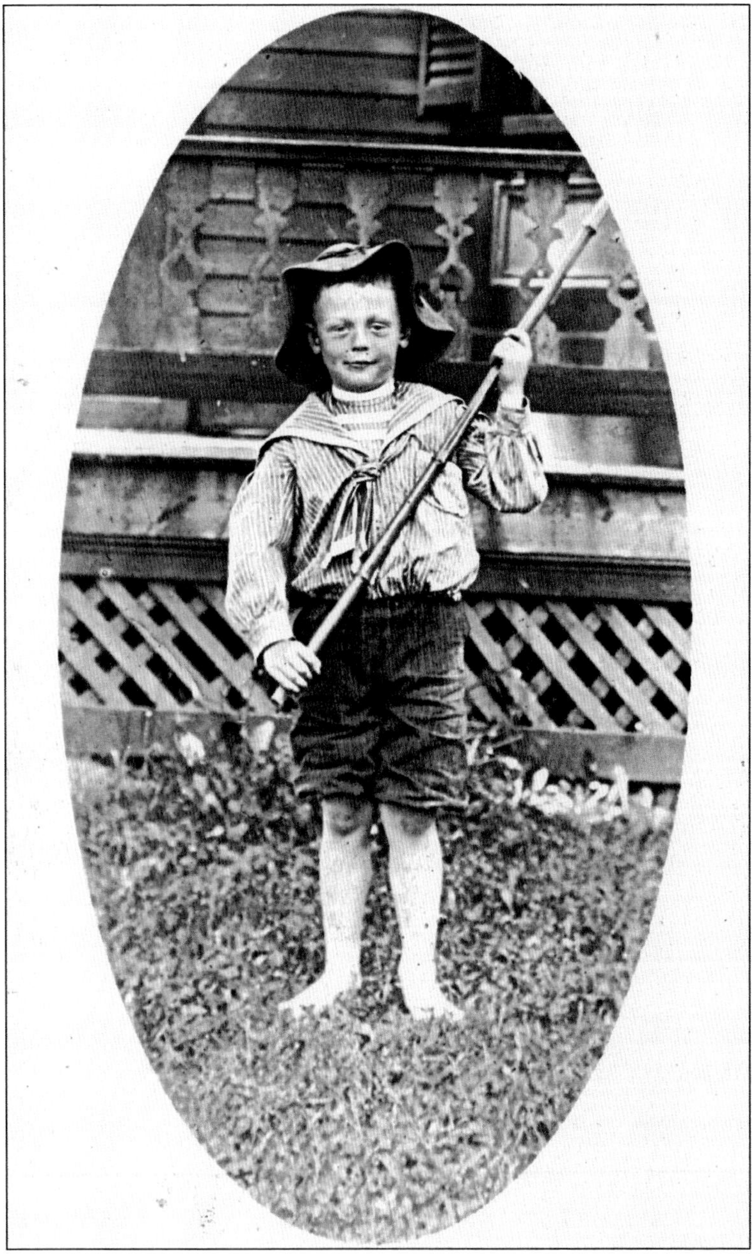

The name of this barefoot boy may be less important than his mischievous smile and relaxed demeanor. A Blue Hill postcard photographer took his photograph for a postcard, apparently around 1910. Has school just let out for the summer? Or maybe he is just happy to be playing soldier with his father's fishing rod. Historian Rufus Candage, in a 1905 essay republished in 2000 by the Blue Hill Historical Society, relates some of his 19th-century experiences at the old schoolhouse on the road to Parker Point. Pupils ranging in age from 4 to 20 shivered in the winter as cold winds blew through the building. Teacher Moses Pillsbury was not amused by a practical joke involving a dead crow being thrown down the chimney and into the schoolhouse stove. Later a young male student set fire to the school with the desired result being the building of a new school with better insulation and fewer winter chills. (BHPL.)

Four

AND THE LIVING WAS EASY

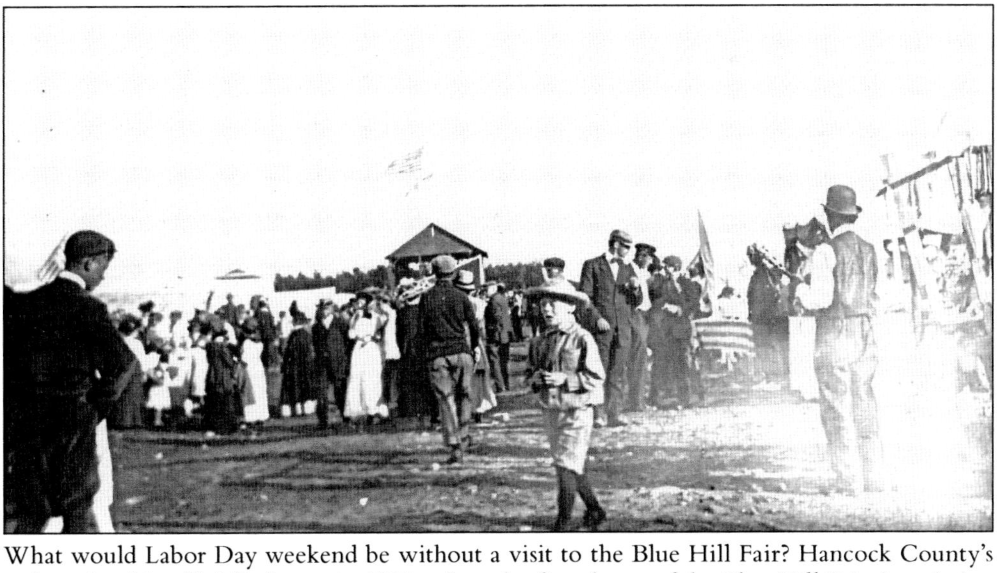

What would Labor Day weekend be without a visit to the Blue Hill Fair? Hancock County's only major fair officially began in 1891, when the first shares of the Blue Hill Fair Association were sold. The event moved to the fairgrounds in 1892 and with the exception of the war year 1944, has met there every year since. The old red wooden grandstand is still being used (see page 45). (BHPL.)

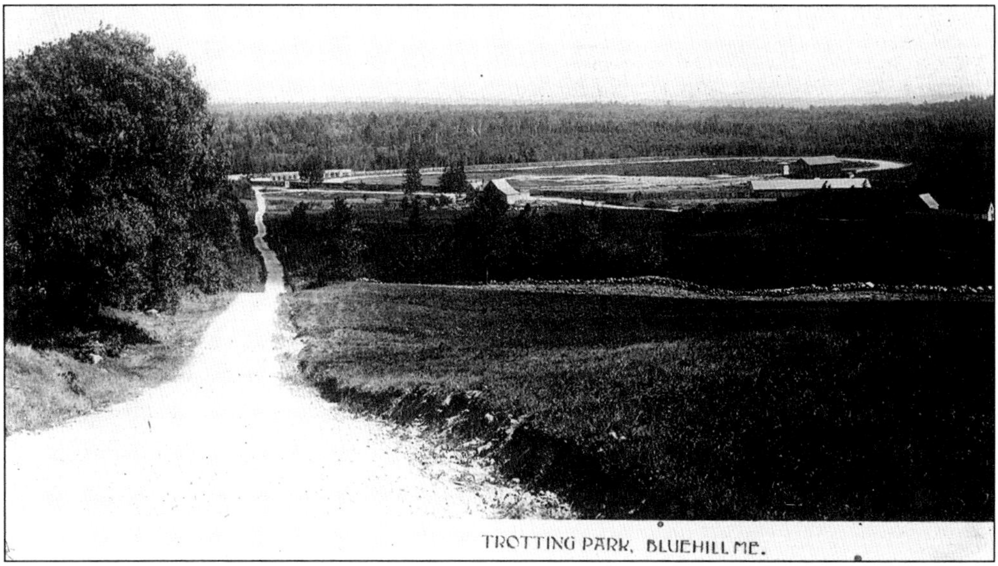

Blue Hill's Trotting Park, seen in this old postcard picture, served the growing horse racing enthusiasts in Hancock County in the early 20th century. Located at the fairgrounds, this property had a racing oval and stables. Trotting horses gave way to harness racing later in the century. Every summer, Blue Hill, Bangor, Skowhegan, and other Maine fairgrounds host harness racing, which is attended by devoted fans. Some just watch, but many more bet on the horses. (BHPL.)

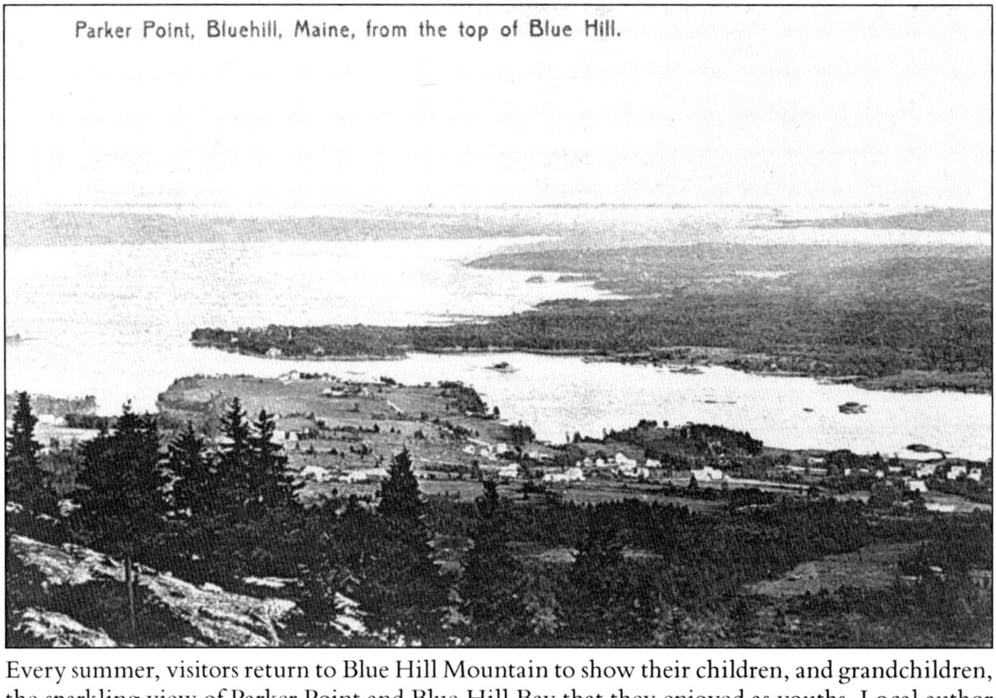

Every summer, visitors return to Blue Hill Mountain to show their children, and grandchildren, the sparkling view of Parker Point and Blue Hill Bay that they enjoyed as youths. Local author Mary Ellen Chase wrote of the mountain in her book *A Goodly Heritage*, "northward . . . at its extreme head [of the bay] rises the great hill, a landmark to mariners past and present and a suggestion to more travelled eyes of Vesuvius beyond the Bay of Naples." (BPL.)

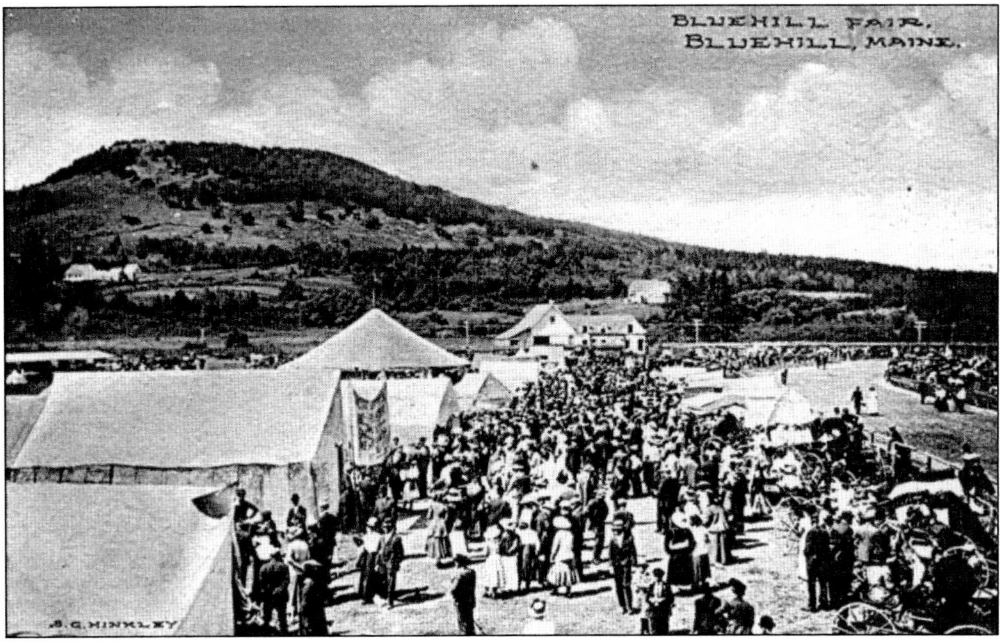

The origins of the Blue Hill Fair can be traced back as early as 1878, the year a Farmer's Club, first met at Tucker's Field in Blue Hill Village. But today's mixture of entertainment and agriculture was born in 1891, when the first shares of the Blue Hill Fair Association were sold. The event moved to the fairgrounds the following year. (BHPL.)

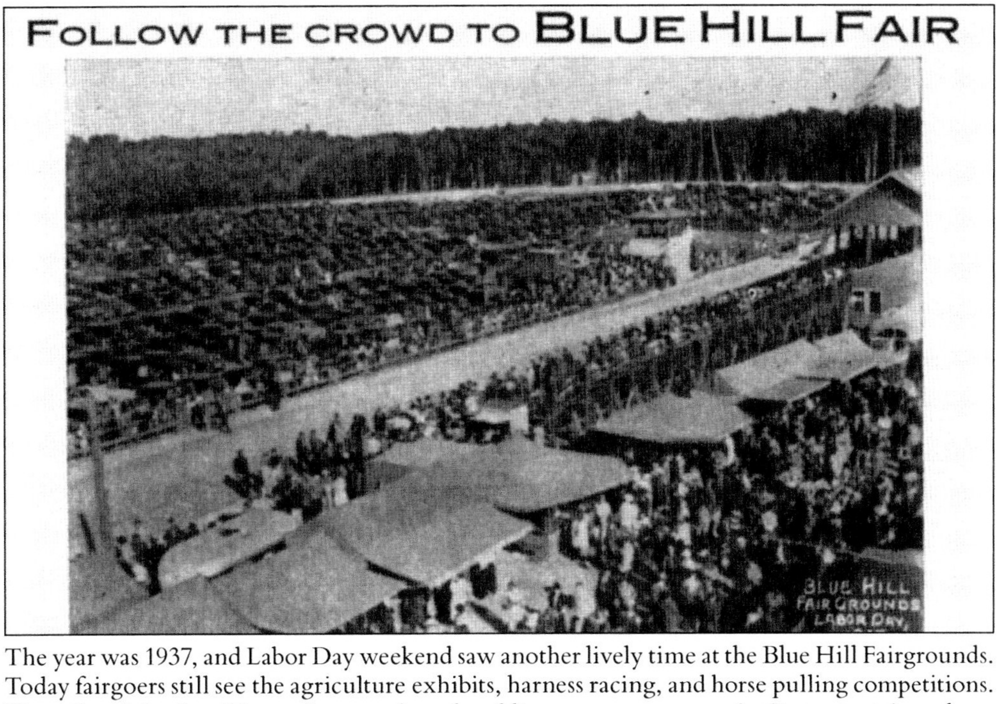

The year was 1937, and Labor Day weekend saw another lively time at the Blue Hill Fairgrounds. Today fairgoers still see the agriculture exhibits, harness racing, and horse pulling competitions. They also sit in the old wooden grandstand and listen to country music. Past entertainers have included Diamond Rio, Colin Raye, B. J. Thomas, and a rising star named Faith Hill, who performed in 1995. (BHPL.)

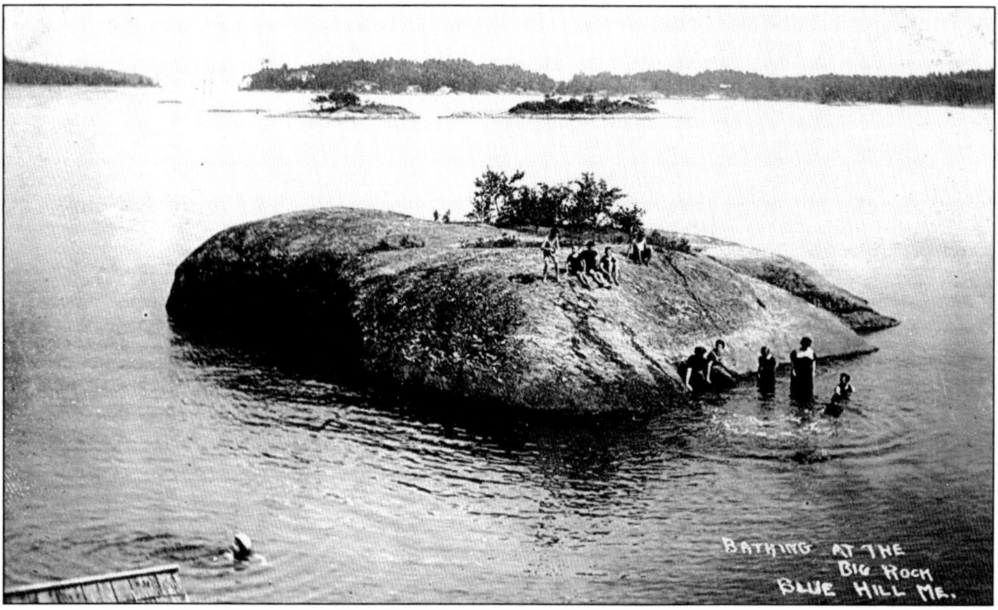

Summertime bathers have been lured to the Big Rock in Blue Hill Bay, a stone's throw from the village, for as long as people have lived in Blue Hill. This view, from around 1915, captures swimmers in long woolen suits enjoying what appear to be warm waters and a smooth ocean bottom. Local historian and author Carl C. Osgood recalls another picture: the bay's rocky, muddy bottom that is to be treated with extreme caution. (BHPL.)

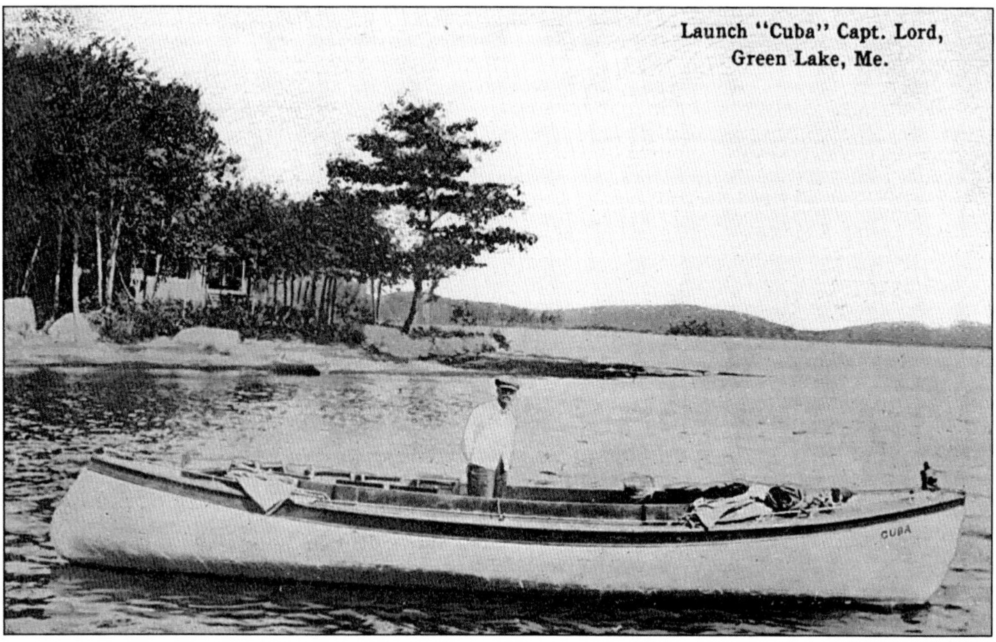

Green Lake in the summer of 1927 was filled with boats of all shapes and sizes. A man identified only as Captain Lord piloted a launch named *Cuba*. Paying passengers traveled across the Ellsworth lake to neighbors' camps and to railroad stations at Jenkins and Nicolin Beaches (see pages 14 and 15). The steamer *Senator* operated here in the 1890s and had at least one famous customer, "Buffalo Bill" Cote, who was en route to a circus performance in Ellsworth. (RRS.)

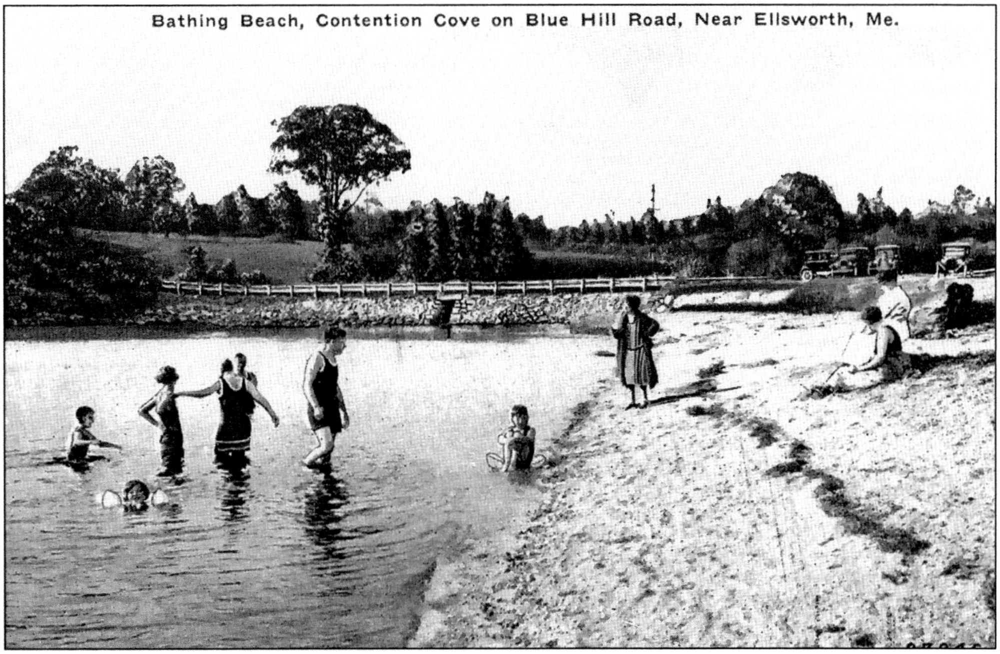

The bathing beach on Route 172, also known as the Blue Hill Road, attracted swimmers on a warm day in the 1920s. It is hard to believe, but that is the narrow road shown in the background, with a long wooden guardrail and stone bridge. Bathers were more discreetly attired at that time than many are today. Contention Cove, an inlet of the Union River Bay, is visible in places from today's improved highway. (RRS.)

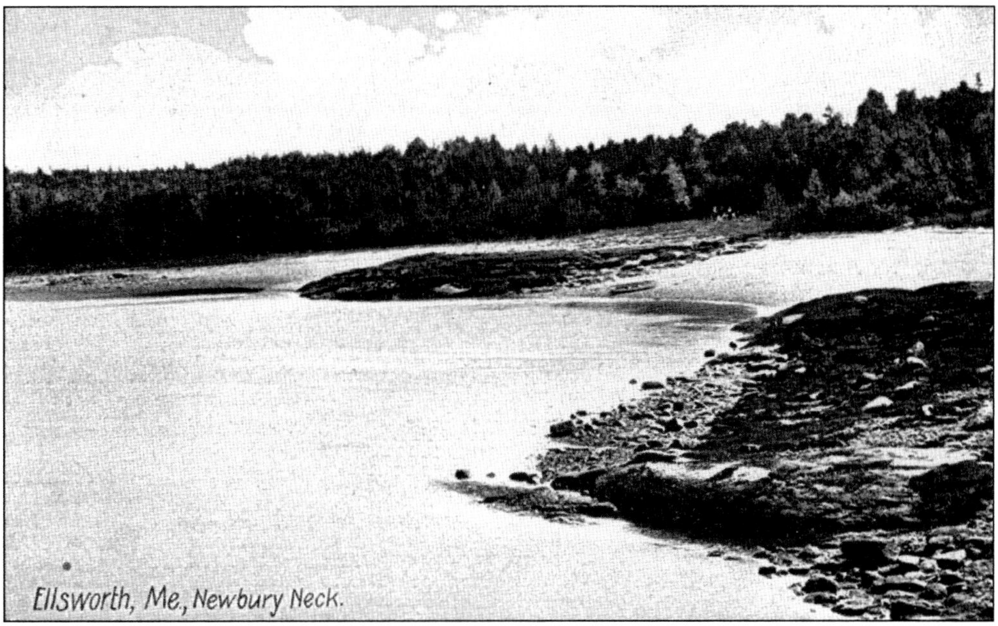

Long and narrow, Newbury Neck hangs like an appendage in the Union River Bay. Located east of East Blue Hill, near the village of Surry, the "Neck" today is a private assemblage of old family homes and newer dwellings purchased or built by people wanting a more relaxed lifestyle. A postcard labeling error (bottom left) locates Newbury Neck in Ellsworth. (RRS.)

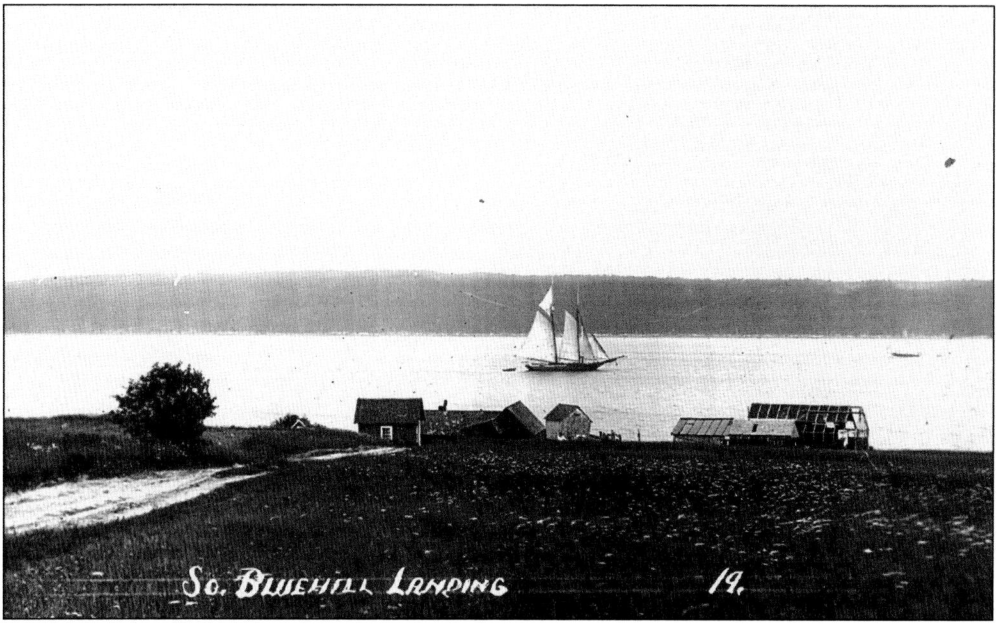

South Blue Hill's boat landing, about 1913, was a tranquil study for a postcard photographer. Long Island stretches out in the distance, and a boat sails in what locals called the "Neck." A factory was located near the wharf, where steamers arrived several times a week in the warmer months, coming across the bay from Rockland and other towns. (BPL.)

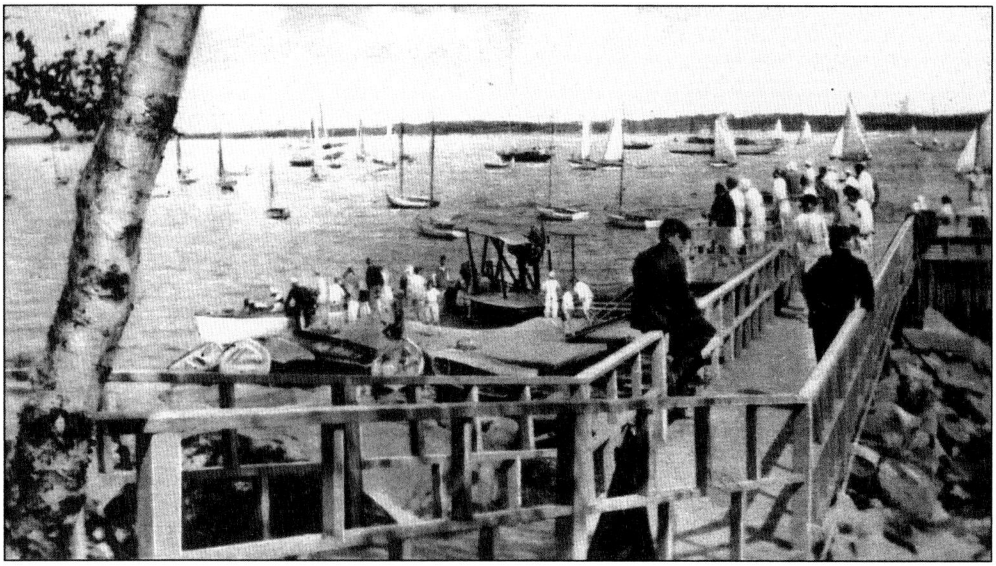

The Kollegewidgwok Yacht Club has taught generations of youth in the Blue Hill Peninsula how to sail. But how should one pronounce the tongue-twister? Henry Becton Jr., the club's commodore, writes on its Web site, "Say 'college,' then 'widge' then 'walk,' all as one smooth mouthful, without accenting any one syllable. There are dissenters, even among members, who say 'college-ah-widge-ah-walk,' but as the years go by the ahs and uhs are getting scarcer." (RRS.)

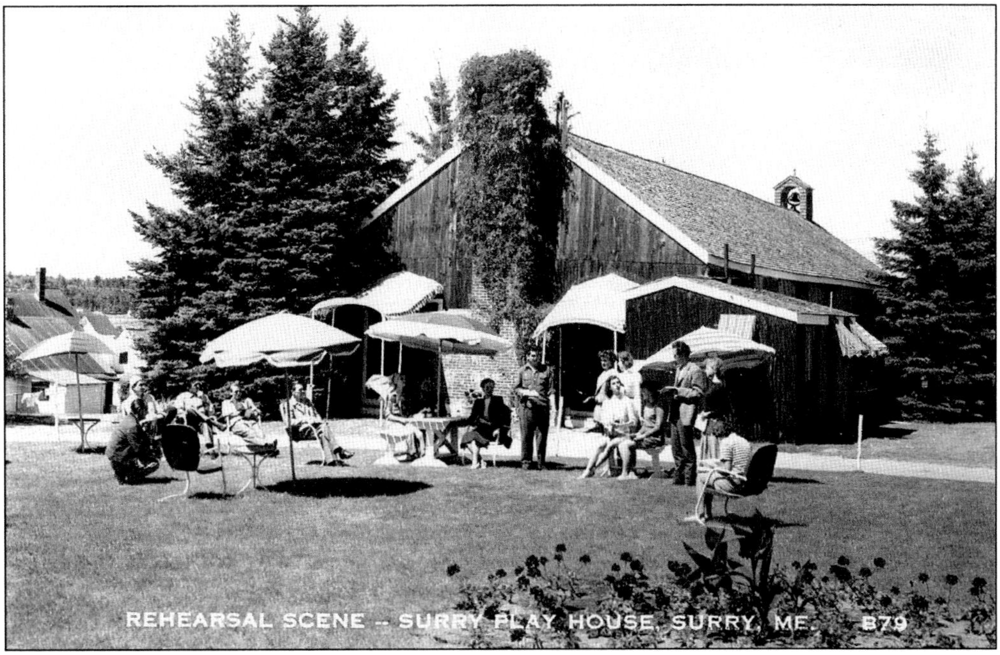

Located in a barn near Contention Cove, five miles from Ellsworth, the Surry Playhouse headlined nationally known actors and local talent from the 1920s to the early 1950s. Joseph Cotton and Henry Fonda acted there, along with perennial favorite Edward Everett Horton. Actor Shepherd Strudwick managed the playhouse for many years. In 1972, actor-director Bill Raiten founded the New Surry Theatre and Acting School in Blue Hill. (RRS.)

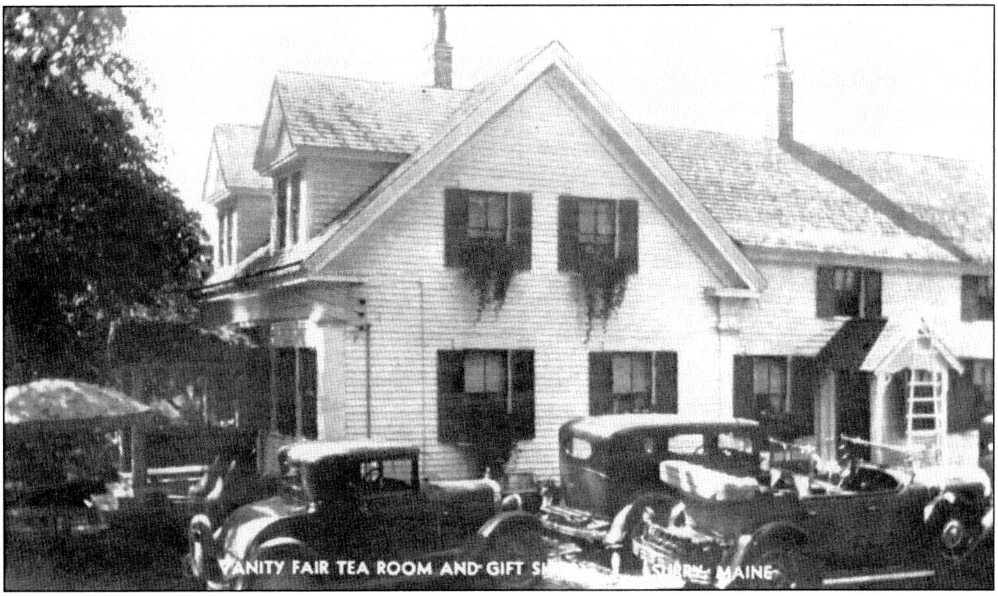

The Vanity Fair Tea Room and Gift Shop, shown here around 1938, catered to patrons of the Surry Playhouse. Managed by a Baltimore owner, the tearoom served Southern cuisine and its season, June 15 to September 15, coincided with the playhouse's. Just as theatergoers have met famous actors in the Shanty coffee shop next to Lakewood Theatre in Madison, the same no doubt happened at the Vanity Fair. (BPL.)

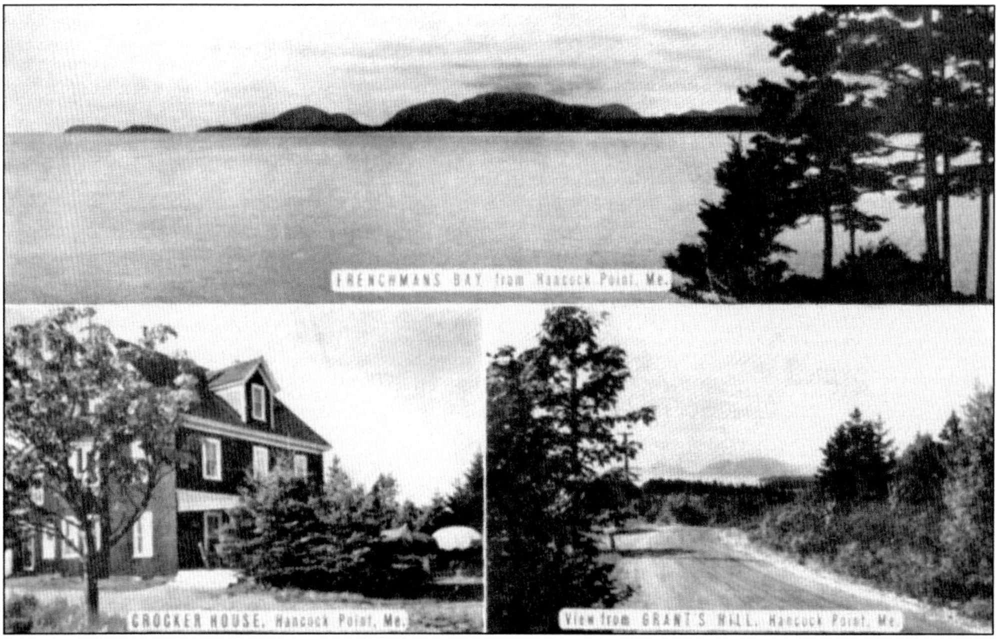

The view from Hancock Point, located on a peninsula southeast of Ellsworth, has changed little in the 60 or more years since this postcard was printed for guests of the Crocker House. Now called the Crocker House Country Inn, the landmark was built in 1884 and restored in 1986. Guests still bicycle around the "Point" to savor the sweeping panorama of Frenchman's Bay and Cadillac Mountain. (RRS.)

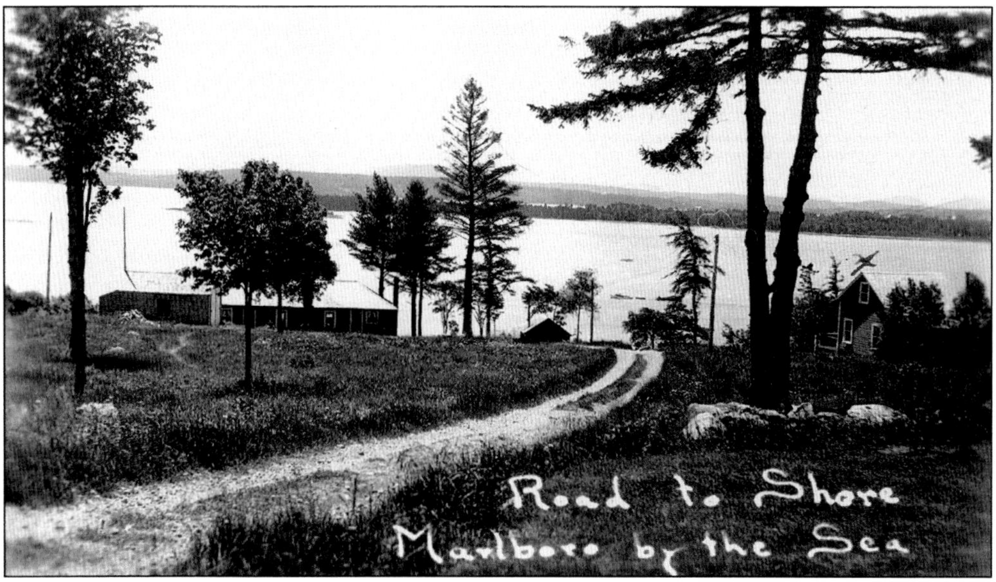

Marlboro by the Sea split after a spat with Hancock in 1933 and became a part of Lamoine, where it has remained ever since. This postcard, with an *X* at the right pointing out a seaside cottage, complete with a view of Mount Desert Island, was mailed on August 29, 1939. A woman named Ethel scribbled this note to a friend: "We have had some nice weather and have had some wonderful drives. Am feeling as good as new. Don't care much for the fog." (RRS.)

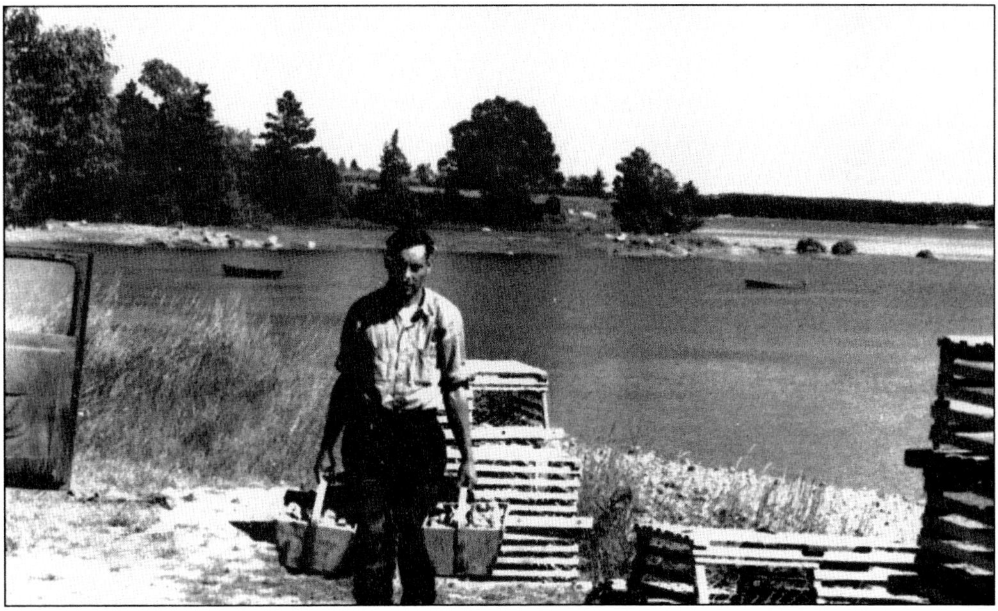

No book about Down East coastal Maine would be complete without at least one picture of a hard-working fisherman who supplied restaurants and homes with fine seafood. This unnamed man, seen around 1948, is shown with the "landing" in East Sullivan as a backdrop. He appears to be carrying hods full of clams, and of course, the wooden lobster traps always add atmosphere to any Maine photograph. (RRS.)

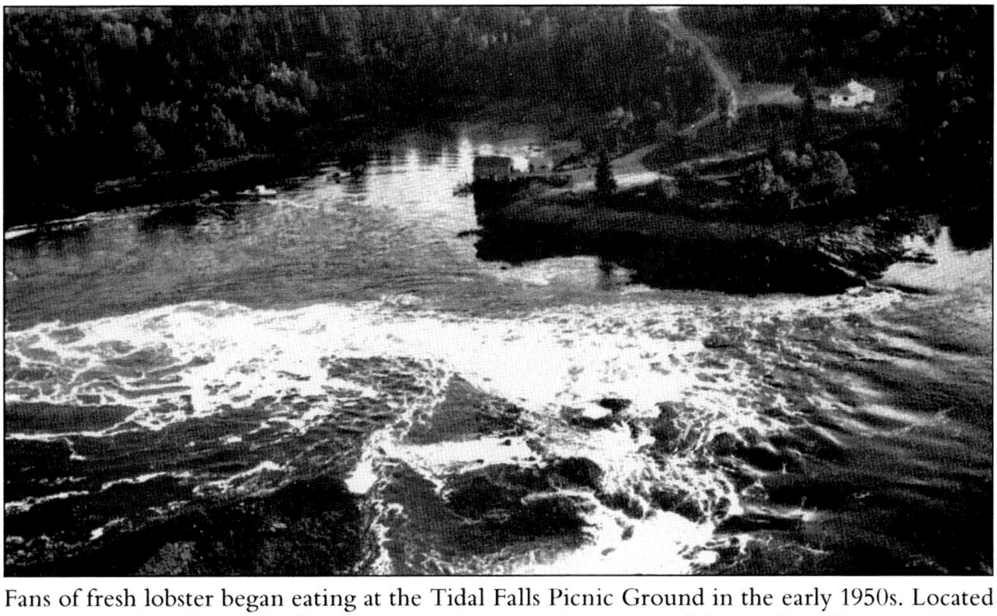

Fans of fresh lobster began eating at the Tidal Falls Picnic Ground in the early 1950s. Located near Route 1 in Hancock, families enjoy the sweeping views of the rushing Taunton River. The property is now owned and operated by the Frenchman Bay Conservancy, which donates all meal proceeds to support the conservancy's conservation of distinctive landscapes and natural resources of the Frenchman Bay and Union River watersheds. (RRS.)

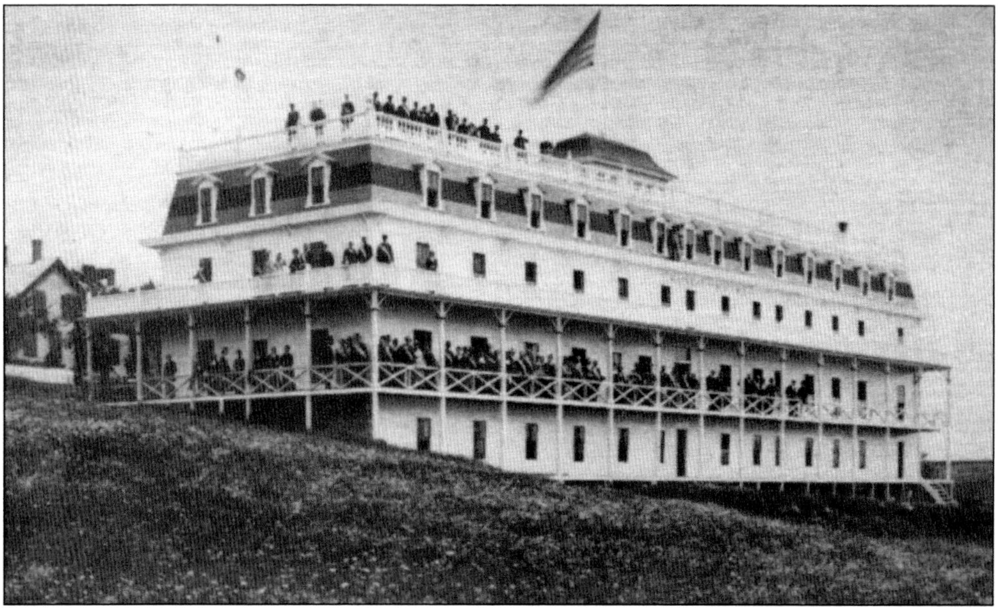

Summer visitors savored the salt air and the 650 feet of piazzas of the Waukeag House, located in Sullivan Harbor. Historian Connee Jellison writes that it was once described as "a fine summer hotel, containing 60 rooms and furnished in good style." It was renovated in 1882 and had a series of owners before being bought by the Dunbar family. It was torn down in 1895, leaving a void for visitors who preferred large seaside inns. (BPL.)

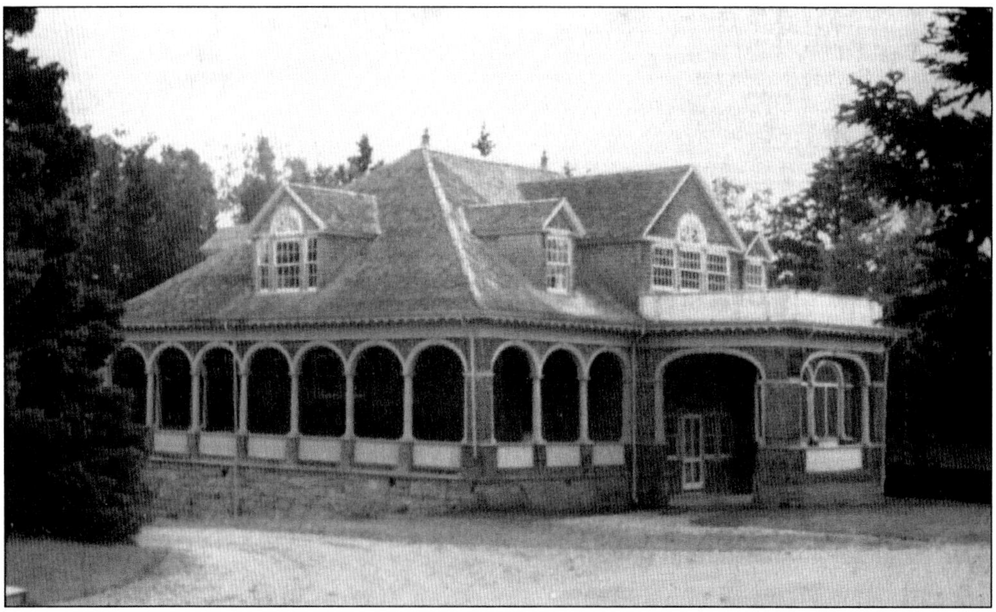

The shingled Sorrento Library, shown here around 1948, is the town's principal landmark. When the neoclassical building opened a century ago, the *Bar Harbor Record* reported, "Of course there are alcoves for books in every conceivable place, both below and in the galleries. The inside finishing is of native wood in natural colors with trimmings of ivory white." Summer residents, many from Bangor, have enjoyed leisurely afternoons at the library. (RRS.)

"About 1½ miles from the harbor there rises to the north a hill which is 950 feet above high water mark," wrote Parson Jonathan Fisher, who settled in Blue Hill in 1796. "The ascent to the rocky summit is quite steep and from the top one is given 'a delightful prospect' of the surrounding land and sea, Mt. Desert Island, Penobscot Bay, the Camden Hills." Cars parked along the Mountain Road on a summer day attest to the continued popularity of the Blue Hill Mountain hike. (BHPL.)

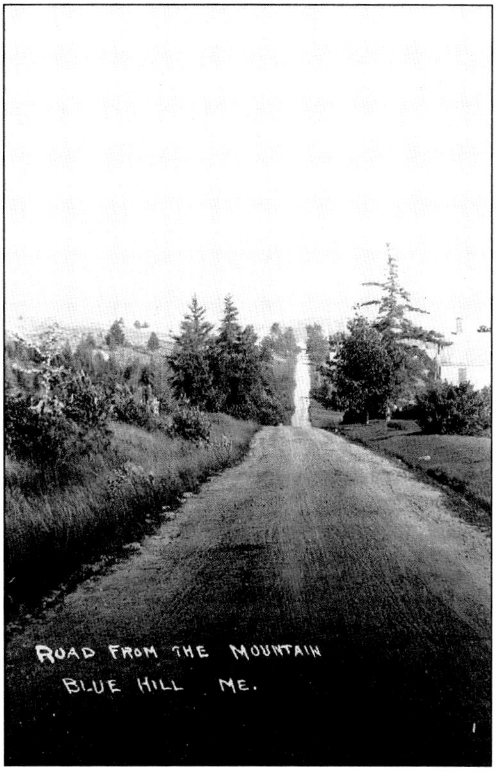

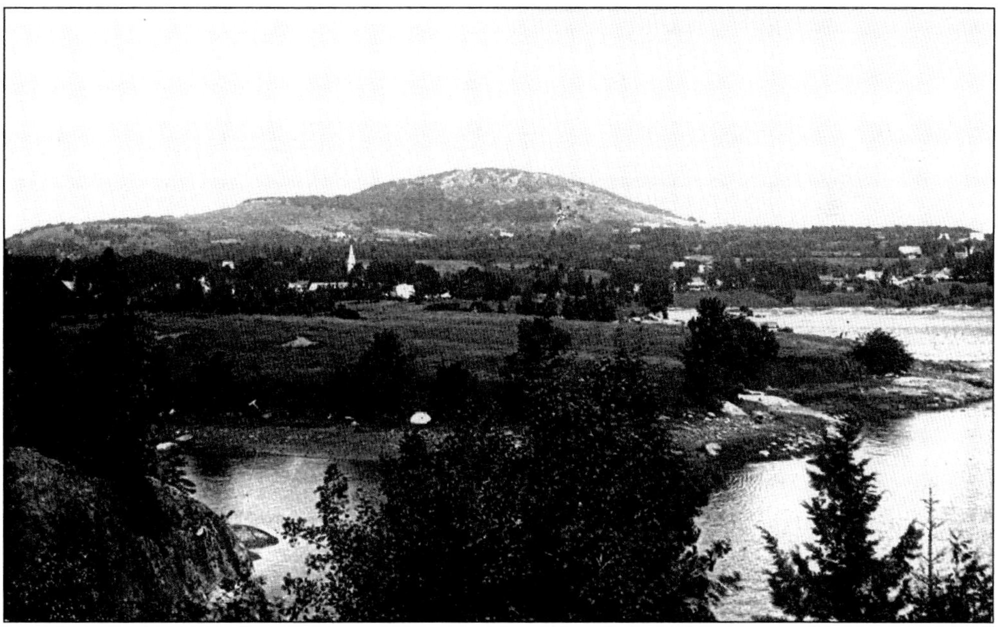

Fitz Hugh Lane immortalized Blue Hill Mountain in his oil on canvas painting in the mid-1850s. This summer postcard view was taken a half-century later but is remarkably similar. The major differences are the church steeple and abundance of houses in the later view missing from Lane's work. Lane captured a tranquil scene, with a horse grazing at the left, a wooden shed in the foreground, and sailing vessels in the harbor. (BPL.)

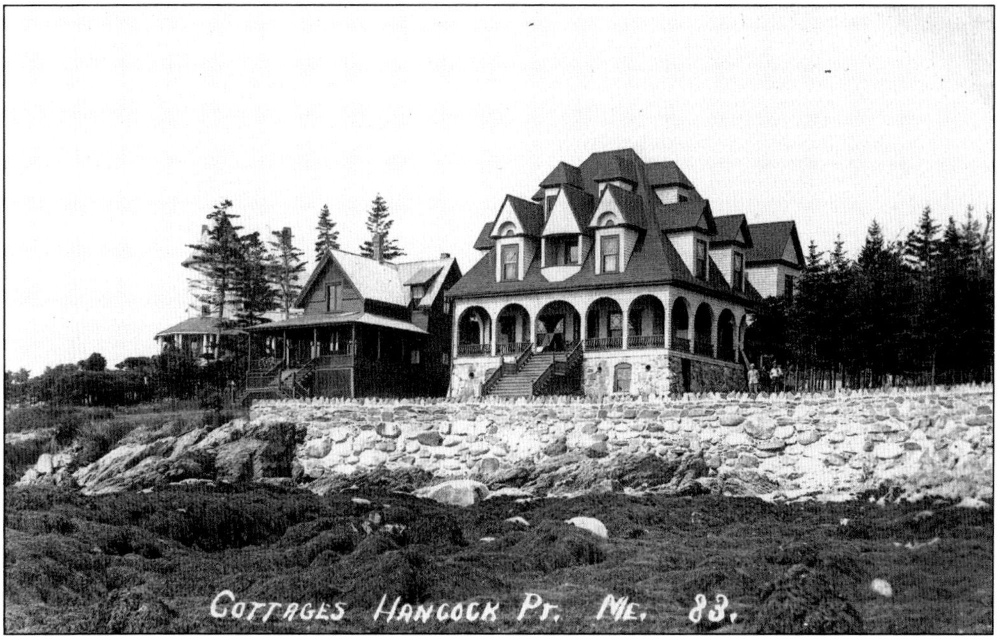

Two handsome Hancock Point cottages made a worthy subject for a postcard view in the 1920s. One of the so-called Swan cottages sits on the rocks at the left, and at right is the large building known as Bellview. Bellview was built as a summer tutoring school for Princeton University students. It replaced the old wooden Maxwell cottage (see page 105). (MHPC.)

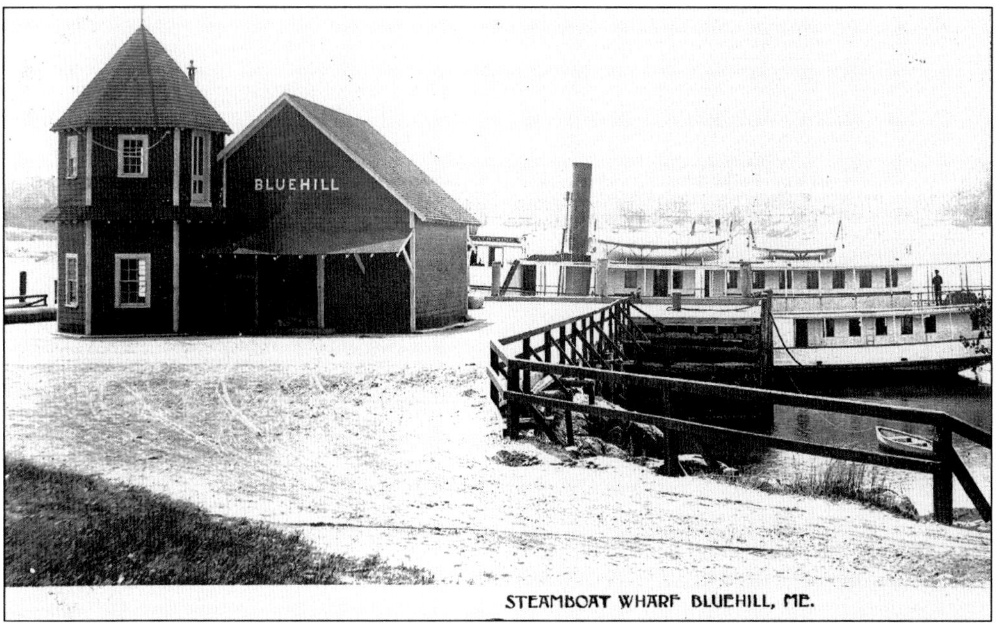

A sure sign of summer was the arrival of the *Boothbay* and other steamers at Blue Hill's steamboat wharf. It was only a short walk or carriage ride into town for the many tourists and summer residents who steamed across Penobscot Bay on the boats. With the demise of Blue Hill's steam era, the *Boothbay* later saw service in 1939 in New York, where it ferried tourists to the Statue of Liberty. (BHPL.)

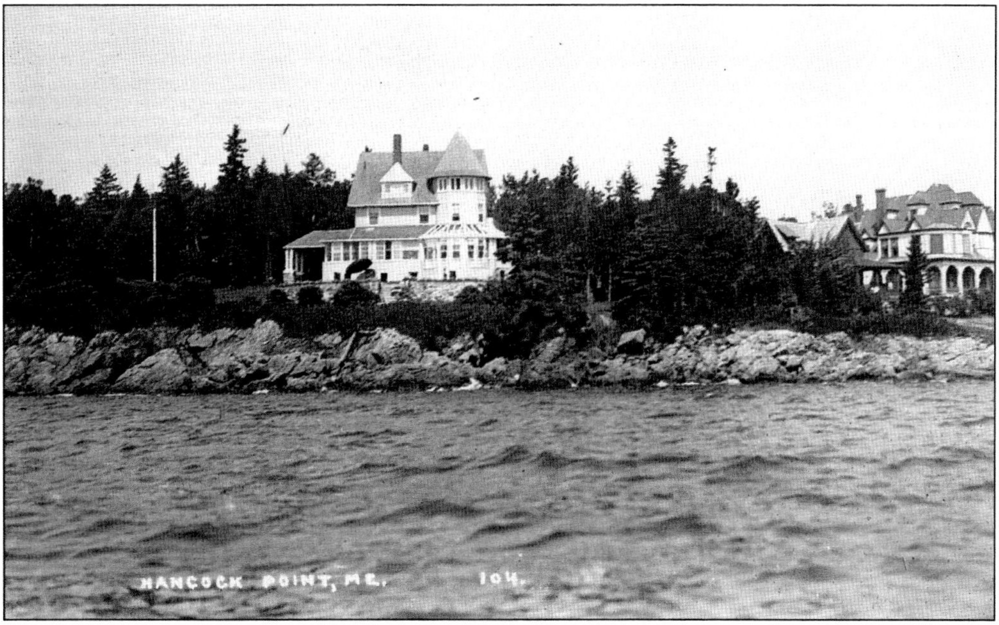

Another view shows the Bellview school at the far right and a large cottage at the left. Bellview was built in 1923 and 1924 and had a slate roof, stonework, leaded windows, and English country manor appearance. With its tennis court and social life, it became an instant showplace at Hancock Point. The Robinson cottage was adjacent to Bellview. (BPL.)

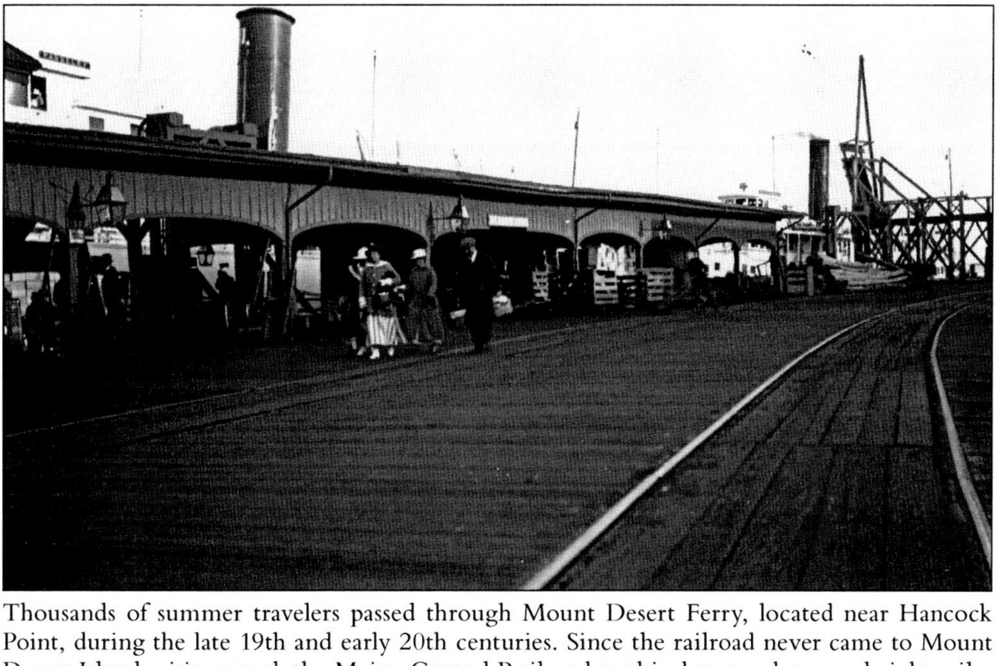

Thousands of summer travelers passed through Mount Desert Ferry, located near Hancock Point, during the late 19th and early 20th centuries. Since the railroad never came to Mount Desert Island, visitors took the Maine Central Railroad to this depot and steamed eight miles across Frenchman's Bay to Bar Harbor. Note the high funnels of the steam ferries docked behind the railroad terminal. (RRS.)

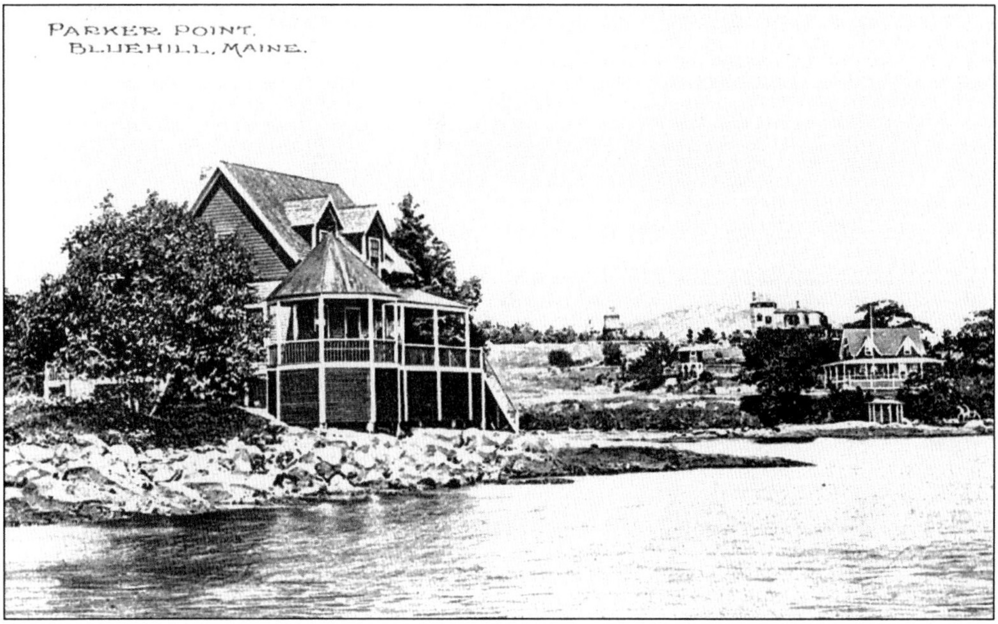

The population of Parker Point, an upper-crust, generations-old Blue Hill summer colony, swells each year as "the summer people" reopen sturdy old family cottages and enjoy again the comforts of coastal life. Writes Esther E. Wood, "Between the first-generation summer people and the natives there was little affection. Only with the passing of the decades has there developed a mutual dependence and affection." (BHPL.)

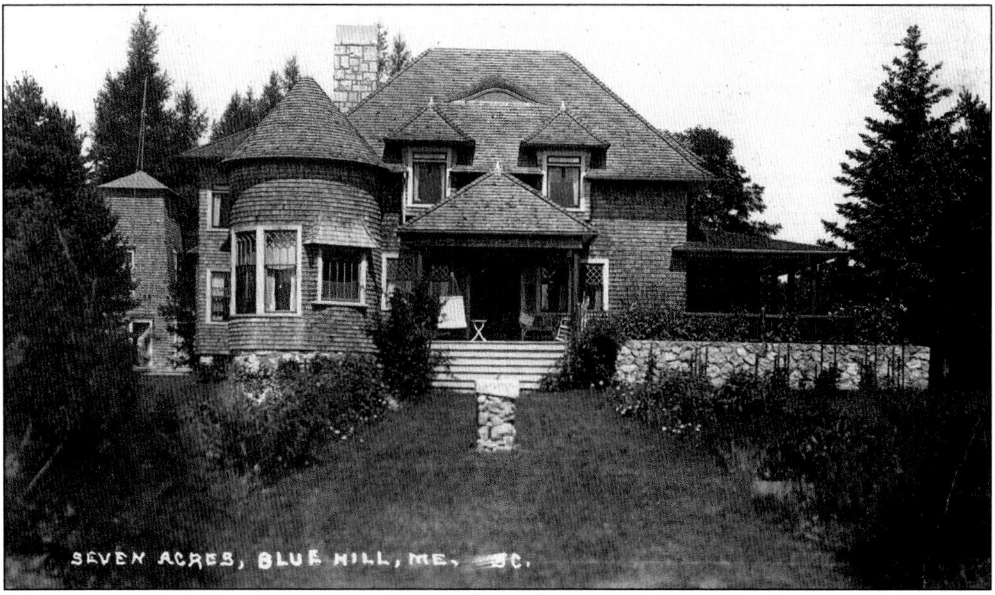

Seven Acres was one of the better-known Blue Hill summer cottages. As seen here about 1915, the 1895 cottage was shingled, with a large stone chimney and a round room to the left of the side porch. Of the early summer residents originally branded as "rusticators," historian Esther E. Wood writes, "[In later years] the summer people have sponsored Blue Hill's good causes and brought great music to town. Today, their golf carts roll where once rolled hay carts and their pleasure craft ride at anchor where schooners and steamboats anchored." (MHPC.)

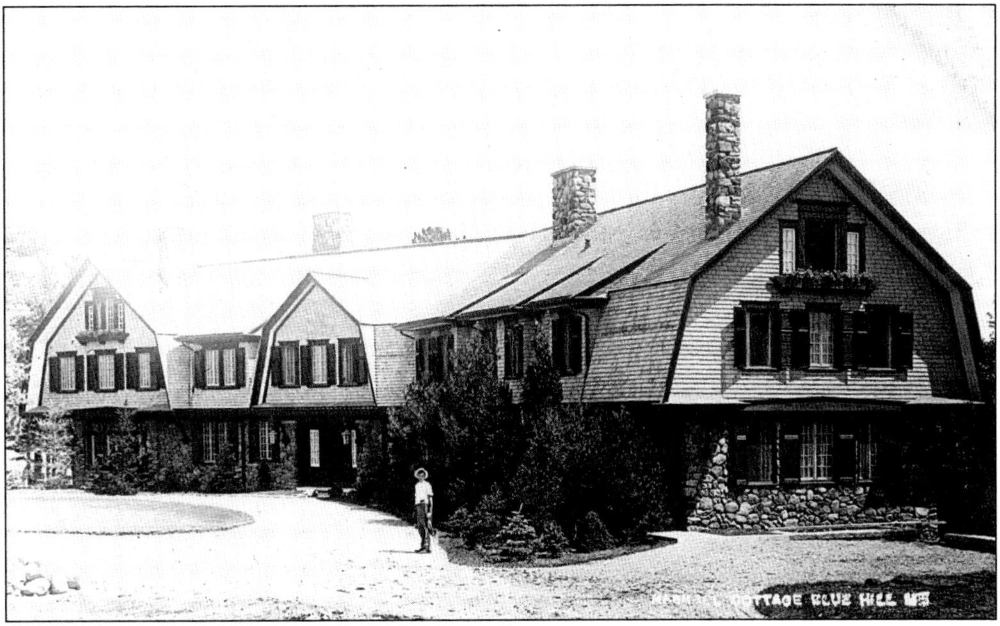

Summer saw a reopening of the grand old Haskell Cottage. The Blue Hill landmark is shown here in the early 20th century, with a wood-shingled roof and stone chimneys. There is also stonework along the ground-floor level. The cottage's gabled roofline is reminiscent of the late-19th-century Franklin D. Roosevelt home, now a popular museum at Campobello Island, New Brunswick, near Lubec, Maine. (BHPL.)

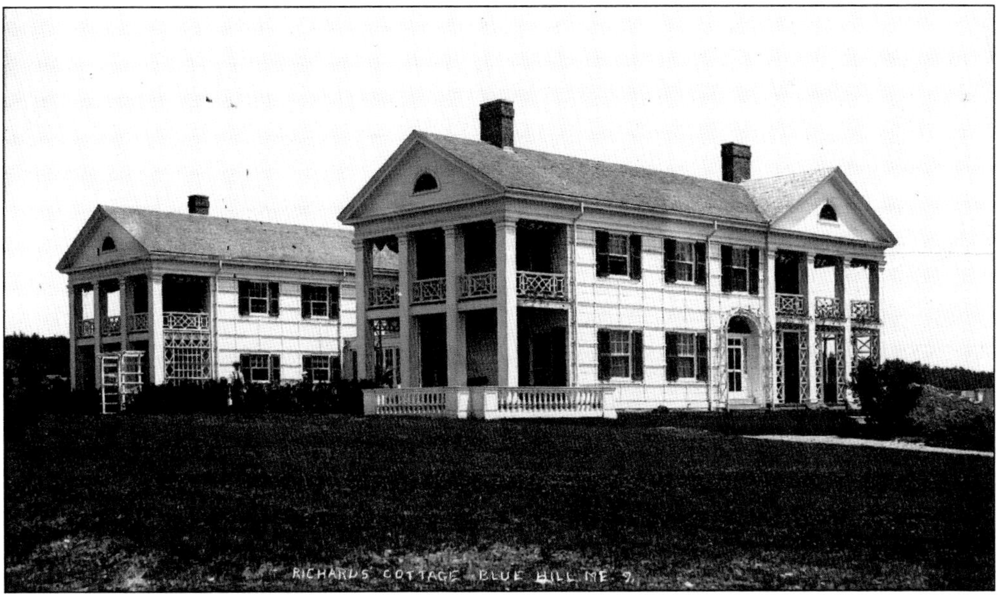

Difficult as it is to believe, this double-style seasonal home was called a cottage. No expense was spared to build the 19th-century landmark, complete with double balconies on both ends of the residence. The upper level of the Richards Cottage balcony at the far right probably afforded a view of Blue Hill Bay. (BHPL.)

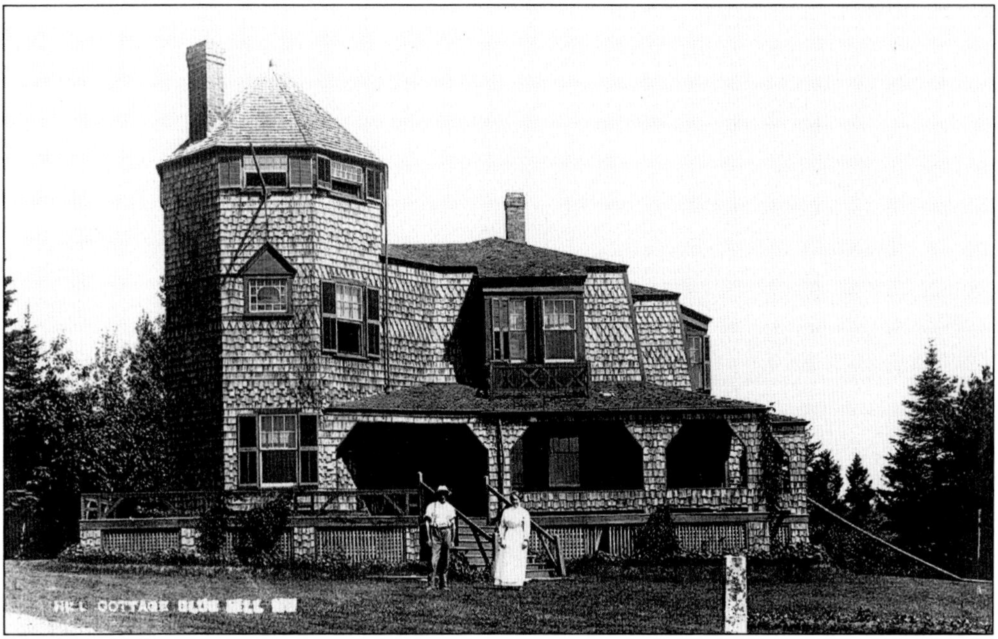

The Hill Cottage in Blue Hill, pictured here early in the last century, was designed in the shingled style created by architect William R. Emerson. Its angular design gave it an unusual appearance; the high rectangular windows probably afforded a splendid ocean view. This summertime scene shows a couple posing in their front yard, no doubt happy to live in such a functional, comfortable cottage. Note the granite hitching post in the right foreground. (BHPL.)

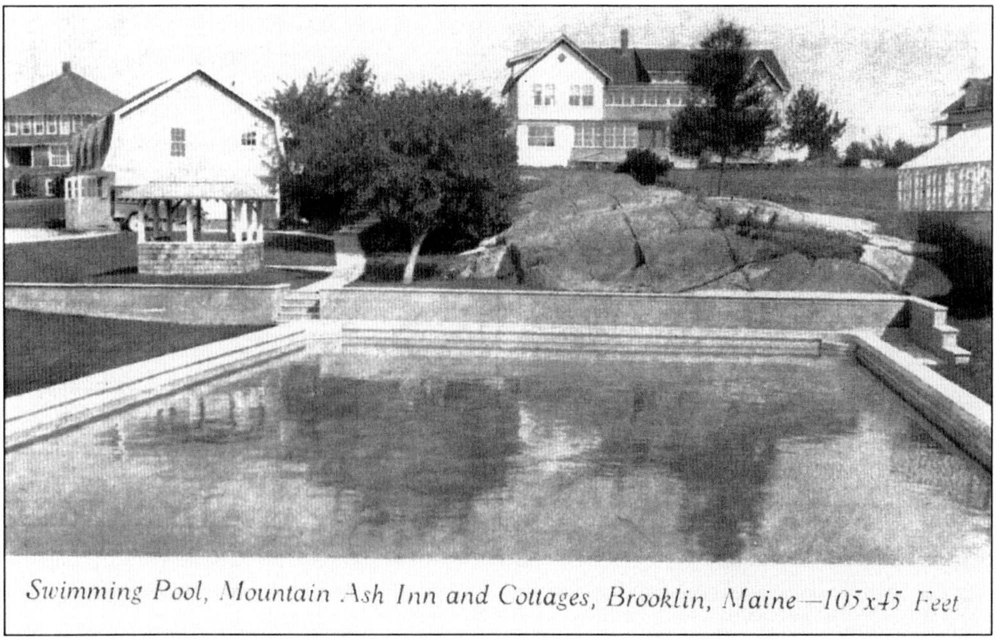

Brooklin's spacious Mountain Ash Inn has been converted into the Student House of the WoodenBoat School. Where tourists once relaxed, aspiring boat builders can use the kitchen and dining hall facilities. Travelers can still stay at the nearby Brooklin Inn, the DragonFlye Inn, and the Lookout Inn. (RRS.)

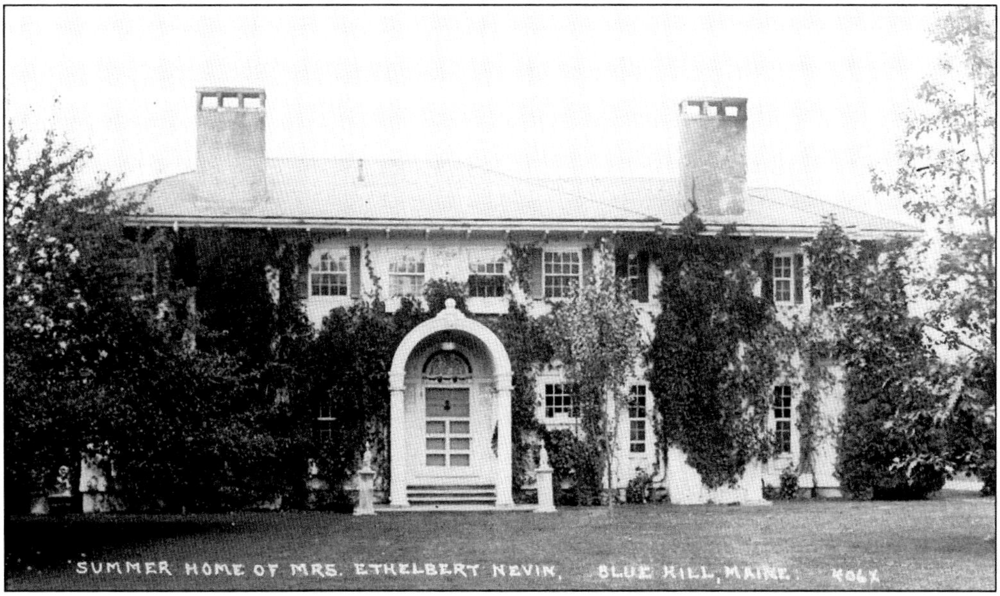

The palatial summer home of Ann Paul Nevin, composer Ethelbert Woodbridge Nevin's widow, was the scene of many dinner parties and other social events. Arcady, as it is called, is located near the Blue Hill Falls Bridge. Wallace Hinckley, the architect, was born and raised in Blue Hill and designed the home in 1913 for Ann. (MHPC.)

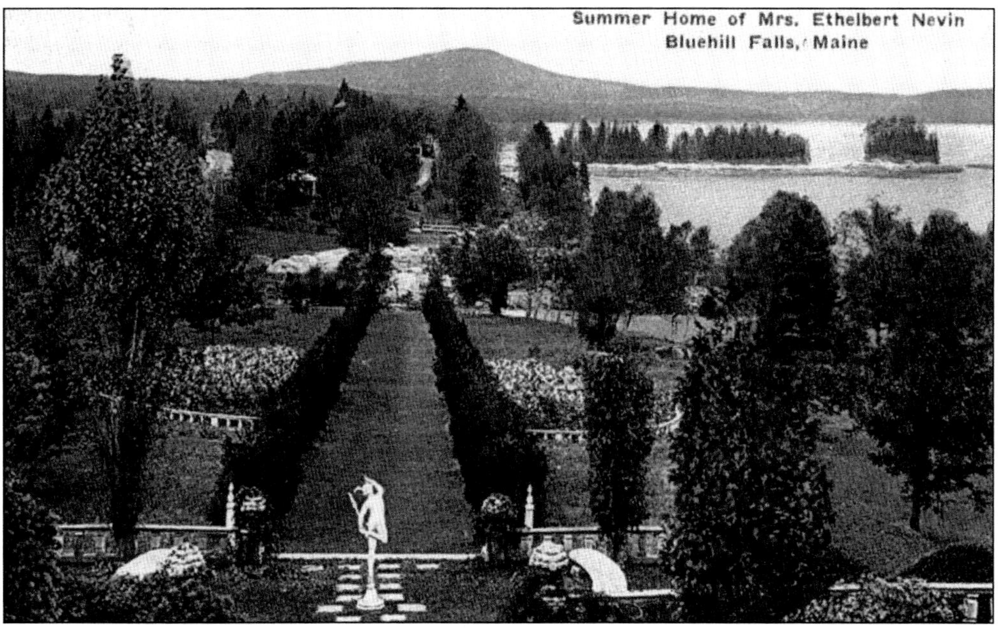

Ann Paul Nevin's estate was the pride of Blue Hill. She and her two children maintained the summer residence long after Ethelbert died. A stroll through Arcady's gardens transported visitors to another time and place. With the aroma of salt in the air, guests were transfixed by the color and the sight of Blue Hill Mountain looming in the distance. (RRS.)

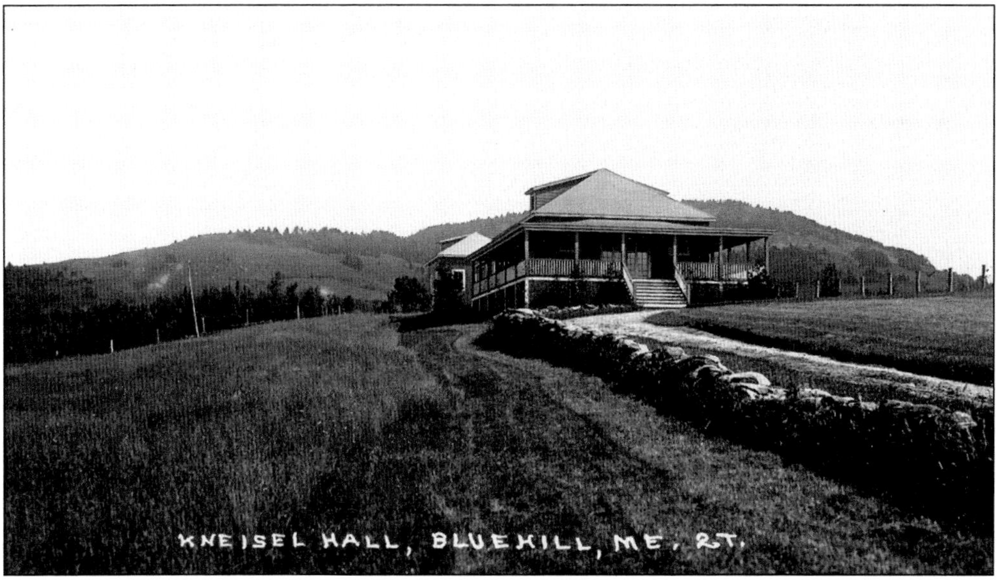

Perched on the southern slope of Blue Hill Mountain, Kneisel Hall has been home to quality summer chamber music for generations. An Austrian violinist named Dr. Franz Kneisel (1865–1926) made this simple building his seasonal studio while in Blue Hill. Public weekly summer concerts are performed on the 20-acre campus, which consists of the concert hall, two dormitories, the Chamber Music Center, five practice studios, a dining hall, and a recreation hall. (BPL.)

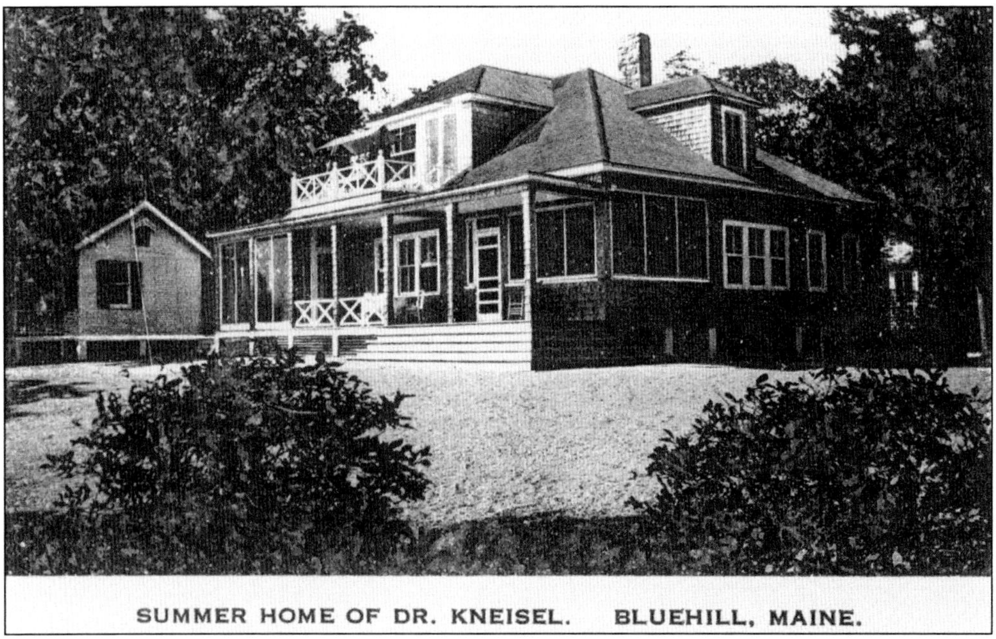

Kneisel was concertmaster of the Boston Symphony Orchestra and founder of the highly praised Kneisel Quartet. When he was not rehearsing in his hillside studio, he relaxed and rehearsed violin solos in this summer home. In 1902, he began bringing some of his most gifted students to Blue Hill. Other musicians of the Kneisel Quartet followed, thus establishing the teaching tradition that thrives every summer at Kneisel Hall. (BPL.)

Five

Highways and Downtowns

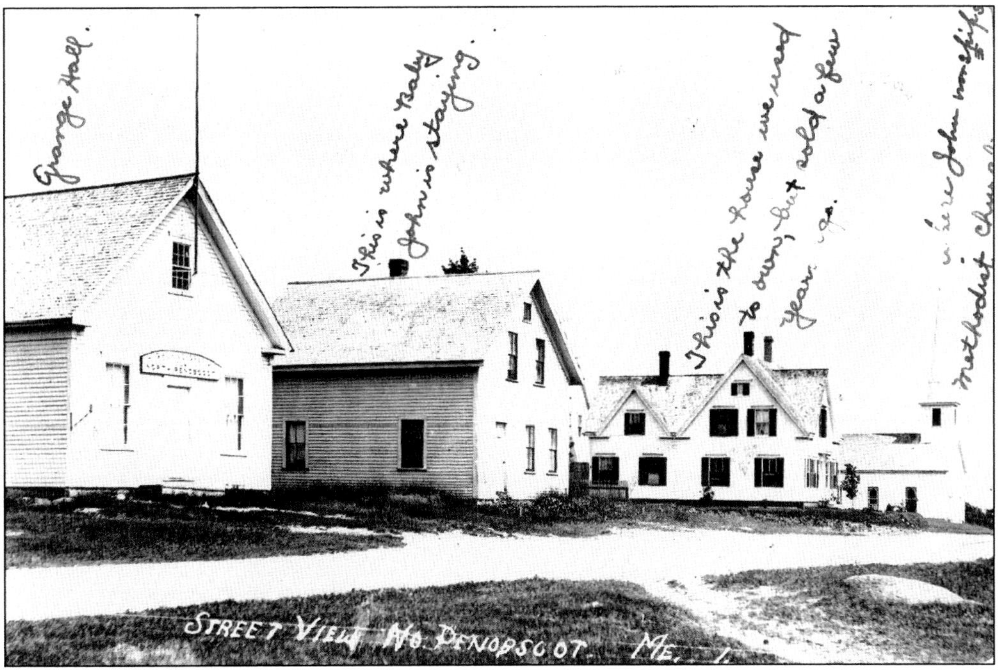

Four white wooden buildings in North Penobscot were the inspiration for this unique postcard, postmarked August 14, 1913. The correspondent penciled in the location of the Grange hall, the house where "Baby John" is staying, "the house we used to own," and the Methodist church where John (probably the baby's father) worships. (MHPC.)

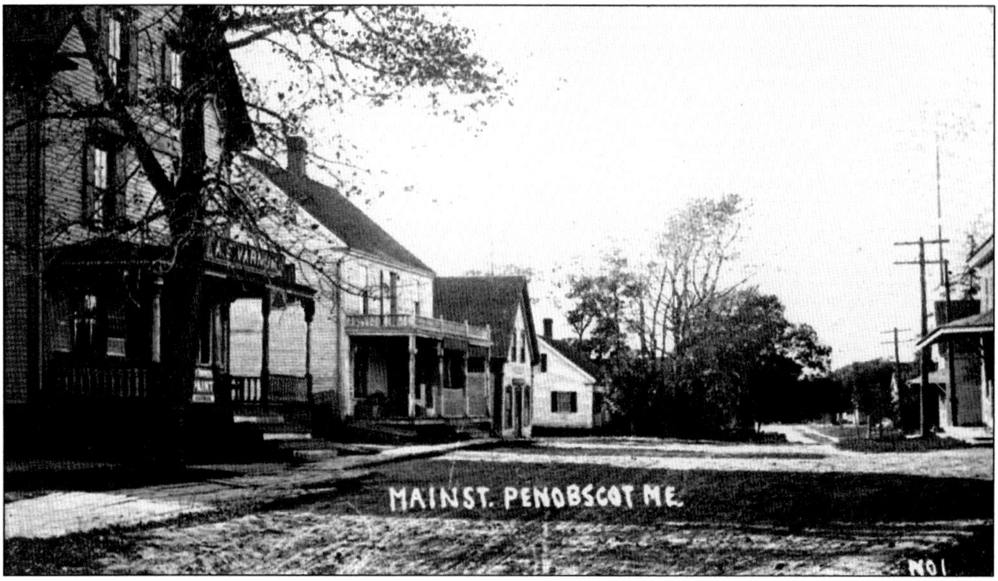

Tucked off in western Hancock County, the town of Penobscot was settled in the 1760s, when it encompassed all of Castine and the eastern part of Brooksville. It is the county's only town with a Native American origin, named for the river and bay upon which it is located. The message on this postcard, dated September 10, 1911, mentions that the writer is starting for Searsport, located across Penobscot Bay, tomorrow, and that he saw two rainbows. (BPL.)

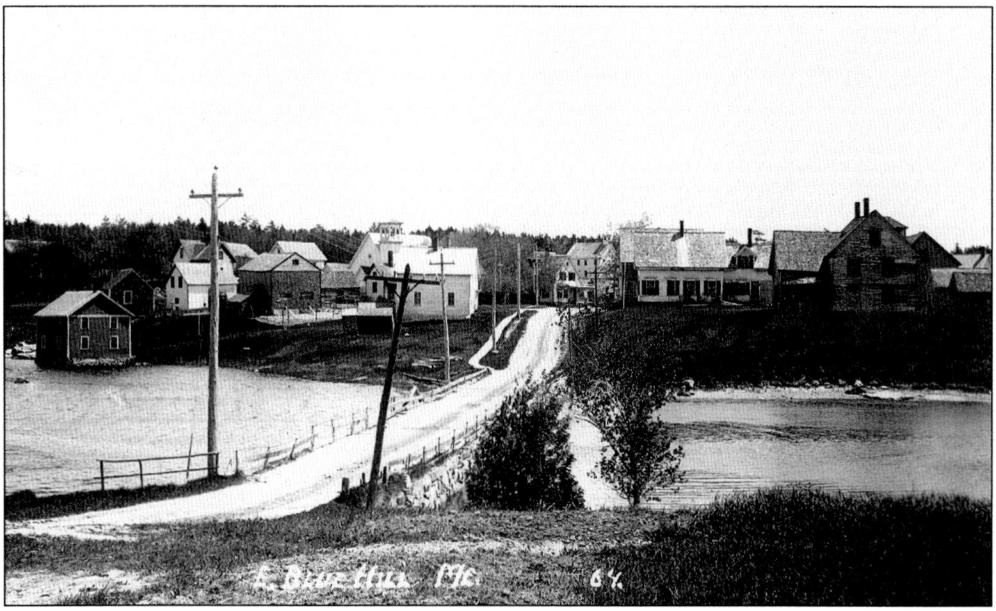

Hidden away on Route 176, East Blue Hill is still a quiet village, but not as quiet as it appeared the day this scene was taken, around 1915. Esther E. Wood, who retired to this village after a long career teaching at the University of Southern Maine, writes that East Blue Hill is where McHard's Stream flows into the bay, and that "In time each settlement [in Blue Hill] had a school, store, and a chapel or church." (RRS.)

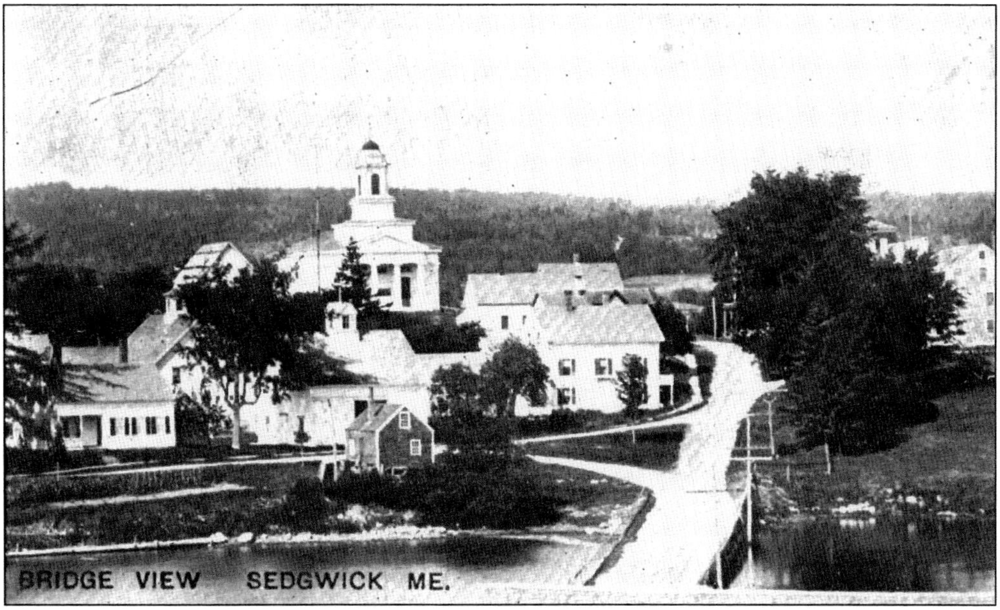

Time has not changed Sedgwick village significantly since this view was made around 1908. The Benjamin River looks about the same, and some of the dwellings in the foreground are still standing. The Baptist church building (see pages 79 and 81) still towers over the town. Built by 1837, it replaced the first church, completed in 1794. The town has retained its relaxed charm. (RRS.)

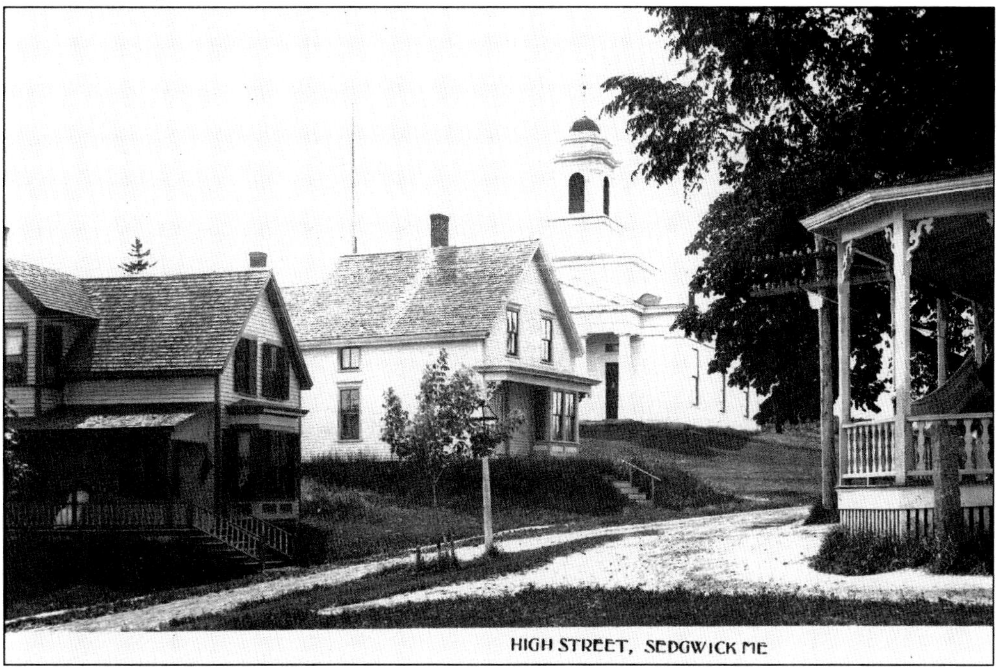

Sedgwick's first permanent settler was Andrew Black in 1759. Others soon followed. The early years were not blessed with prosperity. Official records reveal that all unattached and unmarried females who could not find anyone to support them were advised to leave town. The 1790 census lists about 80 heads of families as living in Sedgwick. (MHPC.)

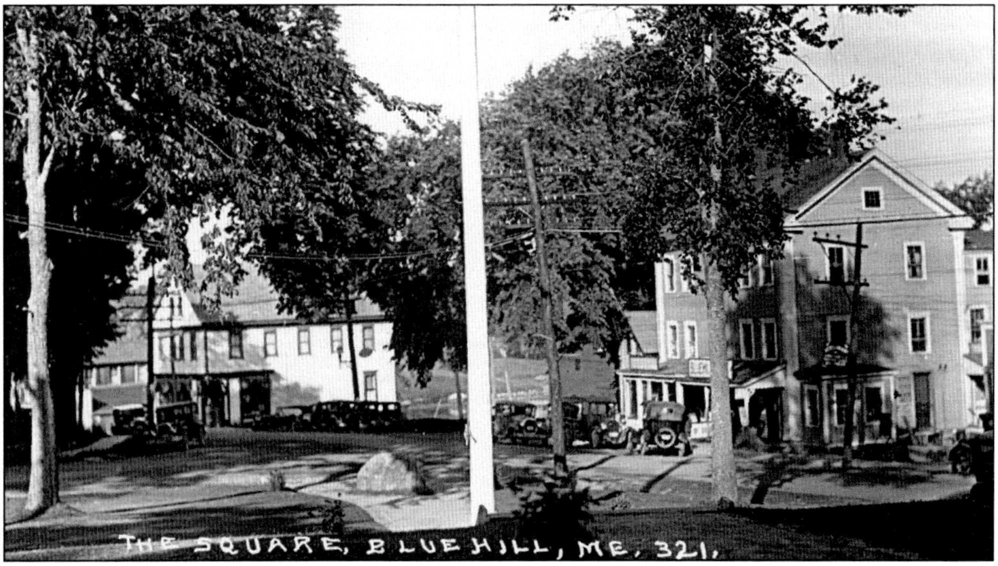

Blue Hill's village square in the 1920s was highlighted by a tall flagpole and business blocks. A popular destination, judging from the early automobiles parked in front, was the three-story block at the right known as "the Exchange," located at Main and Union Streets. Around 1900, Mrs. H. B. Nash sold boots, shoes, fancy goods, and millinery items there. In the 1880s, locals called this hotel the "Copper and Gold Exchange," which profited from the town's short-lived mining boom. A bank later occupied the site. (BPL.)

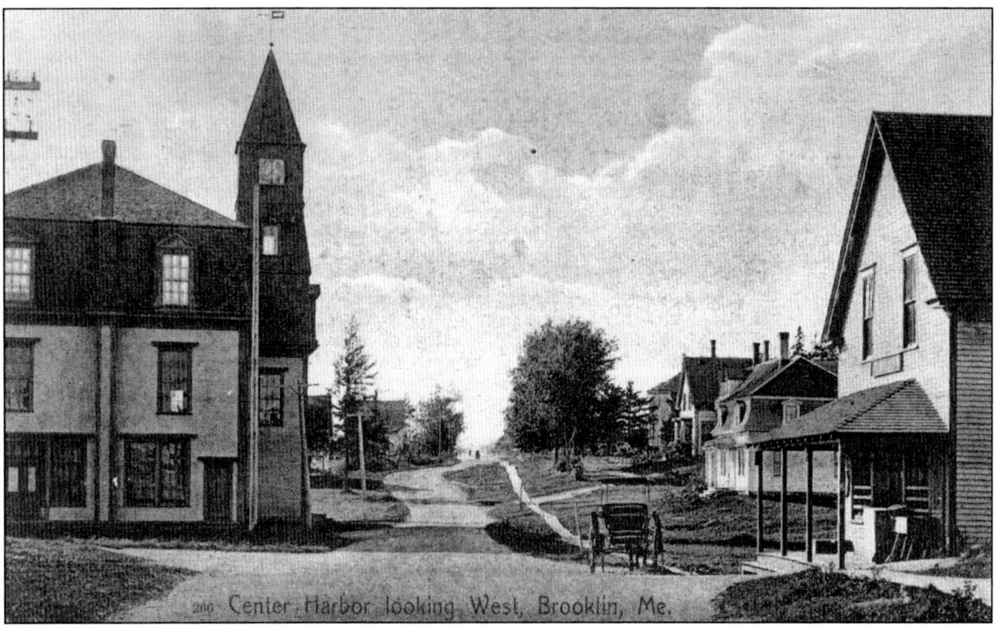

The Odd Fellows Block dominates this *c.* 1910 view of Center Harbor in Brooklin, once famous for its sardine factories. S. G. Stevens's sardine cannery was one of the first companies in Brooklin to pack sardines. Despite their remote location, other fish canneries thrived and put Center Harbor on the map beginning in the early 20th century. Over the years, writes local historian Jane Hooper, these plants changed hands, changed products, and eventually were abandoned. (MHPC.)

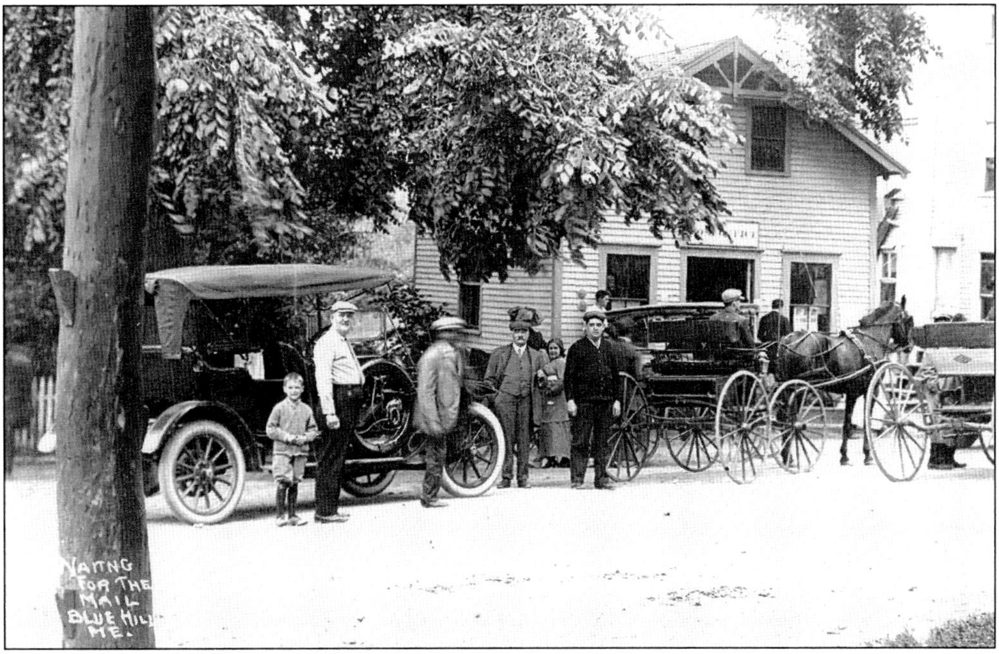

Dating to about 1912, this view shows people, and the automobile and wagons they arrived in, awaiting the mail at Blue Hill's post office. The little boy at the far left clutches his hands in anticipation of receiving a letter or maybe a shiny new picture postcard. Many homes did not have telephones, so the daily mail was eagerly awaited. (BPL.)

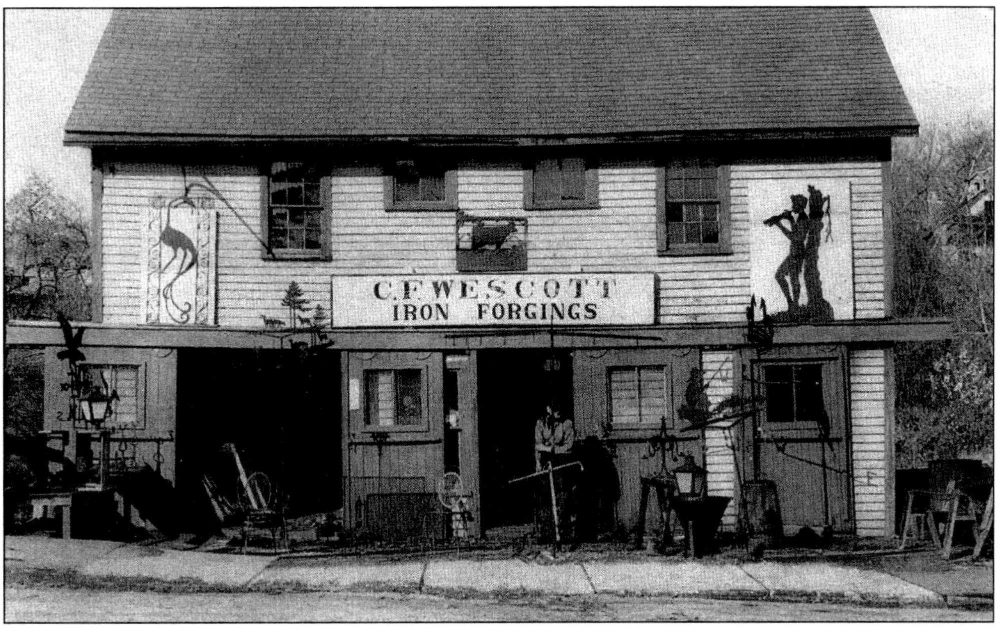

C. F. Wescott's iron forgings was located in an old wooden building, well known to any tourist who has driven over the Main Street bridge in Blue Hill. Wescott and his array of iron works are long gone, and the building has been occupied by a craft shop and restaurants. The Firepond Restaurant used to be located here. In 1960, Maine governor John H. Reed planted a chestnut tree in front of what then was called Hammer and Tong Iron Forgings. (BHPL.)

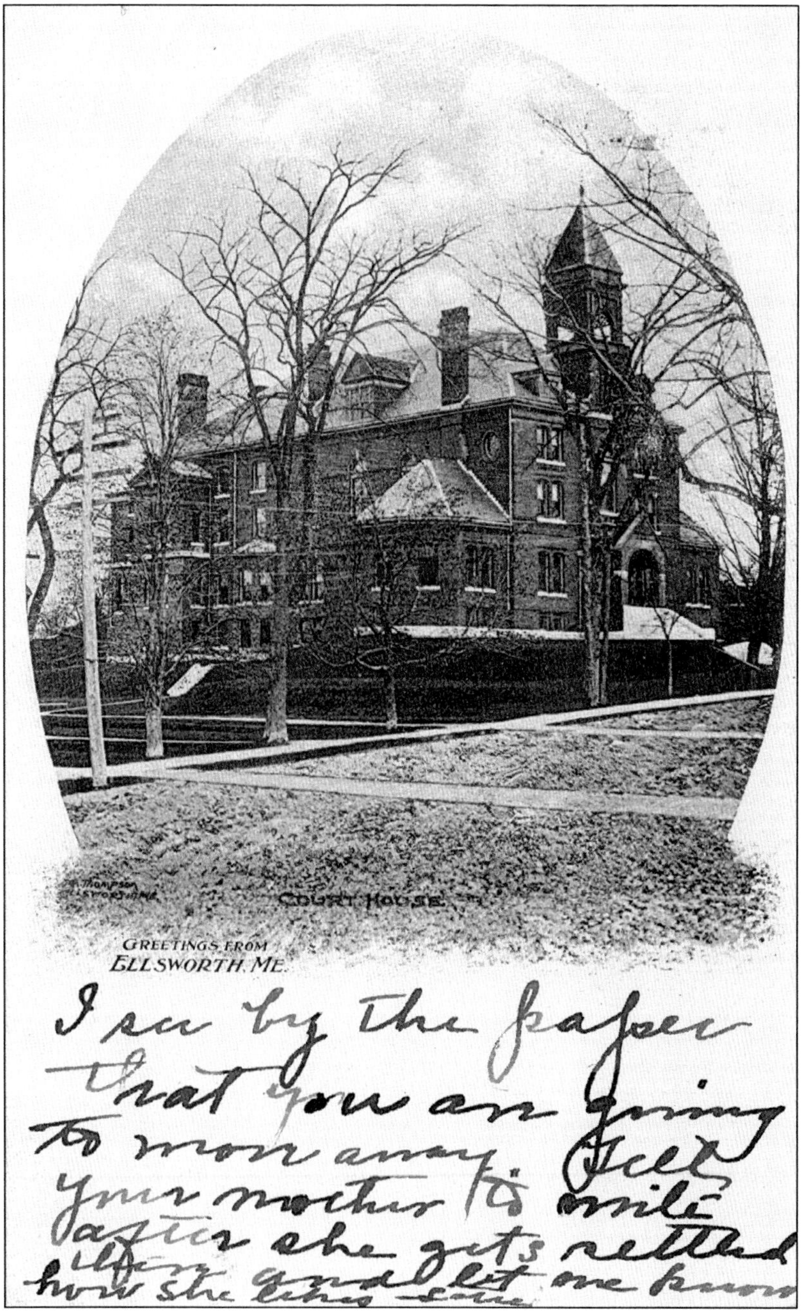

Many famous cases were tried in the old Hancock County Courthouse, built in 1886. To celebrate the opening of the new building, the first term of the supreme judicial court was held in Ellsworth in April of that year. Located on State Street, it was another example of an Ellsworth landmark destroyed by fire. In May 1929, two local firefighters were killed while battling the blaze. Court sessions were held at Hancock Hall on Main Street, but fortunately the present-day courthouse had already been built on the same site in 1931 when the Ellsworth fire of 1933 destroyed the hall and other buildings. Unlike the old courthouse, the "new" one is built of classical granite and brick, with six tall granite Doric columns adorning the facade. (RRS.)

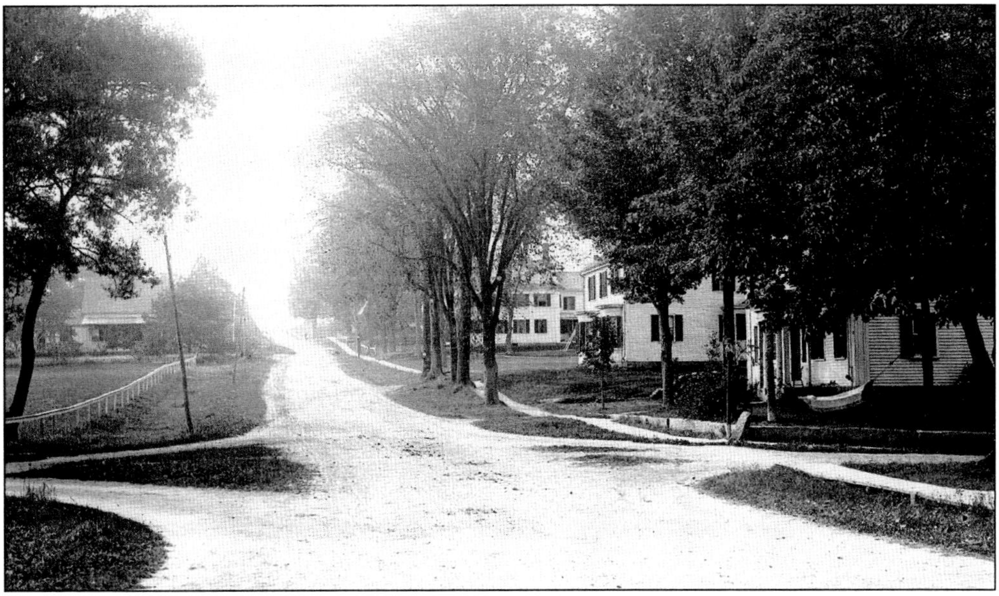

Blue Hill has long been famous as a village of white homes, historic churches, and elm-lined streets. This early view of Union Street, known to locals as the "road to Orland," reveals a canopy of elms stretching into the distance. While the stately old residences have survived, some of Blue Hill's elms have not. Despite efforts to save them, some trees have succumbed to Dutch elm disease. (BHPL.)

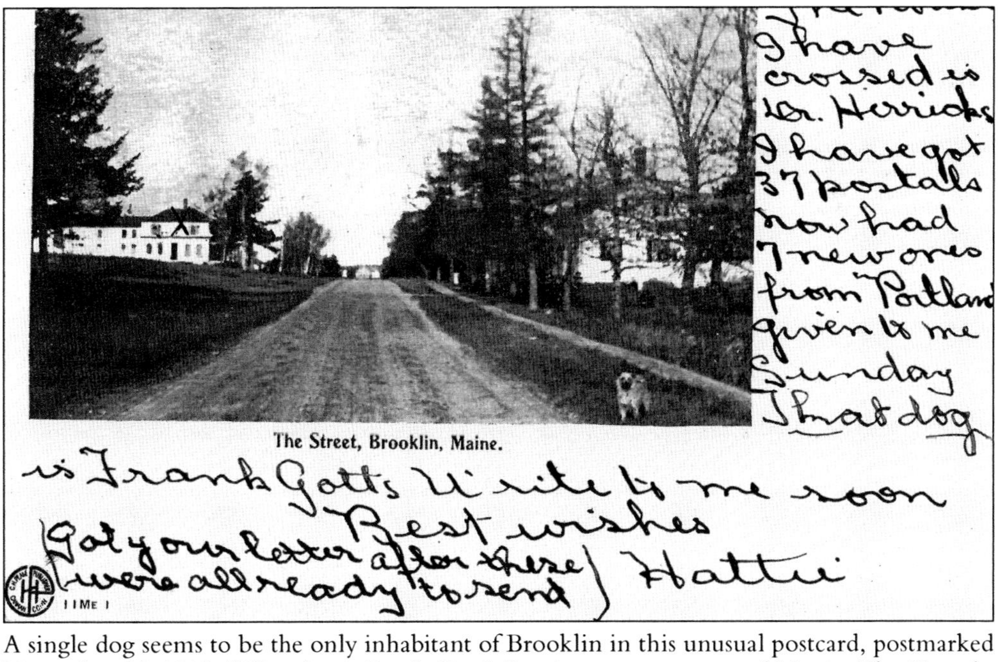

A single dog seems to be the only inhabitant of Brooklin in this unusual postcard, postmarked November 29, 1905. "That dog is Frank Gott's," writes a woman named Hattie. The *X* marks the house on the left where Dr. Herrick lives. Situated on Route 175, Brooklin originally was a part of Sedgwick but was set off from that town in 1849 and incorporated under the name of Port Watson. A month later, the name was changed to Brooklin, because a brook separates the two towns. (RRS.)

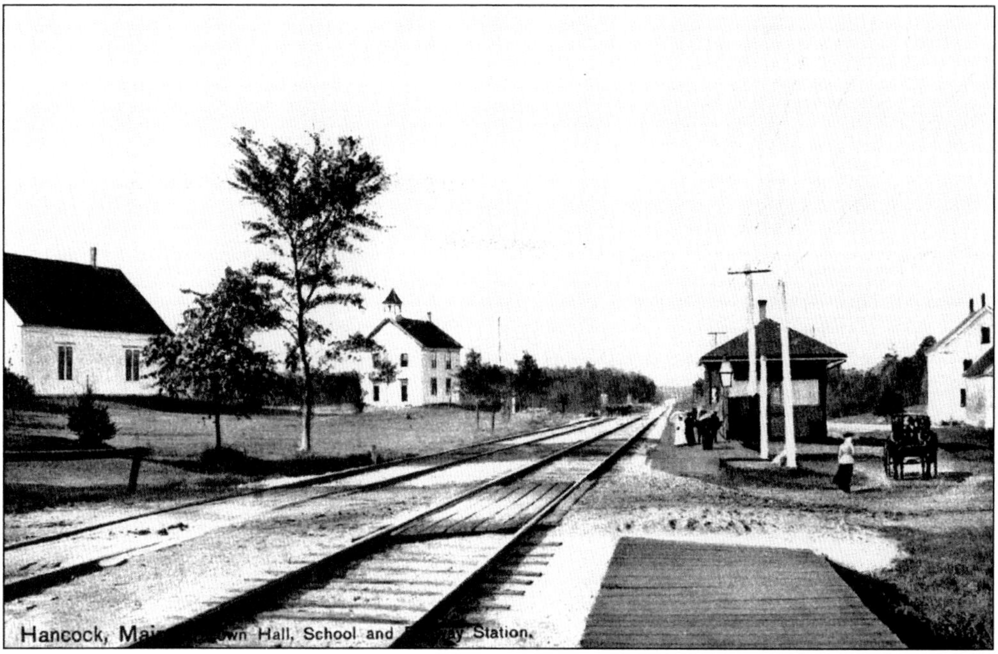

This was a familiar scene to railroad travelers heading Down East around 1918. Passengers at Hancock Corner bought their tickets and waited for the Maine Central Railroad train in the small wooden building at the right. The people and the horse and wagon most likely were painted onto the postcard to liven up the scene. The other two buildings, the town hall (left) and the corner school (background), are still standing just off of Route 1. (BPL.)

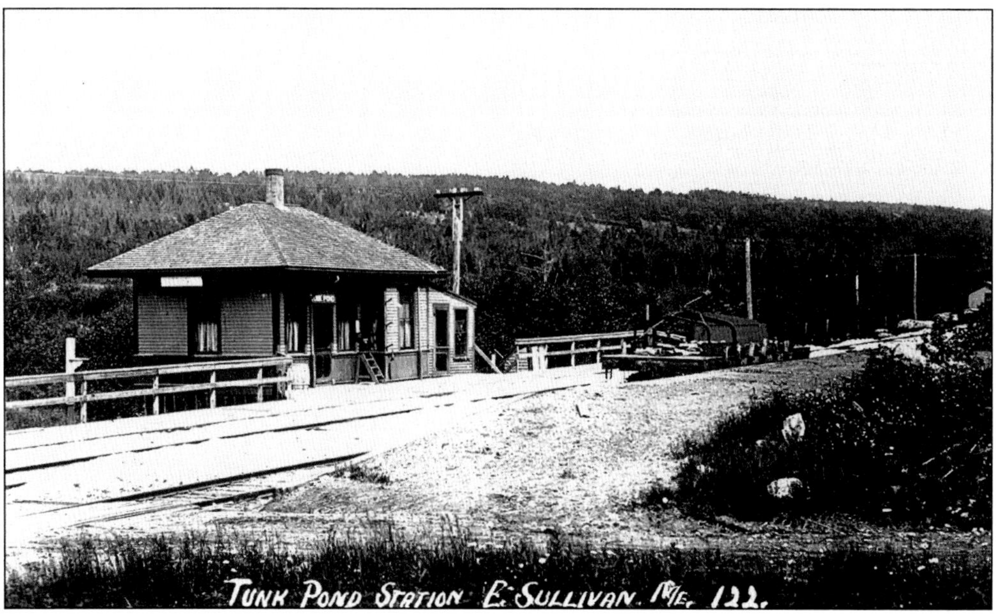

East Sullivan was a bustling place in the days when a railroad stopped in town every day. It even had its own station, as shown in this card, around 1920. The only things missing in this basic postcard are the steam train and the passengers waiting to board. (BPL.)

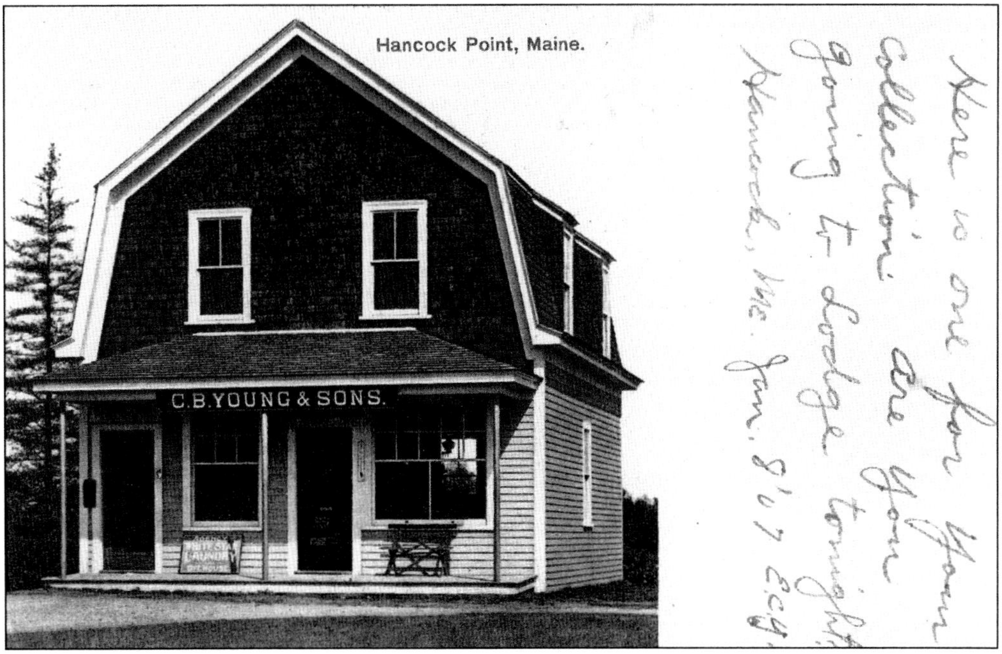

Young's Store served customers at Hancock Point after it was built in 1905. Located near the village green, the store sold canned goods, penknives, flashlights, as well as Texaco gasoline. Herbert Young and his family lived upstairs and a post office, entered through the left-hand door, shared the ground floor. On one occasion a sign in the front window, reading "Fresh eggs and fowl," had to be removed after locals found it a bit too amusing. (MHPC.)

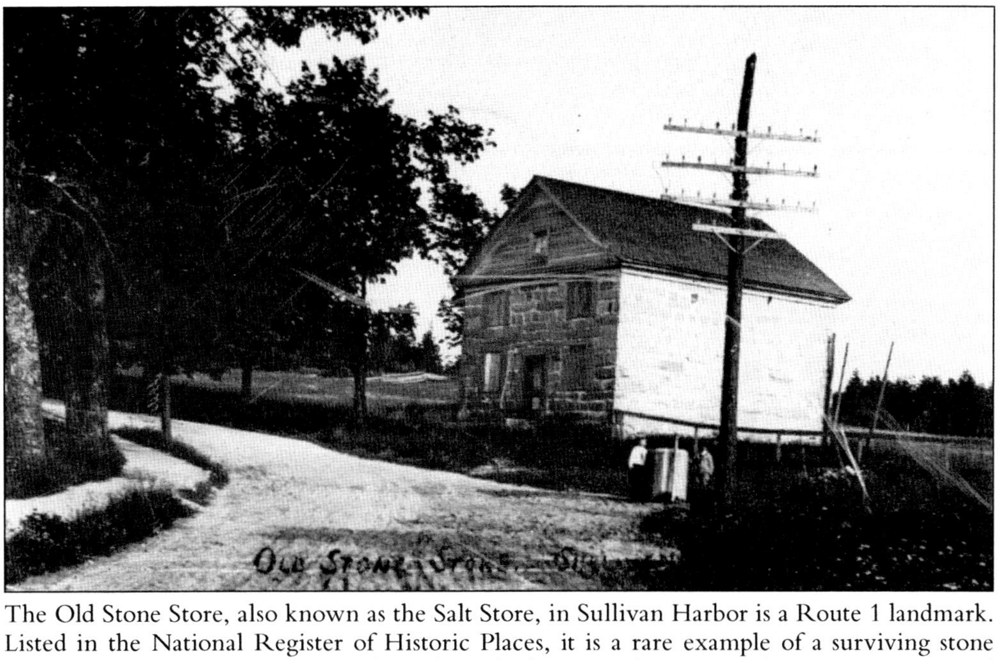

The Old Stone Store, also known as the Salt Store, in Sullivan Harbor is a Route 1 landmark. Listed in the National Register of Historic Places, it is a rare example of a surviving stone building. The town watering trough, in the right foreground, was moved to Sumner Memorial Park when Route 1 was rerouted. A *Bangor Daily News* article in the 1980s speculated that the former store is haunted. (MHPC.)

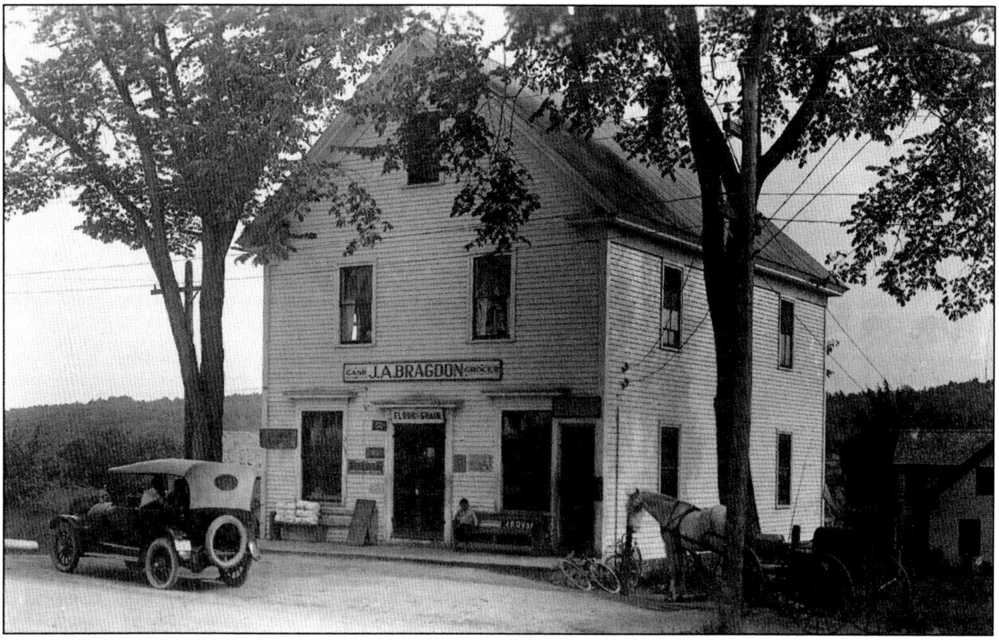

Surry was a tiny village of less than 500 souls in the 1920s. Settled around 1767, and named for Surrey, England (someone dropped the *e*), the fishing town owed its existence to the sea. This scene, taken on Route 172, shows J. A. Bragdon's cash grocery store. Typical of many communities, the post office shared space in the town's only store. A sign over the front door advertises flour and grain. (MHPC.)

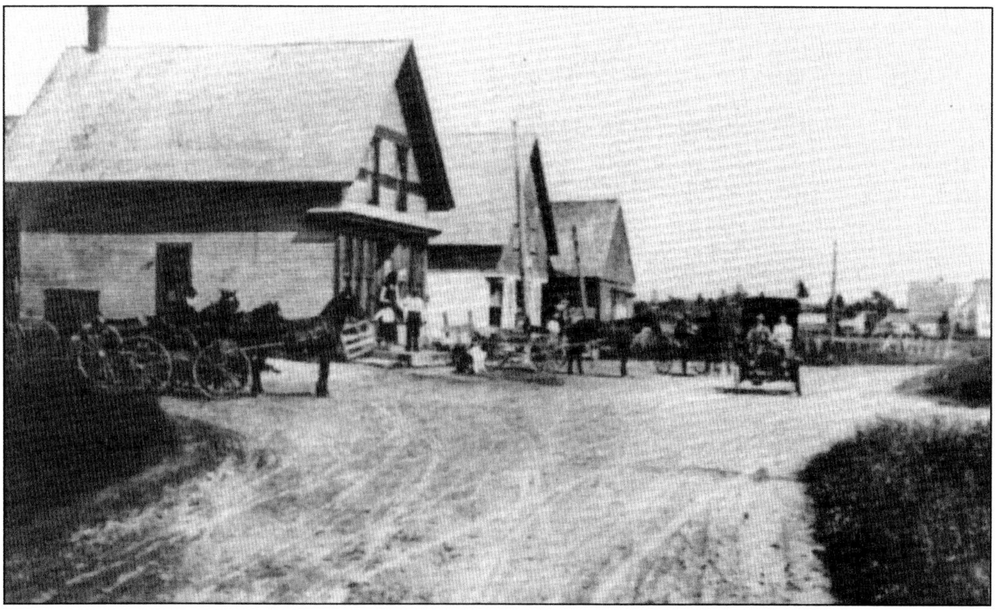

A tin lizzie is shown making its way down dusty Route 1 in East Sullivan. Or maybe the early automobile was superimposed onto the card by an overzealous postcard maker. The first cars in town typically were owned by doctors and other prominent residents. This view shows the corner of Route 1 and the Tunk Pond Road. Hanna Brothers Store and post office, much later in the century, became an antique shop, which burned in a spectacular fire. (BPL.)

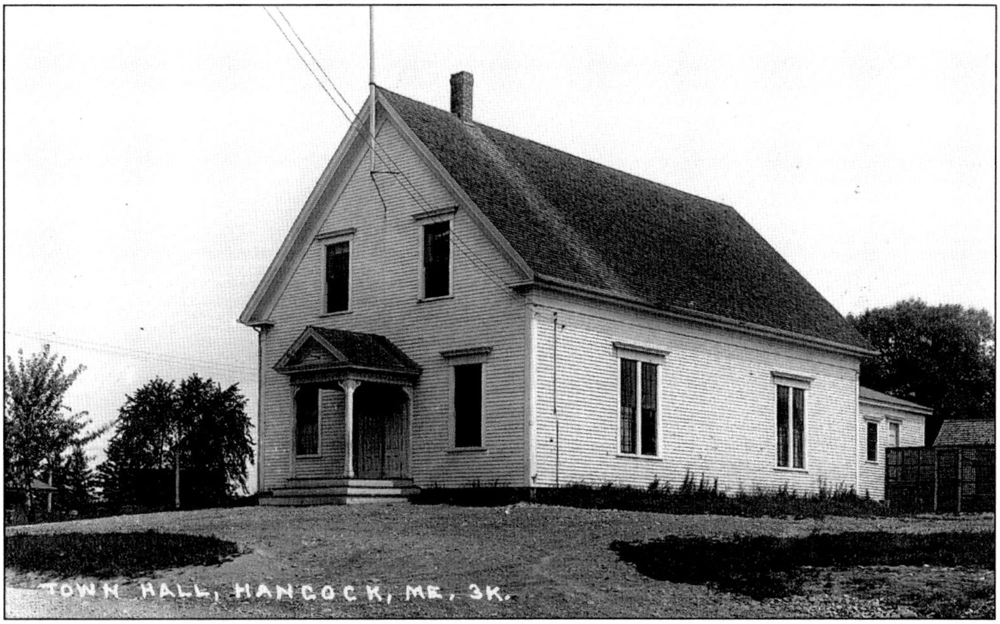

The Hancock Town Hall does not seem to change much. Located at Hancock Corner, just off of Route 1, it is still a town hall after all these years. The Hancock Historical Society's photography collection, picturing seafaring, summer cottages, and notable summer residents, is stored upstairs. Typical of most New England towns, Hancock is governed by a board of selectmen and assessors chosen by popular vote at a town meeting held the second Monday in March. (RRS.)

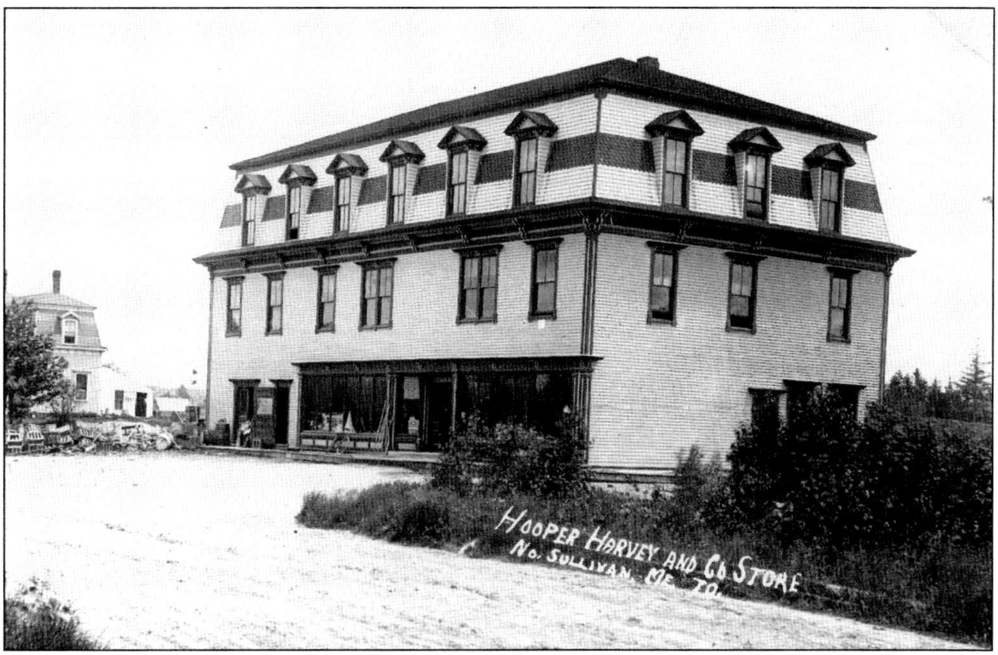

Everyone in North Sullivan shopped at Hooper Harvey and Company store. The long mansard-style roof was distinctive for its band of light and dark colors. Sullivan was once known for its granite industry and fishing fleet, and is still famous as the gateway to the Schoodic Peninsula. (MHPC.)

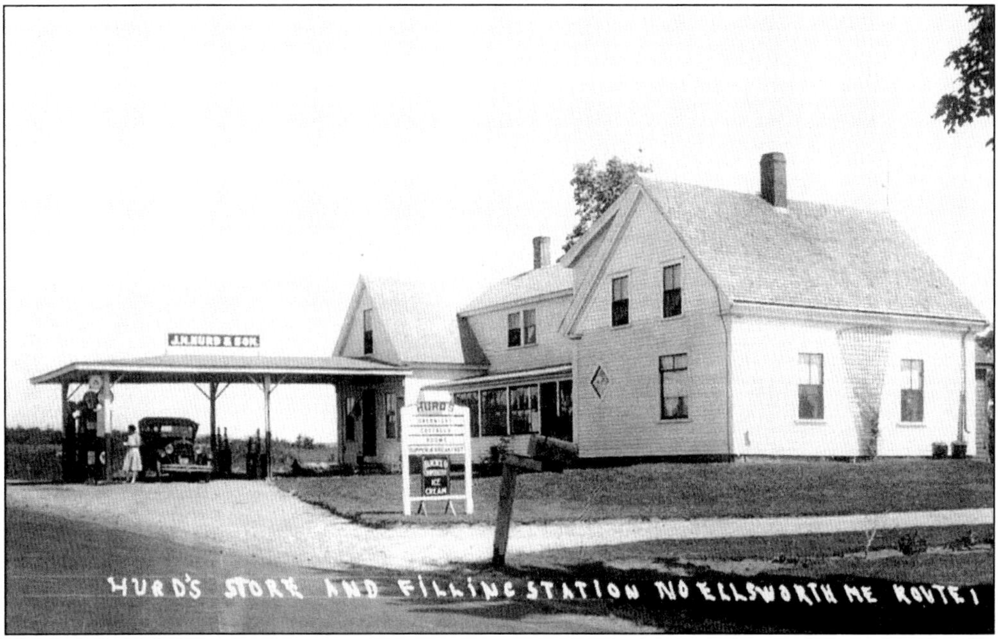

J. N. Hurd and Son store and filling station was a favorite stopping point on the Bangor Road (Route 1A) in North Ellsworth. Shown here in the 1920s, the property also included rooms and overnight cabins, and the Hurds served supper and breakfast. They also sold Hancock County Creamery ice cream. This part of Ellsworth is known as Nicolin (pronounced Nic-OH-lin, reputedly of Native American origin). (RRS.)

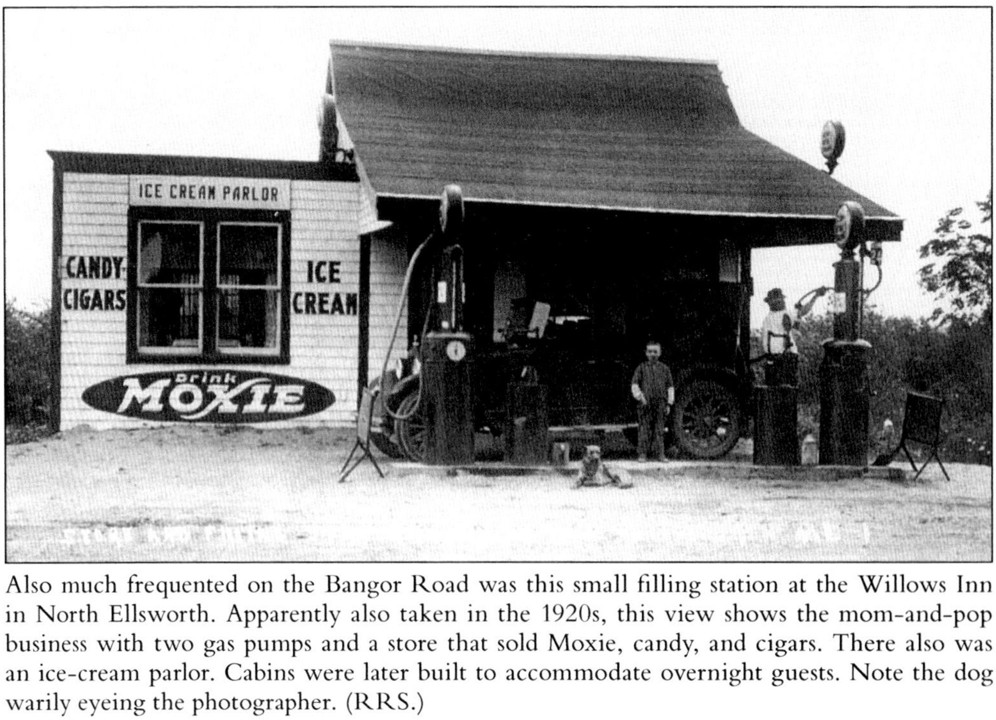

Also much frequented on the Bangor Road was this small filling station at the Willows Inn in North Ellsworth. Apparently also taken in the 1920s, this view shows the mom-and-pop business with two gas pumps and a store that sold Moxie, candy, and cigars. There also was an ice-cream parlor. Cabins were later built to accommodate overnight guests. Note the dog warily eyeing the photographer. (RRS.)

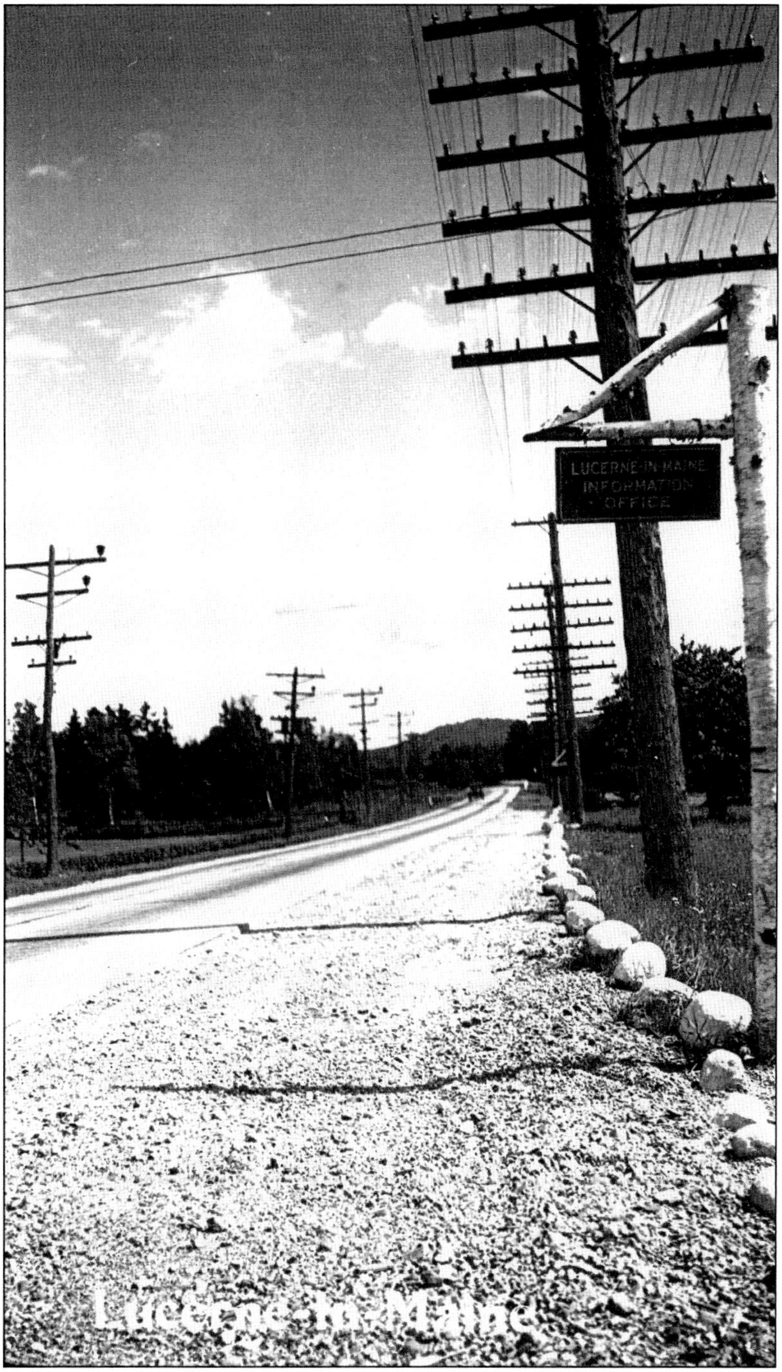

A leisurely drive from Brewer to Ellsworth along Route 1A used to take a long time. In the 1930s, the "Lafayette Highway" was narrow and winding, and there was plenty of time to stop for a picnic lunch and photograph the mountains and lakes along the way. The sign hanging from the birch log reads "Lucerne-in-Maine Information Office." Route 1A today is a veritable superhighway. Construction projects have rerouted sections with many added passing lanes. Gone are the rows of rocks along the roadway and the six-tiered utility poles. (RRS.)

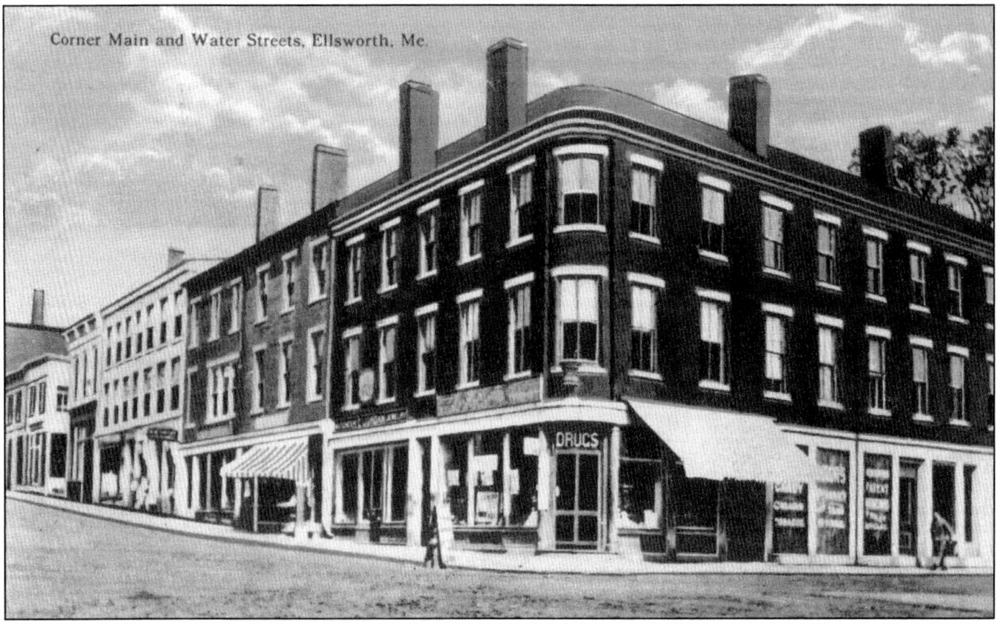

Wiggin and Moore Drugstore was a fixture for decades at the corner of Main and Water Streets in Ellsworth. A mortar and pestle is visible over the pharmacy's front door. Another building in this 1916 view of the south side of Main Street is a granite block built in the 1850s of granite quarried in Sullivan. The *Ellsworth American* and *Bangor Daily News* have offices in these historic blocks, which survived the 1933 fire. (RRS.)

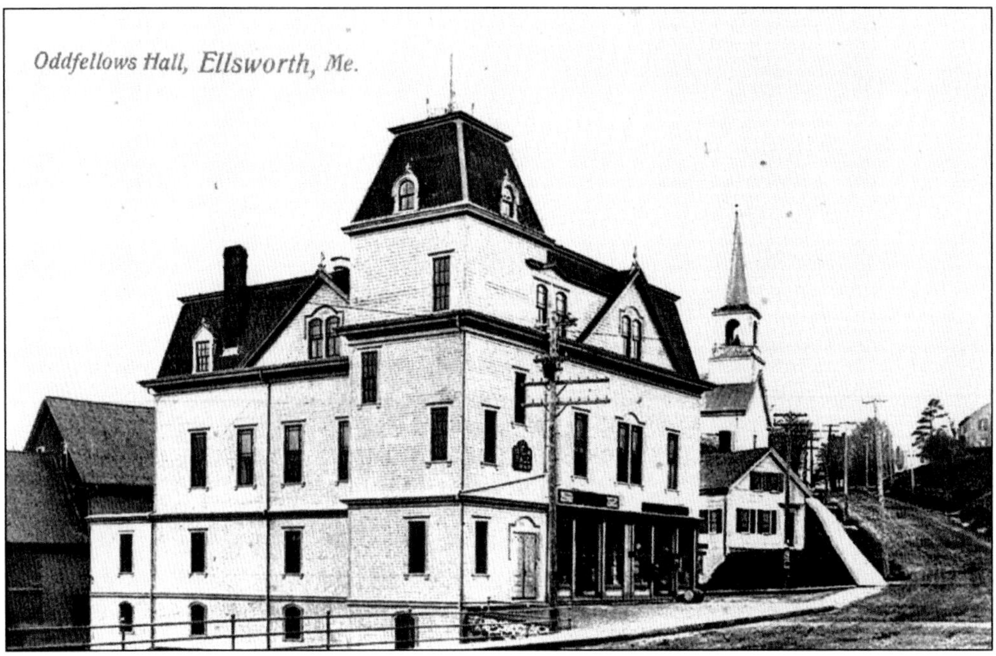

The Ellsworth Odd Fellows Hall still stands by the Main Street Bridge. The Victorian block was built in the late 19th century and is known to today's kitchen shoppers as the home of Rooster Brother. Gone on the west side of the bridge is the Methodist Episcopal church. The church was dedicated on January 12, 1860, and burned in the winter of 1904. (BPL.)

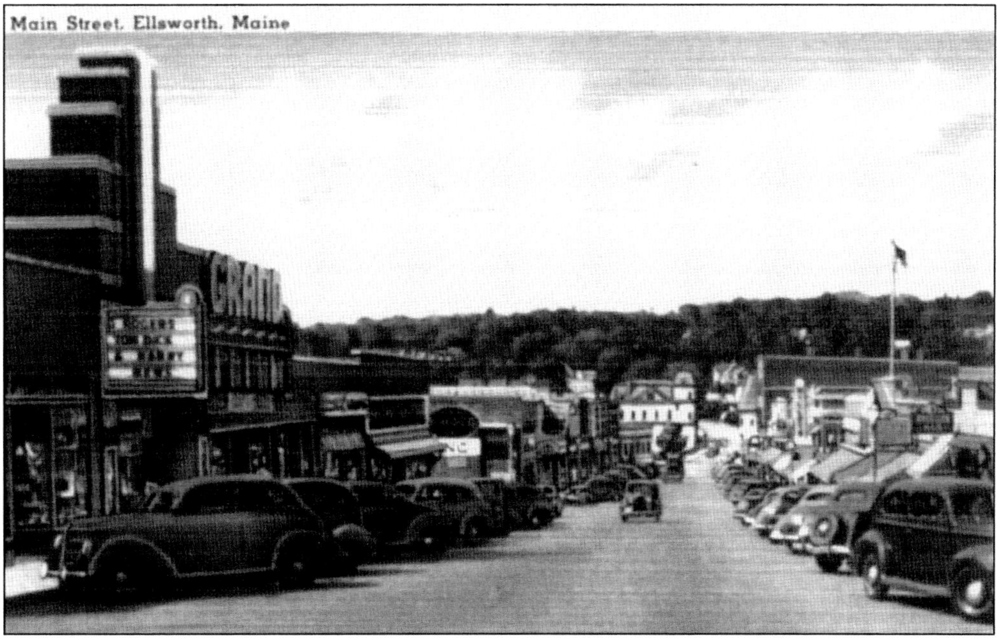

The Grand Theatre on Main Street was nearly five years old when this Ellsworth scene was taken in 1941. Farther down the north side of Main Street are the Joy and Adams blocks, both constructed after the 1933 fire. Willey's clothing store and cafés run by George Panos and the Luchini family were some of the businesses across Main Street. The late historian Hale Joy learned about his community by chatting with his father's Main Street grocery customers. (RRS.)

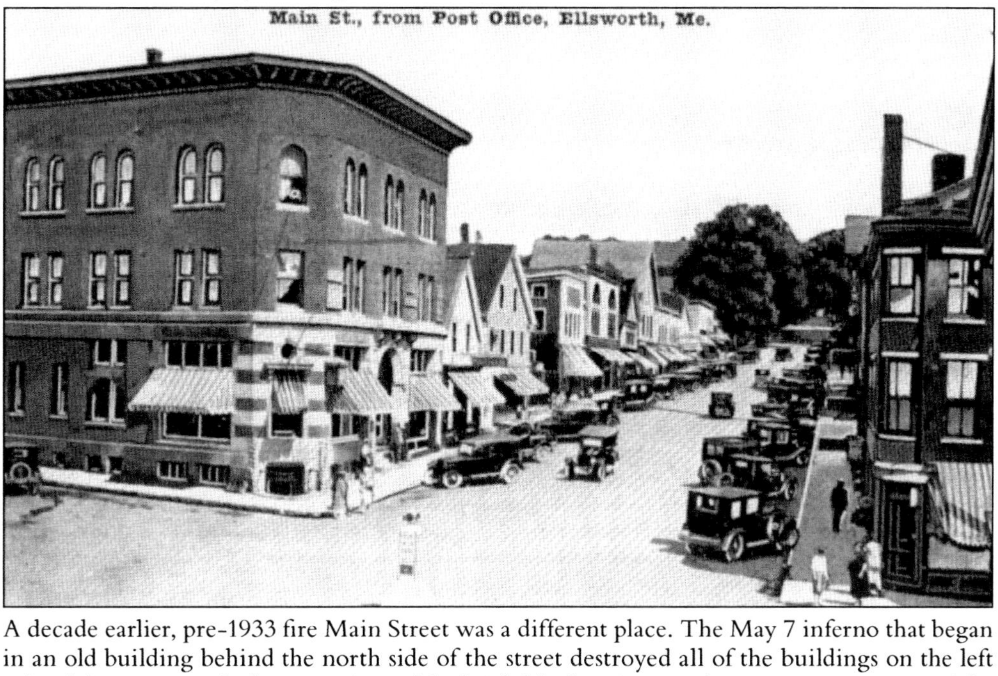

A decade earlier, pre-1933 fire Main Street was a different place. The May 7 inferno that began in an old building behind the north side of the street destroyed all of the buildings on the left side of this view, with the exception of the brick block at State and Main Streets. Some of the merchants doing business in the row of wooden buildings at the left were photographer Irving Osgood and Luchini's fruit and confectionery store. (RRS.)

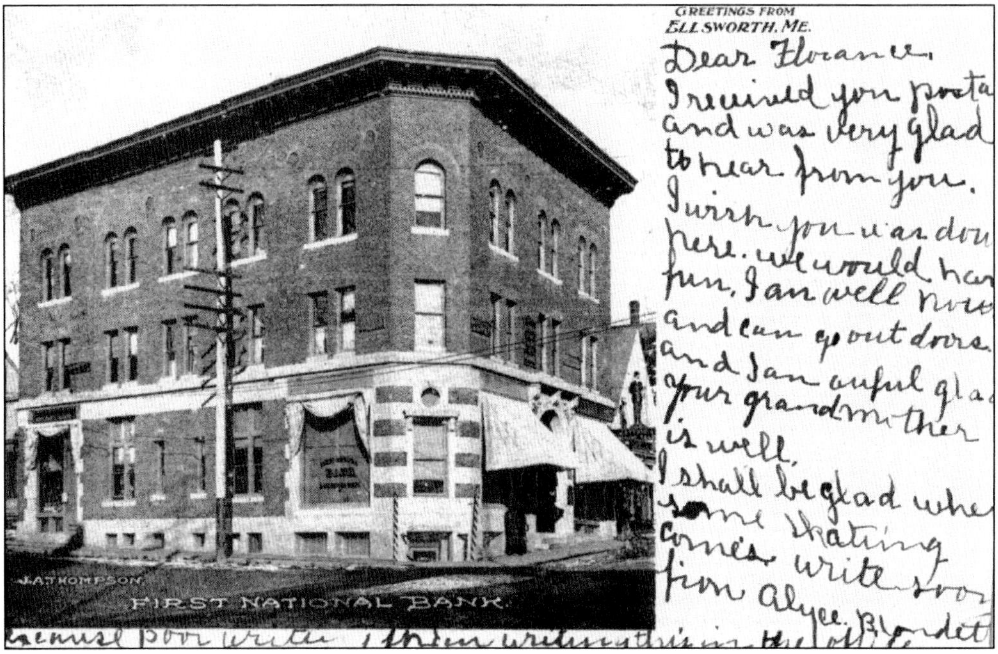

Before the Union Trust Company moved in to this old brick block at State and Main Streets, First National Bank occupied the block. Like other banks, such as Liberty National, the name First National is remembered now by only senior residents. The great Ellsworth fire of May 7, 1933, spared the bank building, but claimed nearly every other building on the north side of Main Street. (MHPC.)

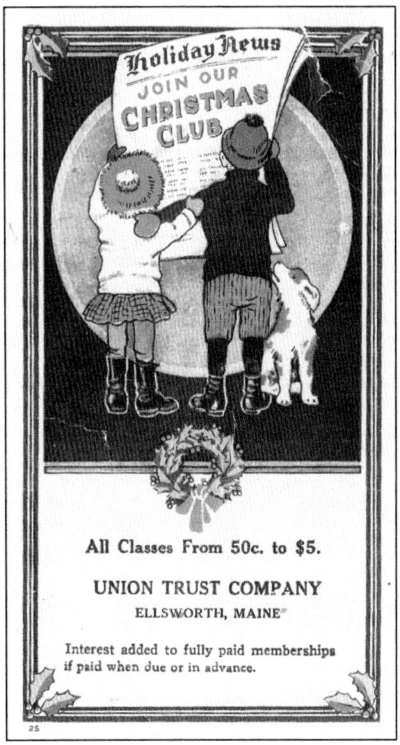

This Union Trust Company advertisement for the bank's Christmas Club is actually a blotter, not a postcard. But it is so cleverly drawn and evocative of its era (the 1930s?) that it is included in this chapter. Union Trust Company has had a strong presence in downtown Ellsworth for many years, branching out into different communities as well. Note the message "All classes from 50¢ to $5," which seems minuscule by today's standards. (RRS.)

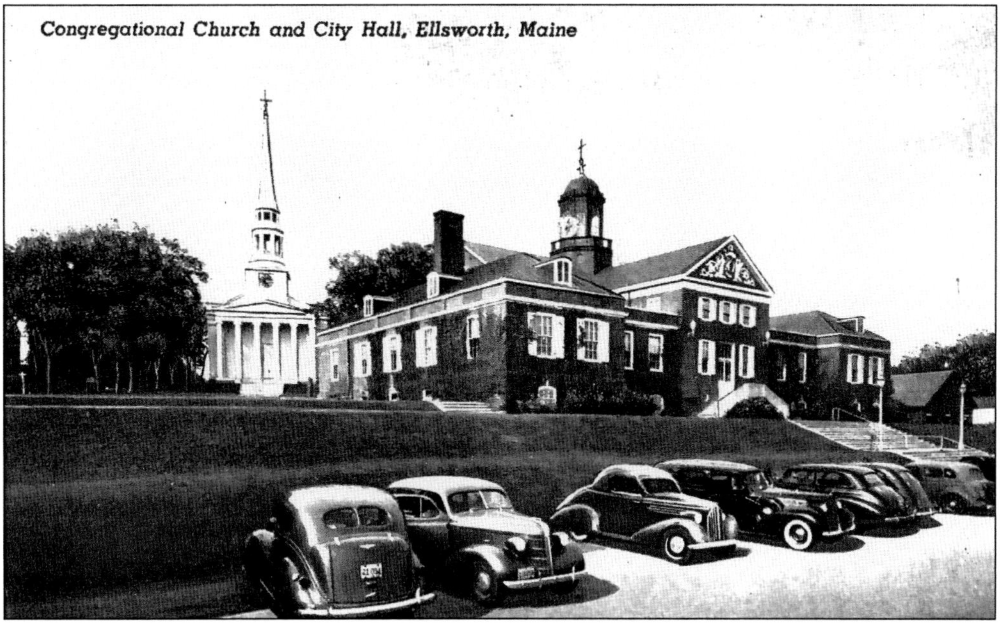

Although they were built a century apart, Ellsworth City Hall and its First Congregational Church stand in perfect symmetry. City hall rose from the ashes of the 1933 fire, which burned the municipal offices in Hancock Hall on Main Street. The church, which has been maintained at great expense over the years, was built in 1847. Local architect Thomas Lord designed it, along with 13 other churches in Hancock County. (RRS.)

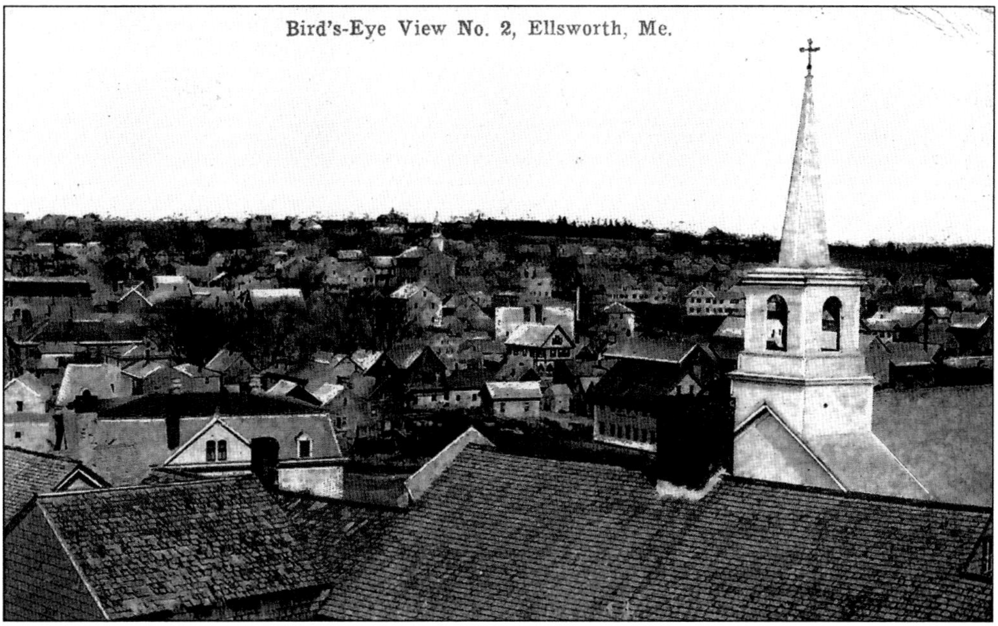

Is this bird's-eye view of Ellsworth recognizable? Much has changed since a photographer snapped this photograph from Bridge Hill around 1910. The late historian Deale B. Salisbury wrote that the view, looking east, shows the old Methodist church on the right and toward the horizon, in the center, the old Baptist church. The roof of the old Ellsworth Odd Fellows Hall is also seen in the lower left. (RRS.)

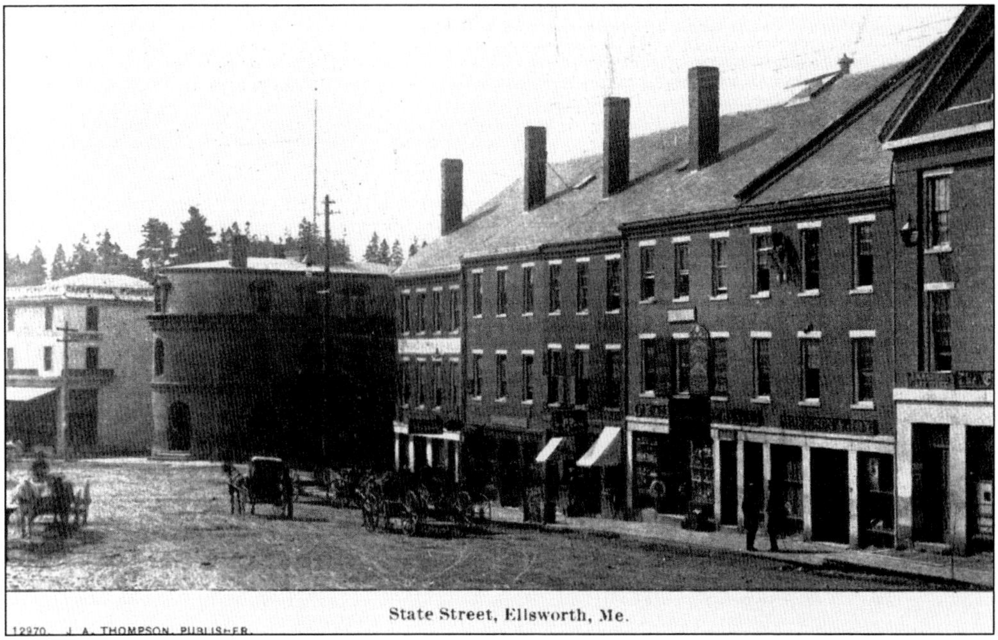

State Street in 1895 was lined with three-story brick buildings. The *Ellsworth American* was published in an office at the far right. In the distance was the corner post office and customs house, which featured a rounded brick design and Ellsworth's only revolving door. Nearby were a GAR hall and the offices of Judge John Peters Jr. (MHPC.)

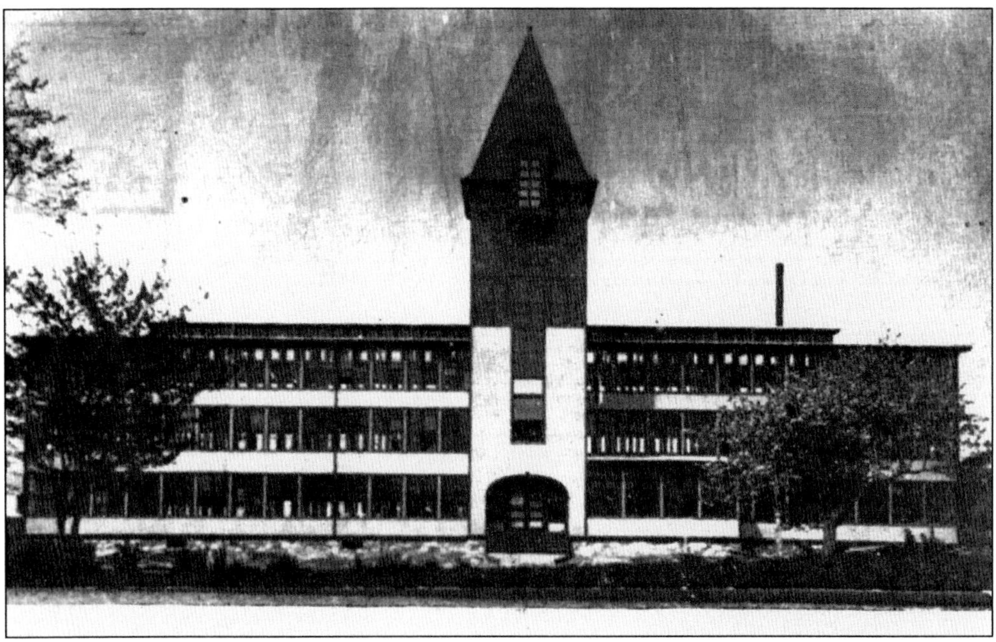

The Dr. Charles C. Knowlton Elementary School occupies the site today, but in another era, this massive mill building made shoes and wood products. Located on State Street, the original $100,000 Pine Tree State Shoe Factory was dedicated on July 4, 1889. It later became the Ellsworth Hardwood Company and turned out such items as pilasters and mop handles. It burned later and was not rebuilt. (MHPC.)

Six

Old Houses of Worship

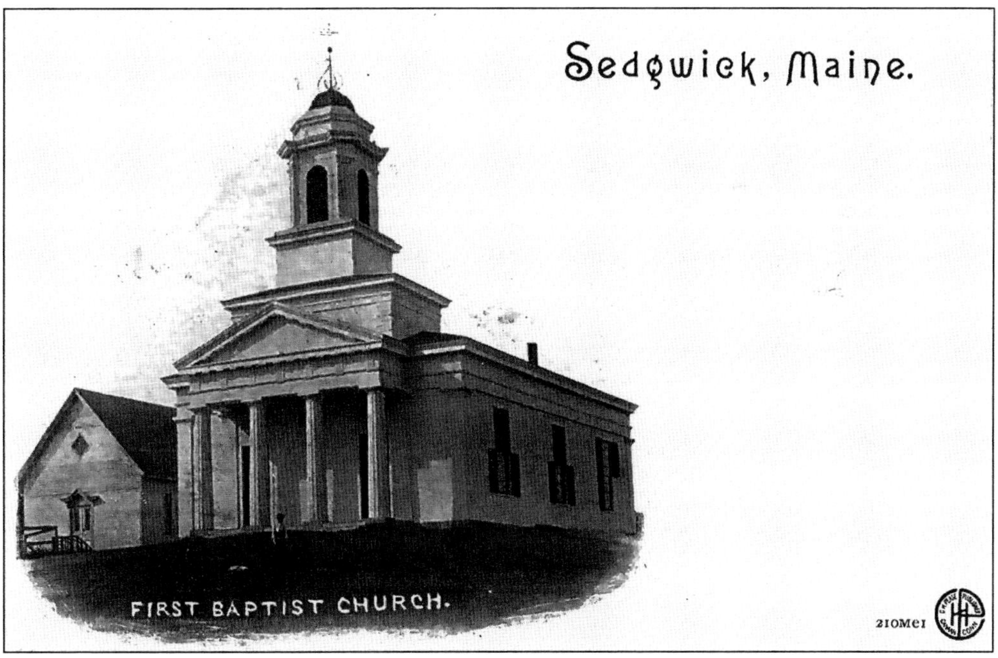

Overlooking the Benjamin River in the village of Sedgwick, the First Baptist Church is a fine example of Greek Revival architecture. It was constructed by 1837, replacing the first church, which dated to 1794. The first minister received an annual salary of £50. In 1973, the church, which was designed by Benjamin S. Deane and also has served as a town hall, was added to the National Register of Historic Places. (RRS.)

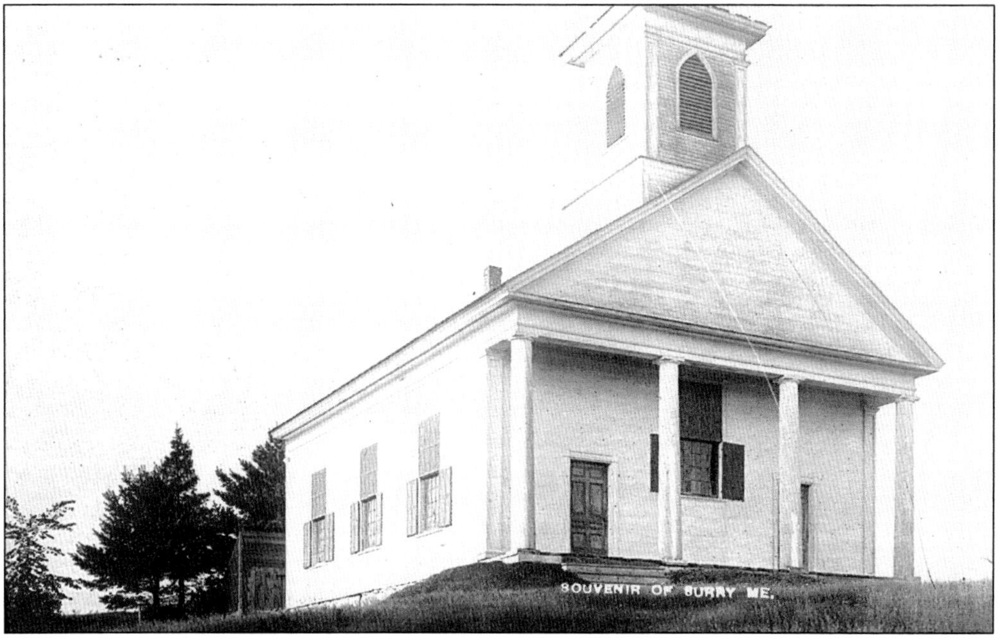

Sometimes postcard objects are not as they seem. A handwritten note, dated March 1, 1914, scrawled on the back of this postcard, reads, "This is a view of the Grange hall at Surry." It certainly resembles a church, leading one to believe that it had been one before the Grange took it over. Today the Arbutus Grange meets every Tuesday at a hall on Route 172. (BPL.)

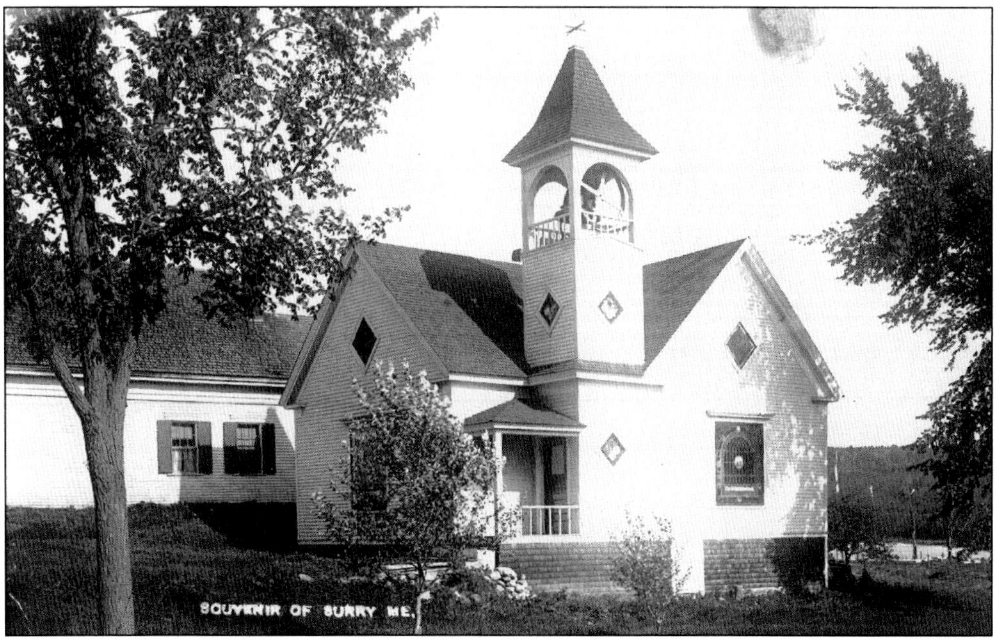

Another Surry church was pictured on a local postcard, dated 1913. Architectural features are the rectangular stained-glass window and the five small, diamond-shaped windows. Rural Hall, located on the Surry Road one mile east of Contention Cove, was listed in the National Register of Historic Places in 2004. (BPL.)

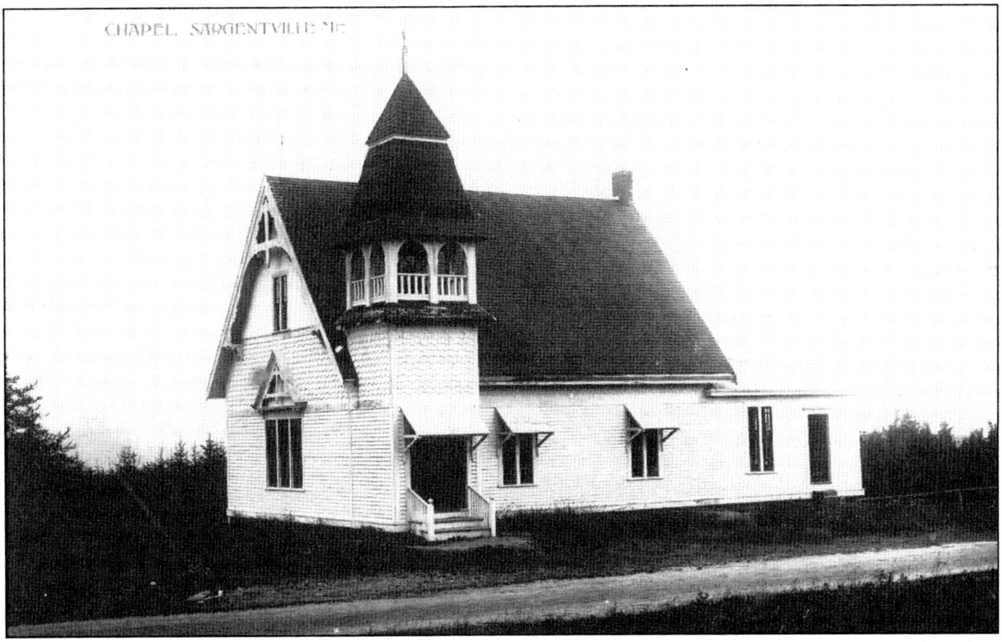

One of Sargentville's churches was a postcard subject in the 1920s. Many coastal Maine churches see increased attendance in the summer, owing to the tourists and seasonal residents looking for a place to worship. Sargentville may be best known as the location of Caterpillar Hill, which affords a breathtaking view of the Deer Isle–Sedgwick Bridge, which spans Eggemoggin Reach. (MHPC.)

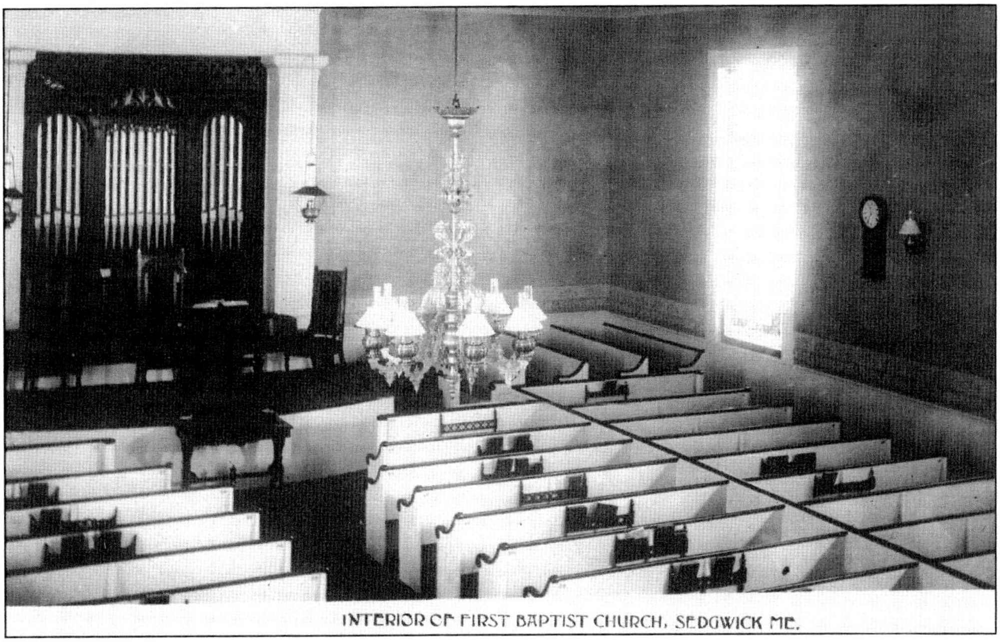

The old wooden clock read 11:30 a.m. when this picture was taken of Sedgwick's First Baptist Church, around 1915. Parishioners sat in white pews, a few of which were perpendicular to the altar. The church had stained-glass windows and an oil chandelier that hung on the high ceiling. Note the hymnals in the backs of some of the pews. (MHPC.)

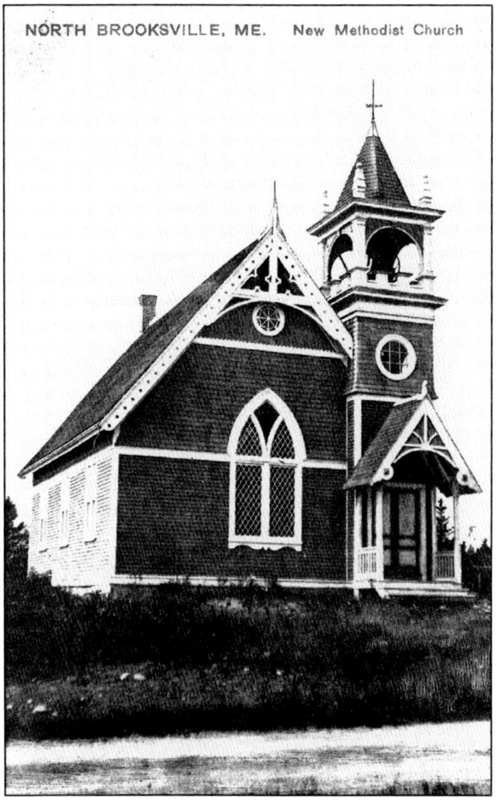

The New Methodist Church in North Brooksville was a handsome building. People no doubt snapped up this postcard showing its lovely architecture, arched window, church steeple, bell, and high wooden cross. Such churches were nice to look at but also served a functional purpose. The seating capacity was often greater than might be expected. (MHPC.)

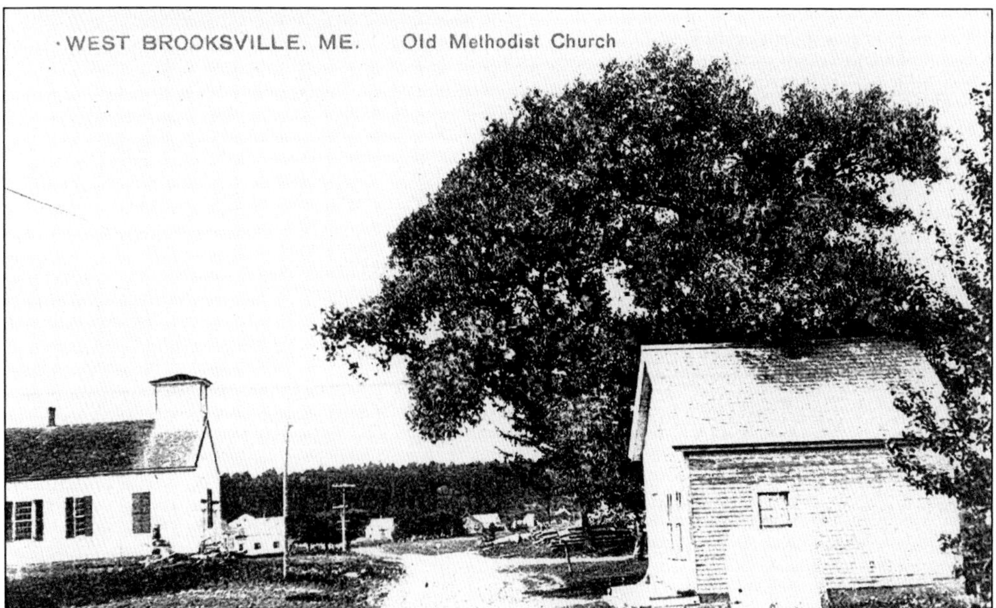

West Brooksville's old Methodist church was a simply designed building, with a flat steeple. A black cross hung from the front of the building. Many such Hancock County towns were populated by Baptists and Methodists, who raised the money to build their churches. Today those churches are the principal landmarks in all of these towns. (RRS.)

The vertical architecture of the Union Church in West Franklin fits the dimensions of this postcard very well. A high steeple is topped by a brass weather vane. A variety of differently shaped windows adorn the old wooden structure. Church doors were typically wide enough to let entire families pass through. And after the church service, the pastor waiting just inside the doorway would not let them out without a kind word and a firm handshake. (MHPC.)

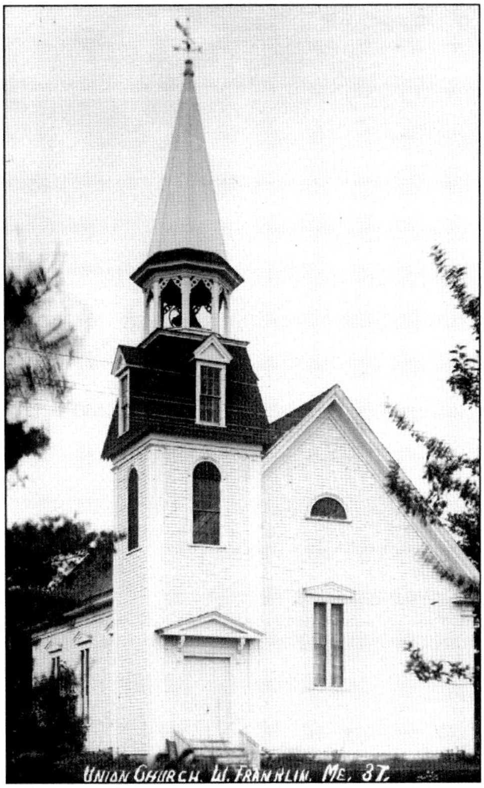

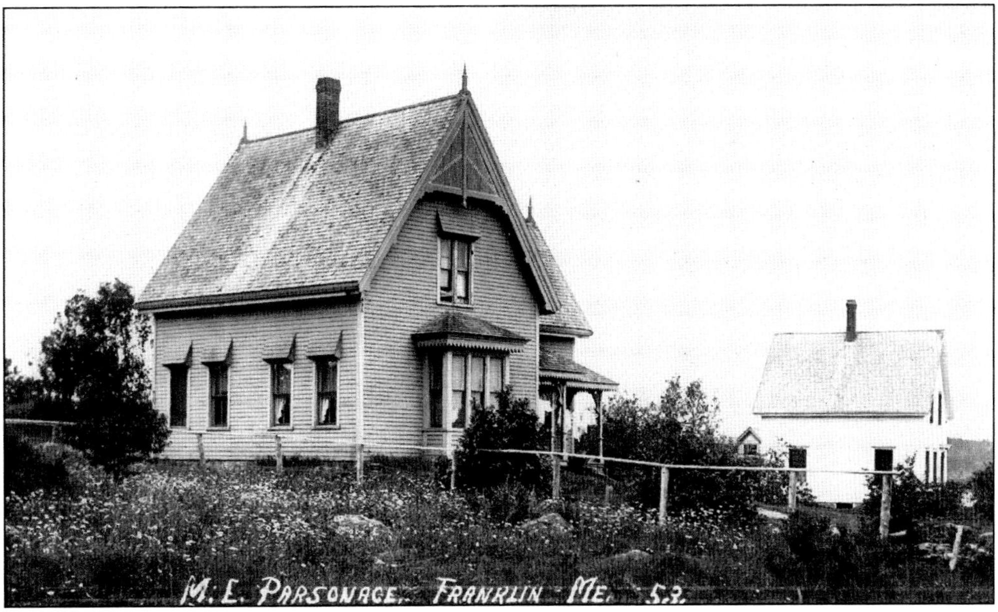

The Methodist Episcopal church parsonage in Franklin is seen in a rural setting in the 1920s. Daisies grow in the front yard, laundry hangs on the front porch, and the property is bordered by a wooden fence. The roofline has almost a churchlike design, not a bad thing to house the local minister and his family. Churches set aside funds for the purchase and maintenance of parsonages, often located next to the houses of worship. (MHPC.)

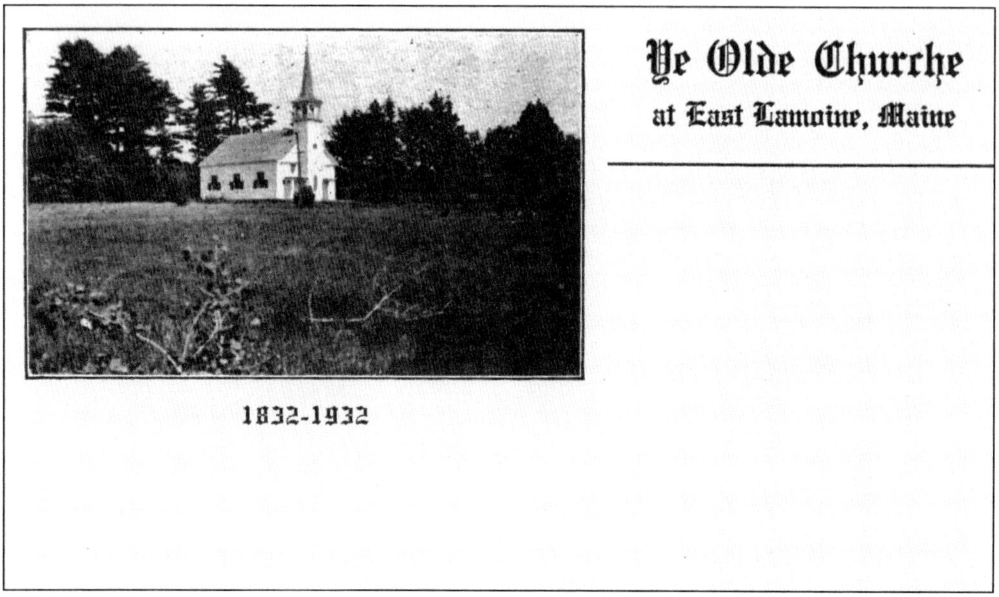

A commemorative postcard celebrates the centennial of "Ye Olde Churche" in East Lamoine. The church was founded in 1832, and this card came out in 1932. The name is quaint in a New England sort of way. But how many townspeople actually referred to the building as Ye Olde Churche? Probably very few, if the truth were told. (RRS.)

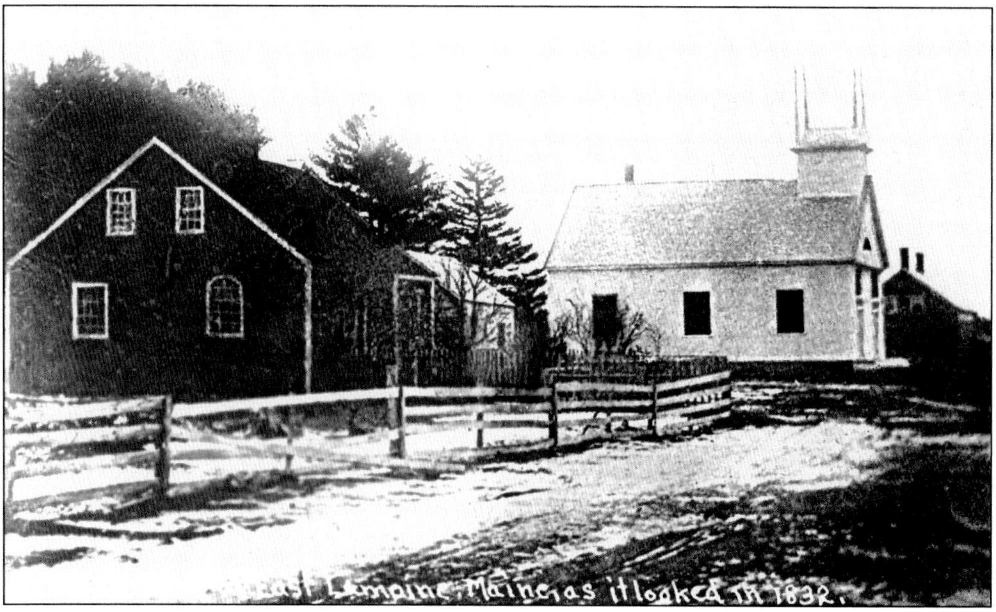

An earlier view shows the same church, or at least one on the same site. The caption states that this is how the church looked in 1832, so it must have remained unchanged up into the early 20th century, the date of this photograph. Note the houses on either side of the structure and the church's small white steeple. (RRS.)

This postcard pictures Church of Our Father in Sullivan as a beautiful little church, with graceful architecture. Today's churches in Sullivan include Sullivan Harbor Church, North Sullivan United Methodist Church, Union Church, and Community Church. An Episcopal Church of Our Father, probably unrelated to the earlier one in Sullivan, is located across the bay in Hulls Cove. (MHPC.)

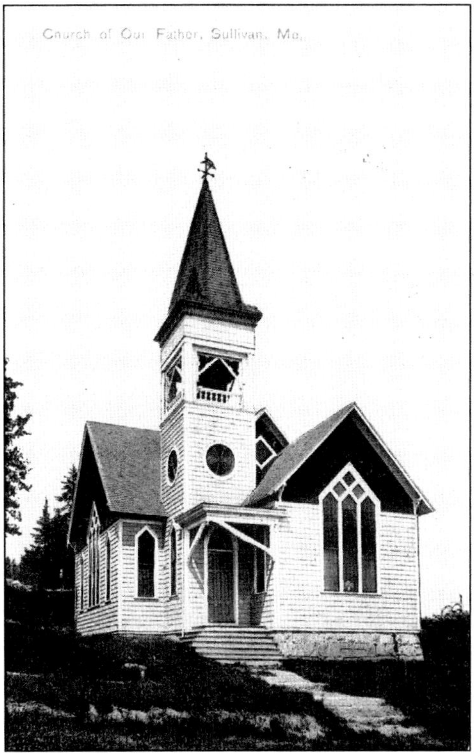

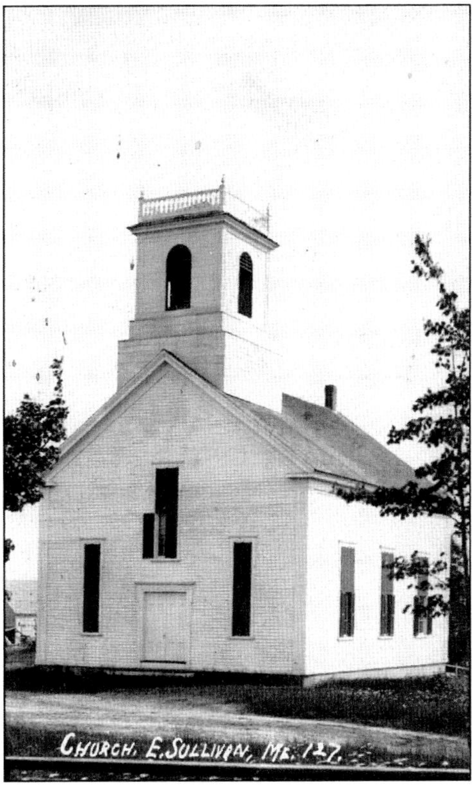

Many churches scattered throughout New England have the same sort of architecture as this church in East Sullivan. There is the familiar broad steeple, with a widow's walk on top reaching toward the heavens. Churches made good postcard subjects, as they were easily identifiable and spoke well of the persons sending them. This one was postmarked in Sullivan on January 12, 1915. (MHPC.)

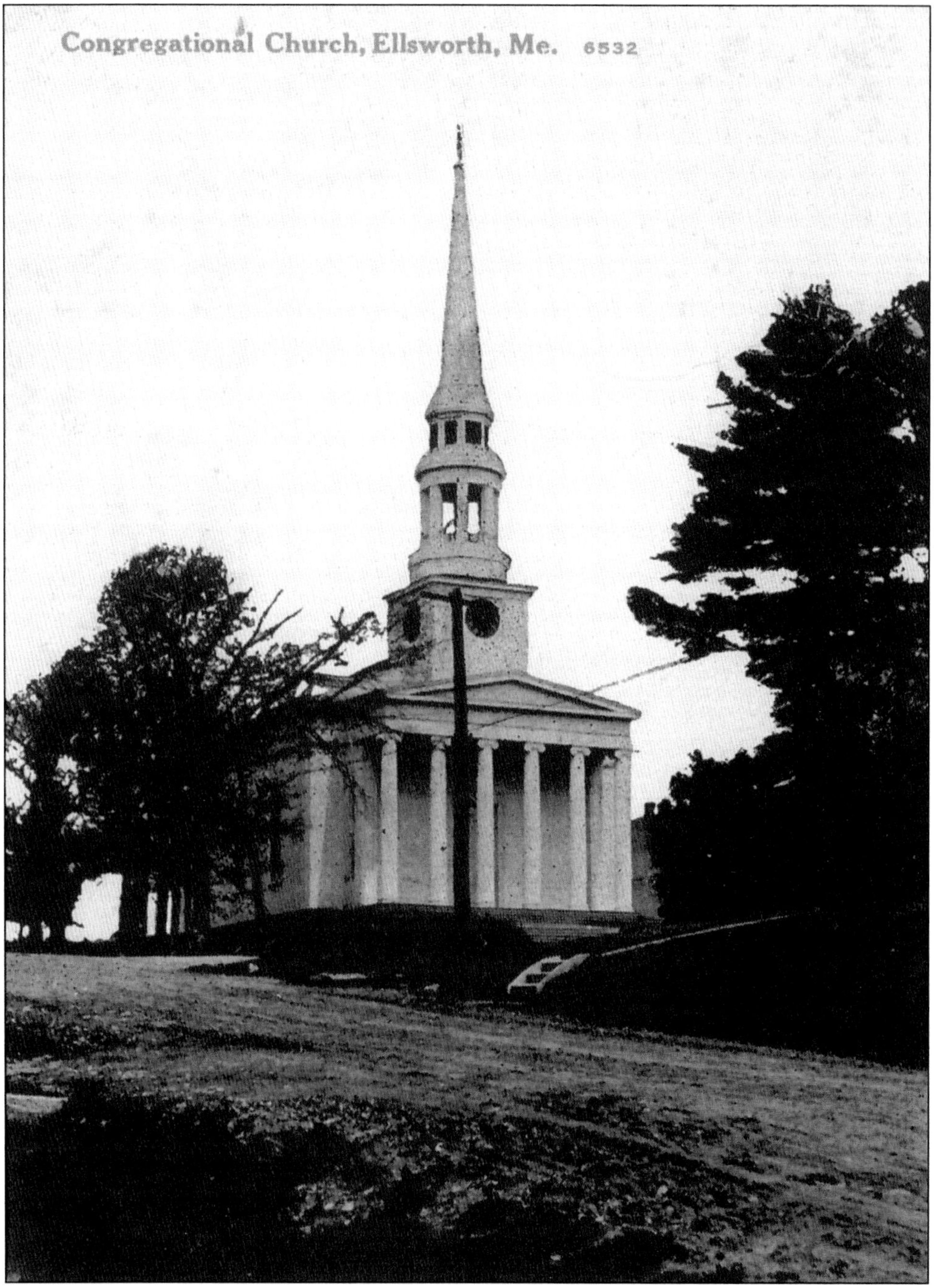

Its tall white spire, clock, and six columns make Ellsworth's First Congregational Church one of Hancock County's most recognizable religious landmarks. The building was constructed in 1847 by the prolific Thomas Lord, who built 14 churches in the county. An original Congregational church was built on this site, later to become Church Street, in 1818. It was torn down and replaced by the present church to meet the growing congregation attracted by the dynamic pastor Rev. Sewell Tenney. In 1972, members voted to join the United Church of Christ. A year later, the building was listed in the National Register of Historic Places. (RRS.)

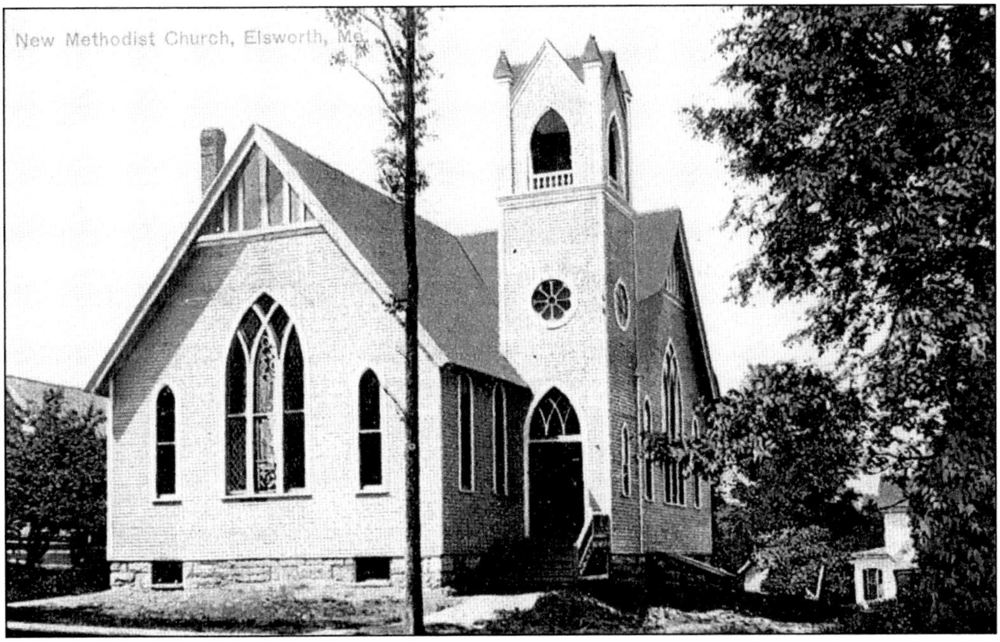

People wept when the Methodist church and parsonage went up in flames during the 1933 Ellsworth fire. The church was located on Hancock Street, and eventually parishioners planned a new church building on the same site. Rebuilding began in 1934, and on December 18, 1938, the new church was dedicated. Residents with long memories recalled the burning of the original Methodist church on Bridge Hill in the winter of 1904. (BPL.)

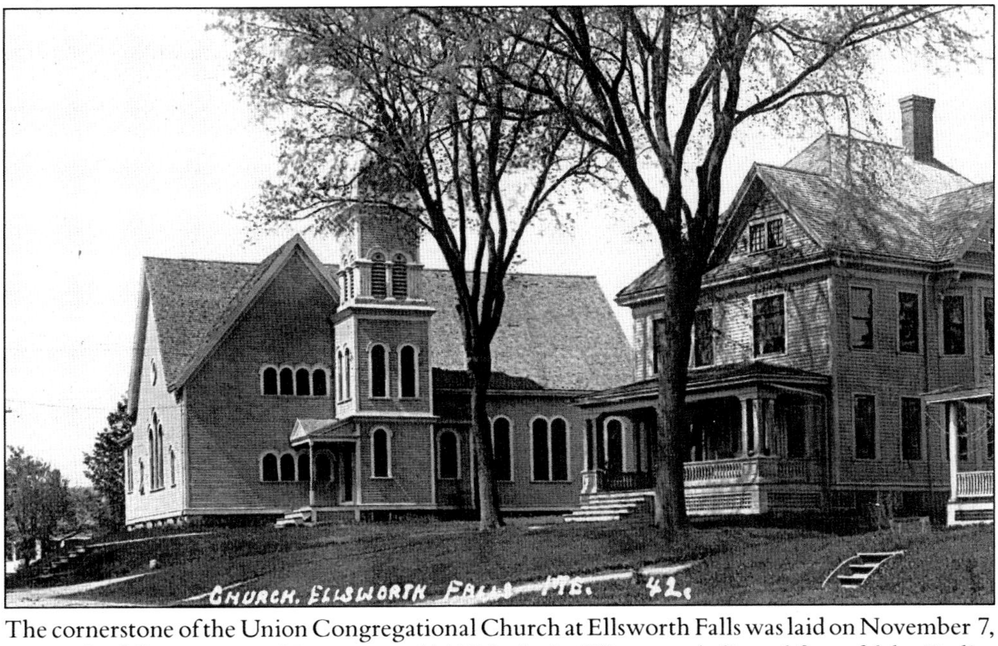

The cornerstone of the Union Congregational Church at Ellsworth Falls was laid on November 7, 1896. The following May 25, at a cost of $4,700, the building was dedicated free of debt. Earlier in the century, local ministers from downtown would come out to the falls to preach, so having a separate falls church was quite an accomplishment. On March 19, 1961, the Union Church voted to join in membership with the United Church of Christ. (BPL.)

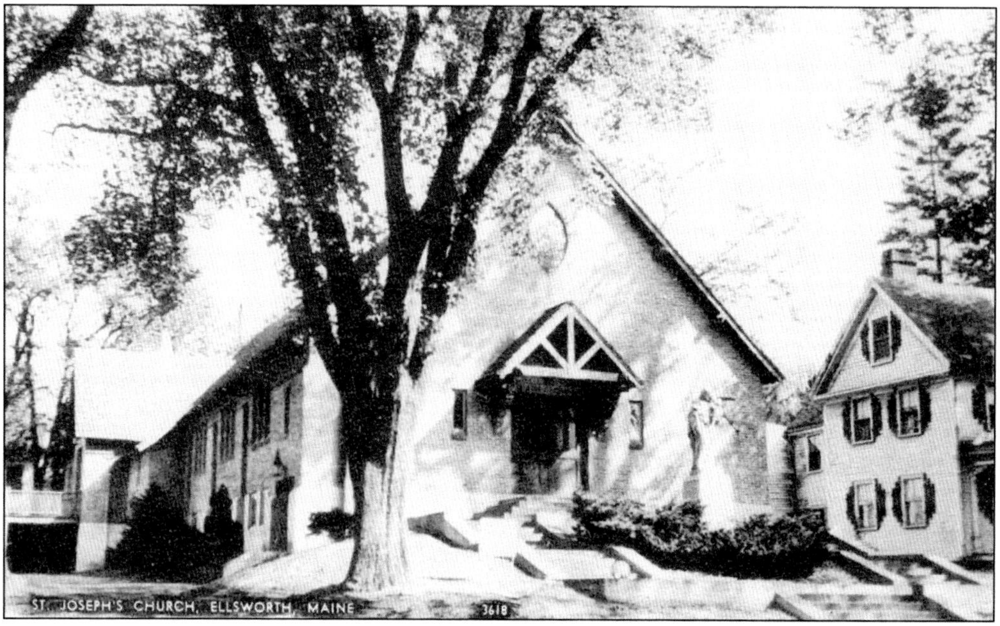

Members of Ellsworth's Catholic community have worshiped at St. Joseph's Church on High Street since it was built in 1939. Before that, the faithful attended services at Catholic churches on Chapel Street, and originally, on High Street, between Elm and Deane Streets. In the summer, a St. Joseph's Church outreach program conducts weekend masses at Blue Hill, Green Lake, and Winter Harbor. (RRS.)

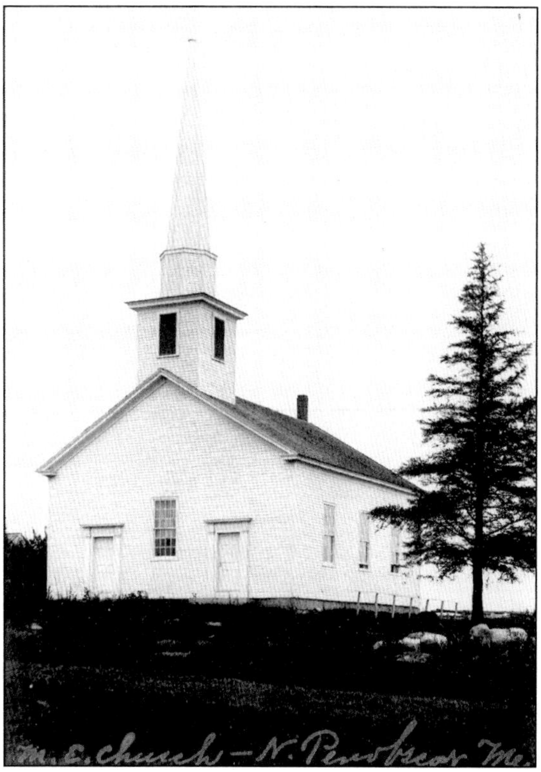

For a century and a half, the North Penobscot United Methodist Church stood on the hill where Route 15 meets Route 199. By 1991, it was decided to move the old landmark to Blue Hill, where it was reconstructed on Route 177 as the St. Francis-by-the-Sea Episcopal Church. Parishioners still worship in the original church pews. Although the building has been expanded and somewhat redesigned, its simple architecture, including the tall white spire, remains. (MHPC.)

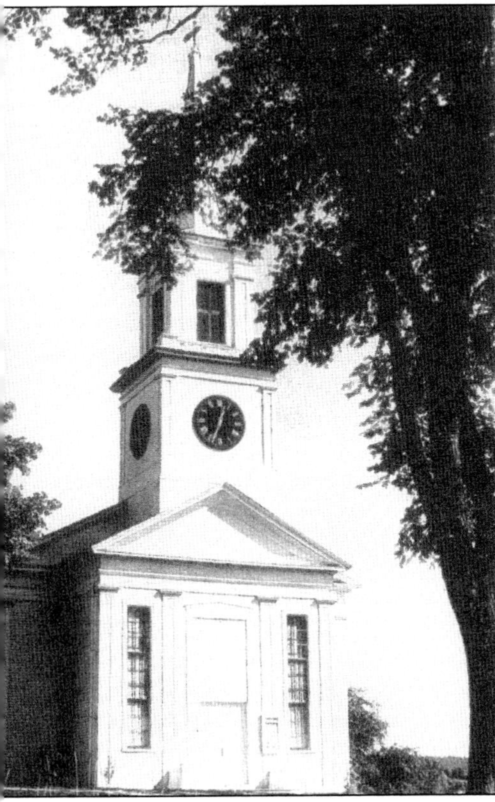

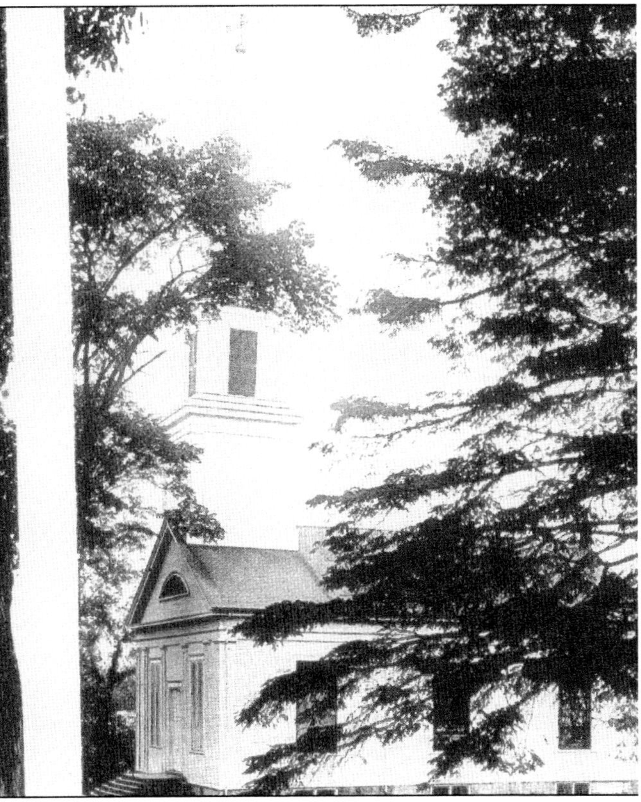

Blue Hill's two crowning glories would have to be the Baptist church (left) and First Congregational Church (right). Reaching well back into the 19th century, the landmarks' tall spires reassured sailors at sea, local residents, and summer visitors that religion played a major role in the town's development. The Congregational church on Main Street was dedicated in January 1843, having replaced an earlier meetinghouse that burned on January 2, 1842. The Reverend Jonathan Fisher pastored the earlier church. The present Greek Revival–style church was built by Thomas Lord and designed by Benjamin S. Deane. A copy of a Paul Revere bell hangs in the church, which has six stained-glass windows. The Blue Hill Baptist Church sits on a hill on Pleasant Street. It was started in 1817, after the town's newly formed Baptist organization had been meeting in barns, houses, and fields. Later work on the church added a clock, a second story, a high pulpit, box pews, and galleries. The bell was hung in 1858, being the gift of the Ladies' Sewing Circle. Thomas Lord remodeled the interior to its present appearance. The chapel was built in 1880, and the oak pews, still in use today, replaced the earlier white ones in 1928. The church was later responsible for three satellite churches, at South Blue Hill (1825), East Blue Hill (1880), and Penobscot (1878). (BHPL.)

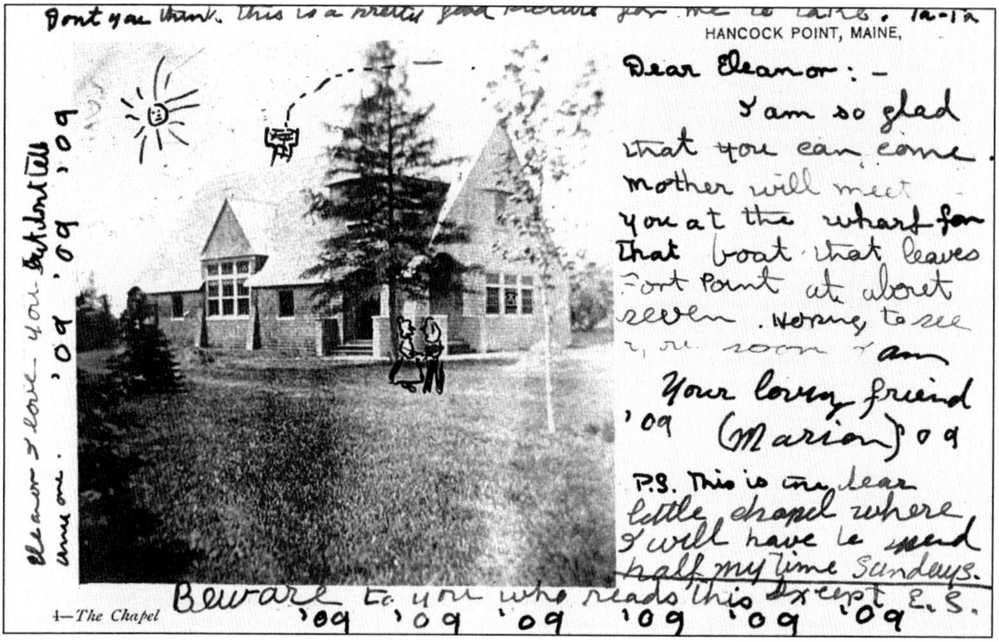

Almost lost in this unique old postcard is the beautiful wood-shingled chapel at Hancock Point. A particularly prolific correspondent named Marion used up every inch in 1906 to catch up on all the news. The chapel was built in 1898–1899 and was maintained by the Chapel Society. Noted for its graceful architecture and lovely windows, the chapel is a favorite place for weddings and non-religious functions. (RRS.)

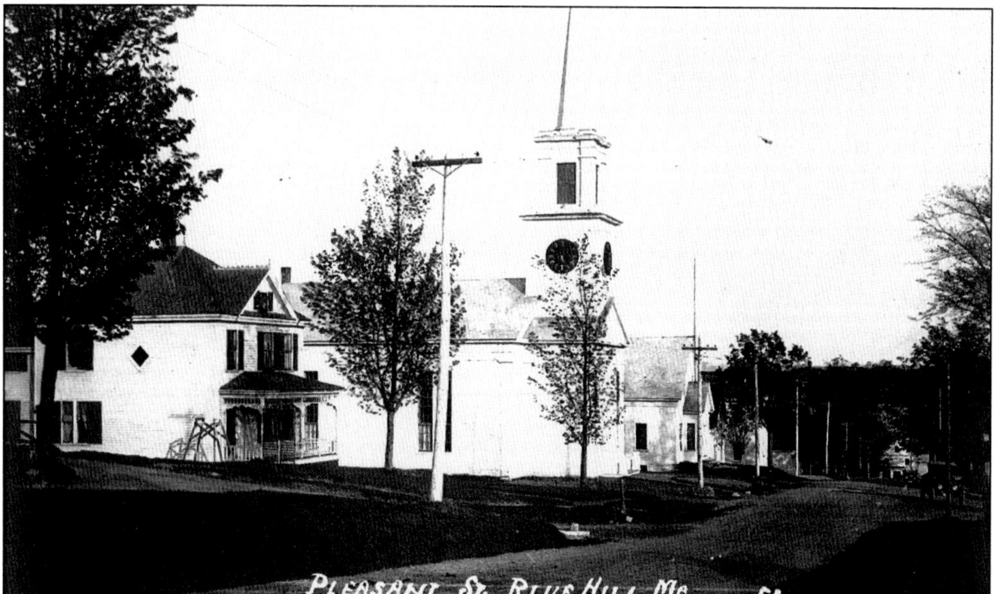

No matter how many times one has driven down Pleasant Street toward Blue Hill village, the sight of the Baptist church still inspires. Originally the minister preached from a high pulpit and parishioners sat in box pews after this landmark was built in 1817. Thomas Lord, renowned for having built 14 Hancock County churches, remodeled the interior to its present appearance in the 1850s. (BPL.)

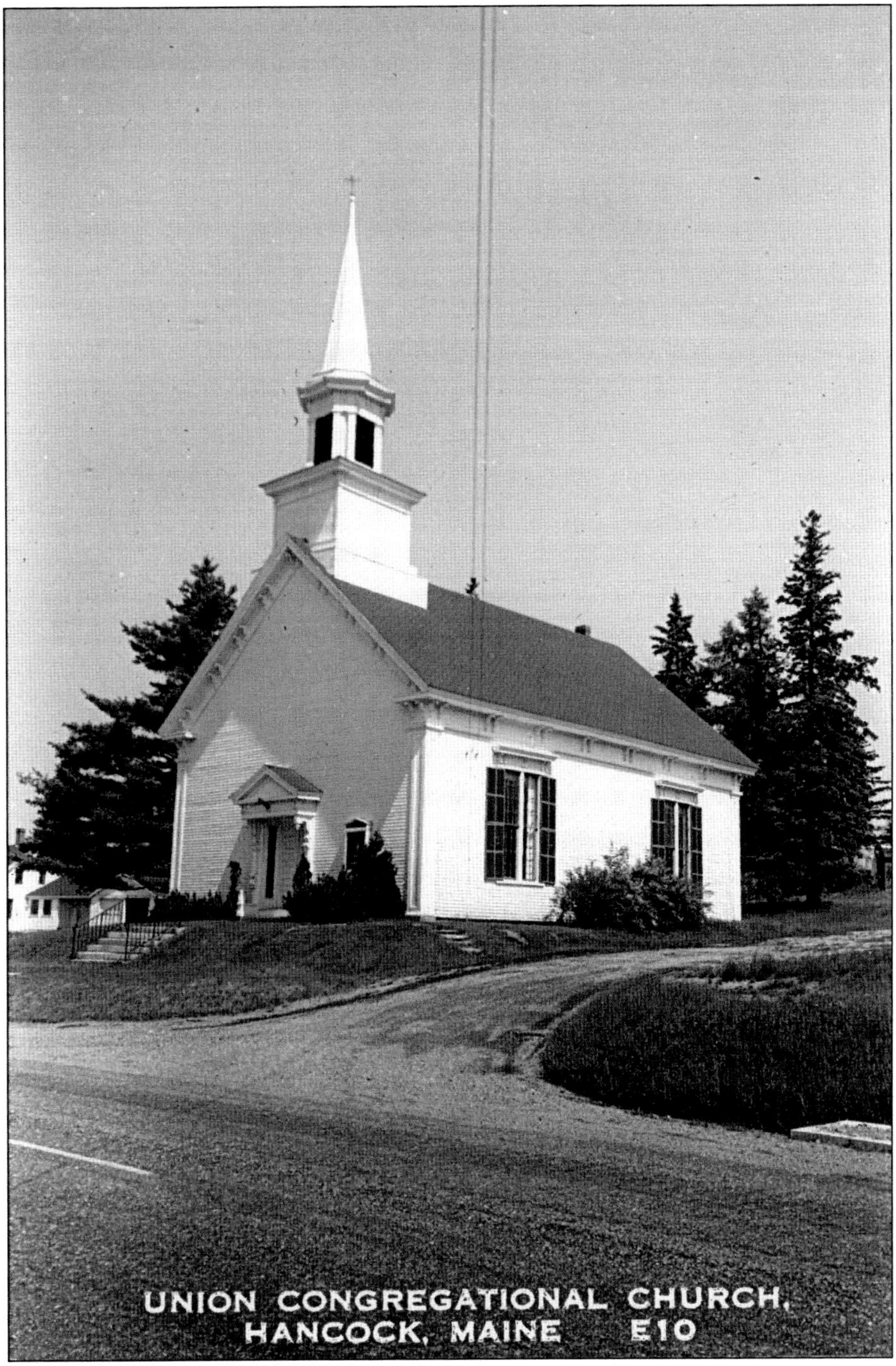

The gleaming white spire of the Union Congregational Church on Route 1 in Hancock has long been a beacon for travelers heading Down East. Originally one of three Baptist churches in Hancock, its members voted to turn Congregational in 1940. Originally called the Church at the Corner, the Union Congregational Church's interior architecture was changed after 1940, including the construction of an altar in 1942 and the removal of the front pews. The vestry was added in 1967, and in 1973, a new steeple replaced the old one. (RRS.)

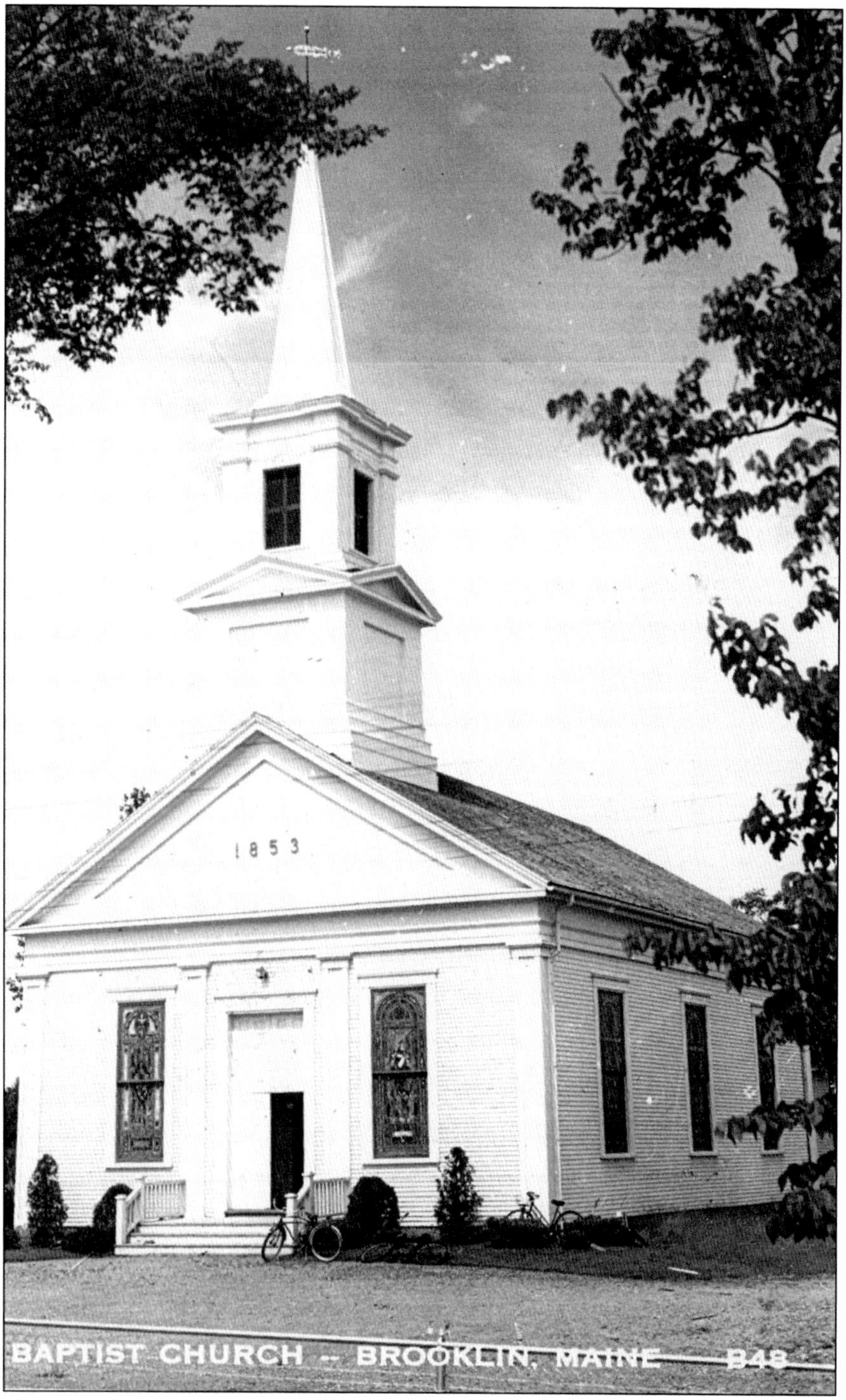

The Baptist church in Brooklin Center is a wonderful example of 19th-century church architecture. It also speaks volumes about the high value the townspeople placed on religion that they would raise the funds to construct such a beautiful house of worship. Visitors often remark about the beautiful stained-glass windows and the symmetrical lines of the 1853 church's architecture. It was located across from the Brooklin General Store. (BPL.)

Seven

Favorite County Landmarks

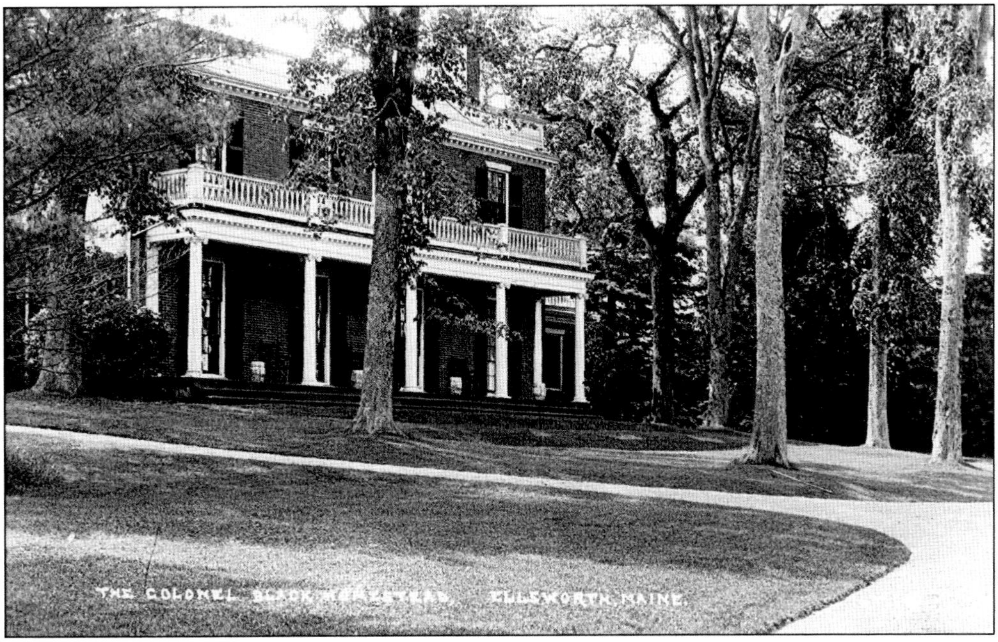

Woodlawn, better known as the Black Mansion, is one of Maine's most treasured museums. Wealthy land agent Col. John Black (1781–1856) had it built between 1824 and 1828 and spared no expense. A curious feature of the Ellsworth mansion is that visitors must enter from the side. Colonel Black probably wanted only windows on the front from which to admire the sweeping view to the south. (Brian Swartz.)

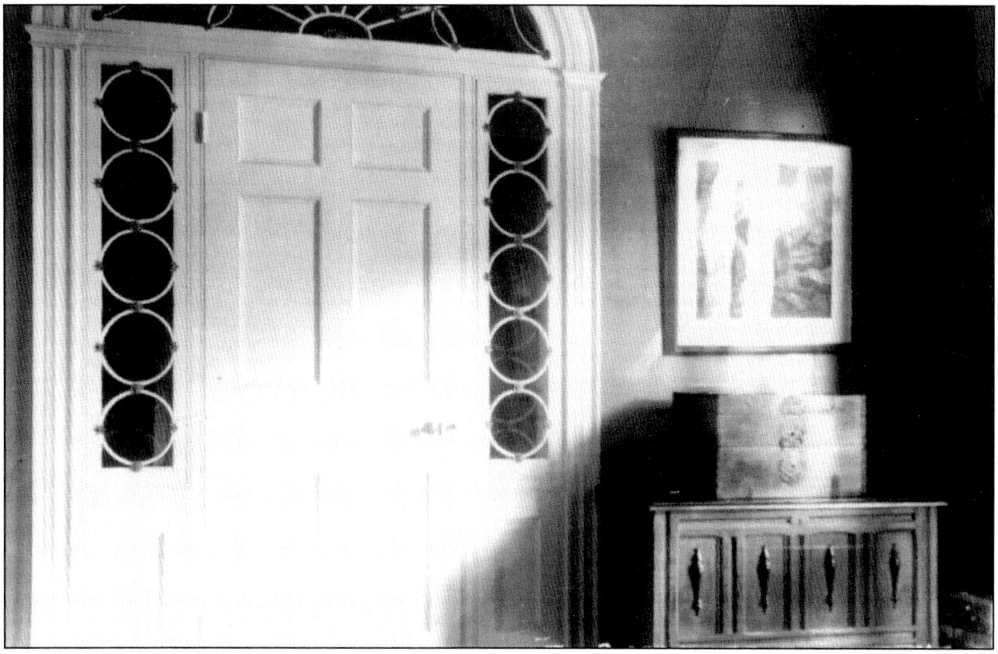

Col. John Black enjoyed welcoming guests at this lovely old doorway. The five round panes of glass on either side, and the ornate fanlight over the door, are original to the house. Woodlawn, as Ellsworth's Black Mansion is known, is open as a museum and open to the public in the summer months. (MHPC.)

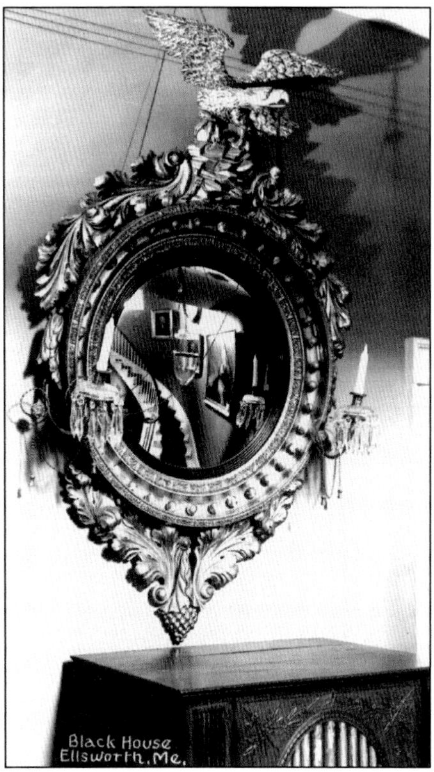

This gorgeous brass eagle mirror has been a favorite subject of postcard photographers. Because of its weight, two strong cables hold it in place. The grand stairway, chandelier, and oil portrait of Colonel Black are reflected in the round mirror. Many of these old black and white views still turn up at antique shops and auctions. (MHPC.)

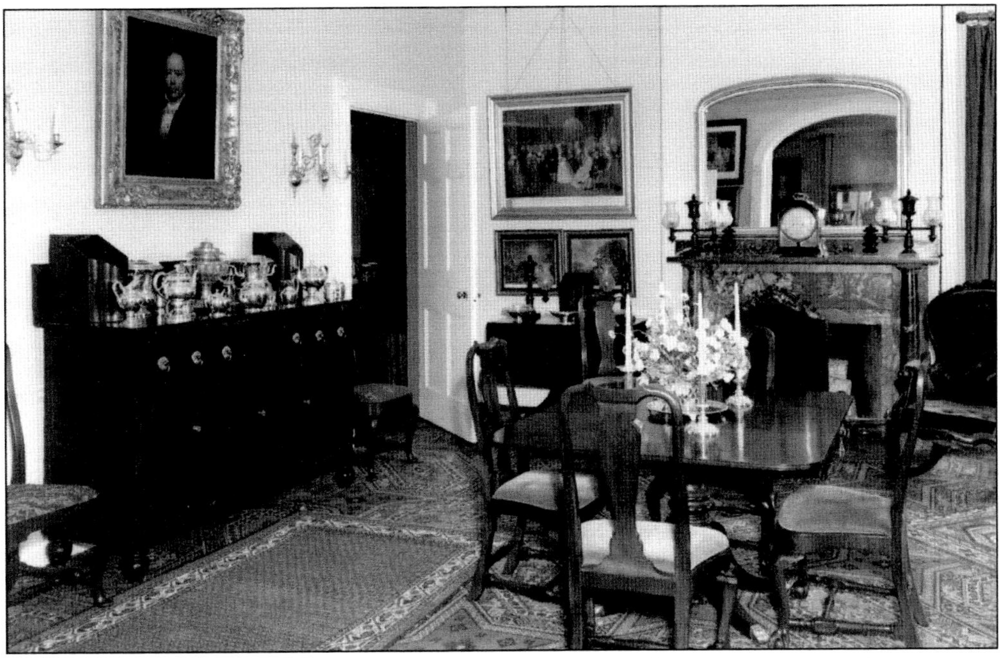

How many dinner conversations were held in this fine old dining room? And what were the topics of conversation? George Nixon Black Jr. saw that his grandfather's classic mansion was left in a trust in the early 20th century. It has been carefully restored and rates as one of coastal Maine's premier historical attractions. The grounds are also open to the public. In 2007, the Shakespearean play *As You Like It* was performed on the property. (MHPC.)

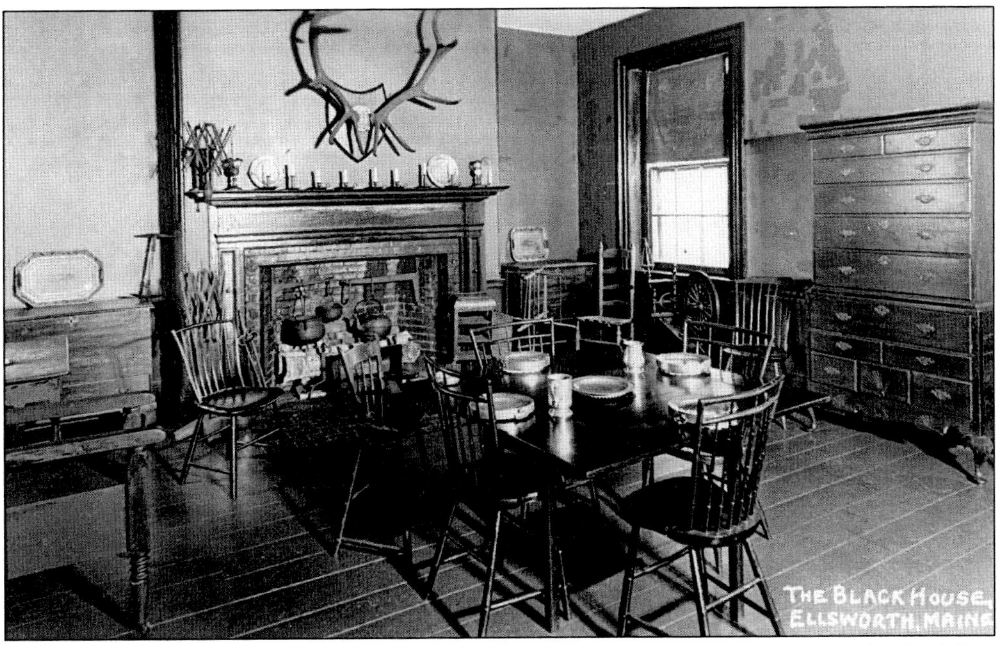

The kitchen of his old mansion is just as Colonel Black would remember it. A wooden high boy sat on the right, a simple table and chairs were there, and a pair of Canadian elk horns hung over the fireplace. Kitchens were popular meeting places for Maine families in early times. (RRS.)

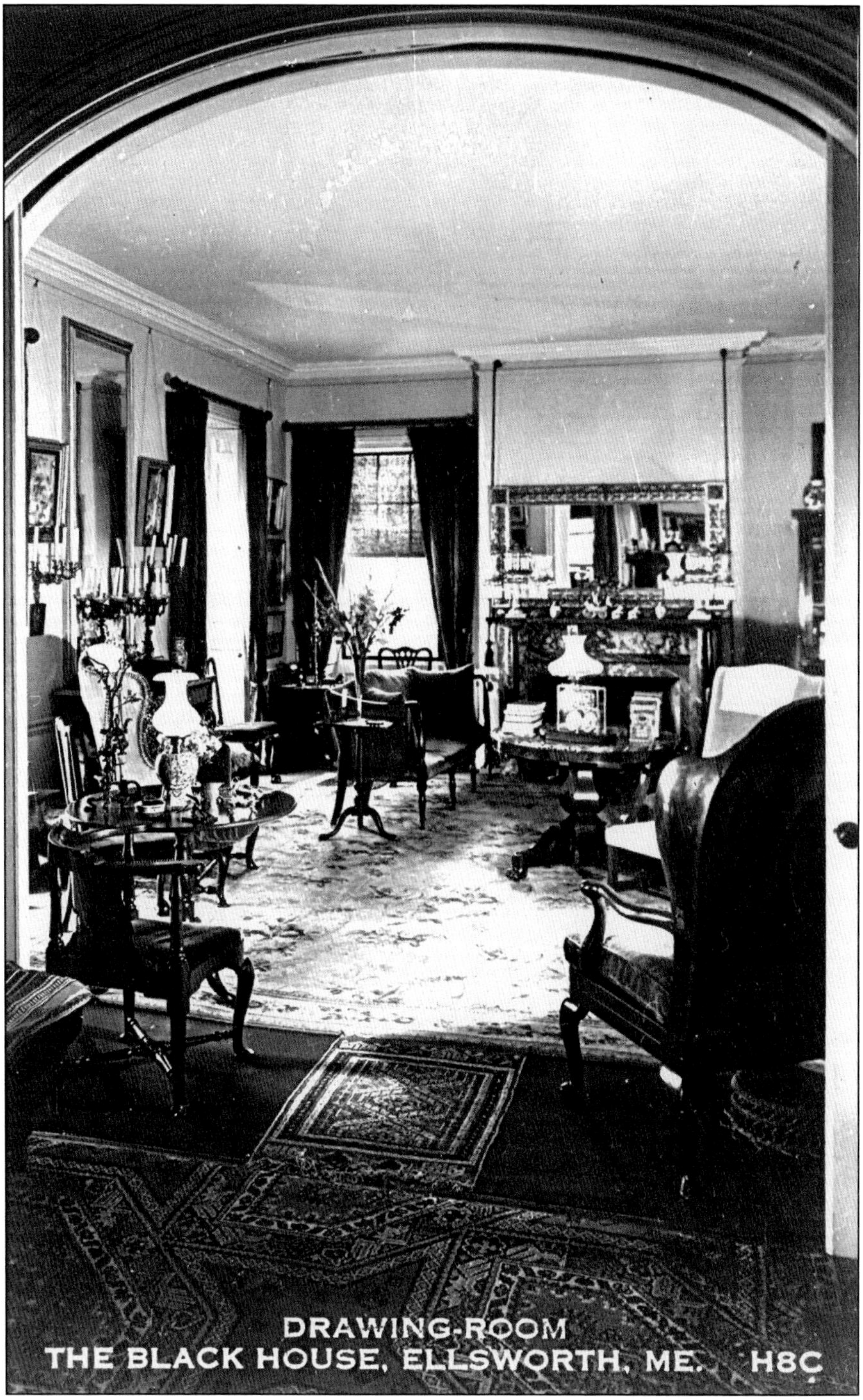

Col. John Black's drawing room must have been a cozy place to relax or carry on conversation during cold winter nights. One can imagine some hard bargaining carried on here, as well. Colonel Black was a driving personality who became the wealthiest man east of Bangor in an era when land speculation could make or break a man. Colonel Black took innumerable chances and won nearly all of them. (RRS.)

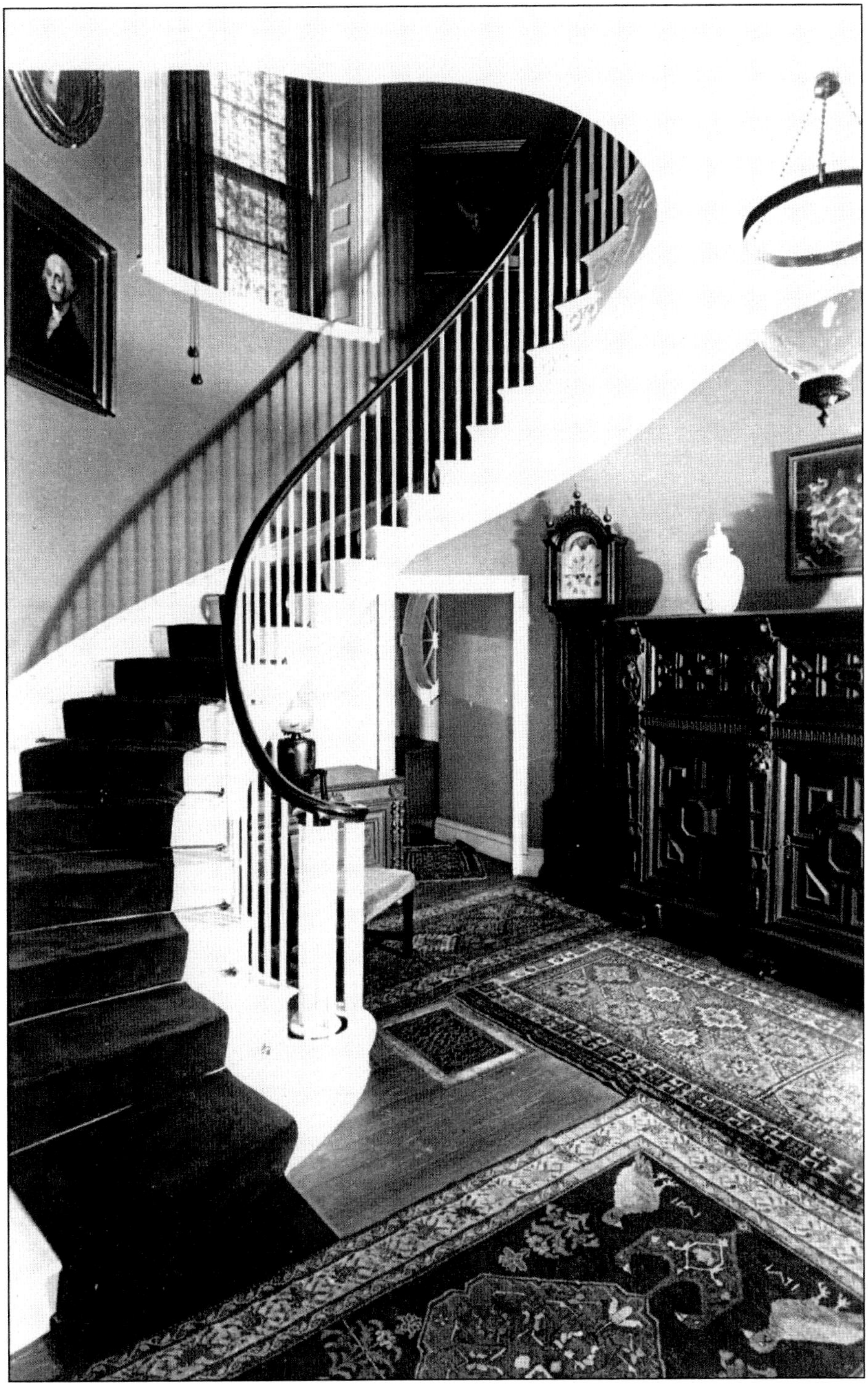

One of the glories of Woodlawn is its lovely curving staircase. A chandelier, grandfather clock, and oriental rugs only add to the elegance. Oil portraits line the stairway walls. The largest pictures Colonel Black's father-in-law, Gen. David Cobb, the first agent in Maine for the Bingham estate. The Gilbert Stuart portrait of George Washington is a reproduction. (RRS.)

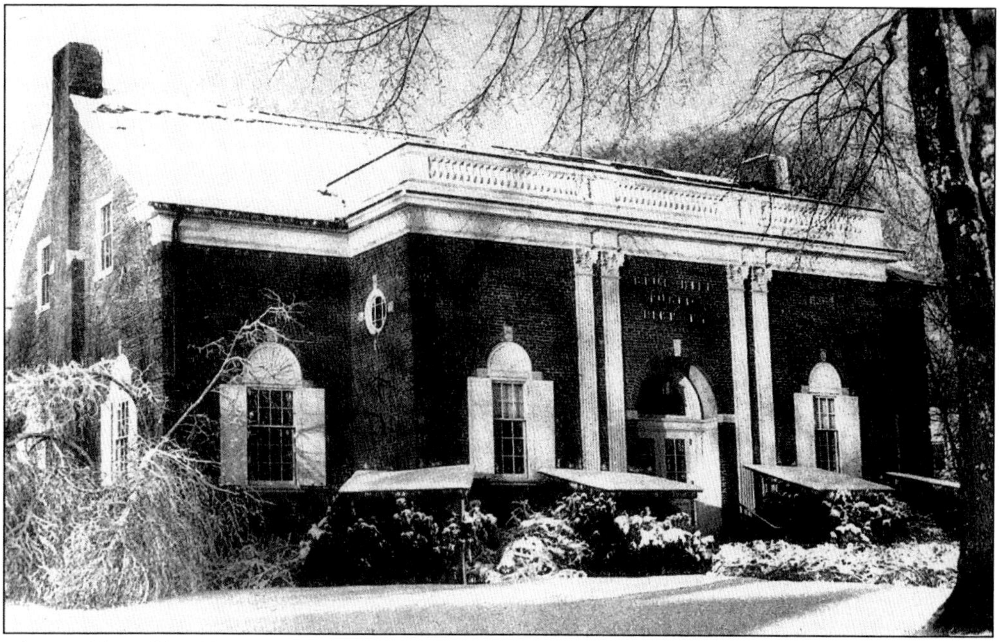

Blue Hill's public library has grown and evolved over the years, but the sturdy brick facade never seems to change. Neither does its librarians' mission to help anyone, local or visitor. The library was opened in 1940 with the help of Adelaide Pearson, who solicited private donations. Also instrumental was Anne Hinckley, who secured aid from the Public Works Administration. (BHPL.)

The Friend Memorial Library in Brooklin is a welcoming place where children and adults can research school projects or hear lectures by regional authors. Author E. B. White and his wife, Katharine, who lived in Brooklin, supported the library in many ways. In 1952, book prizes, courtesy of the Whites, were awarded to 15 students. In 1994, the Friends of Friend Memorial Library planted a garden that brings together things dear to the Whites: flowers, birds, books, and children. (RRS.)

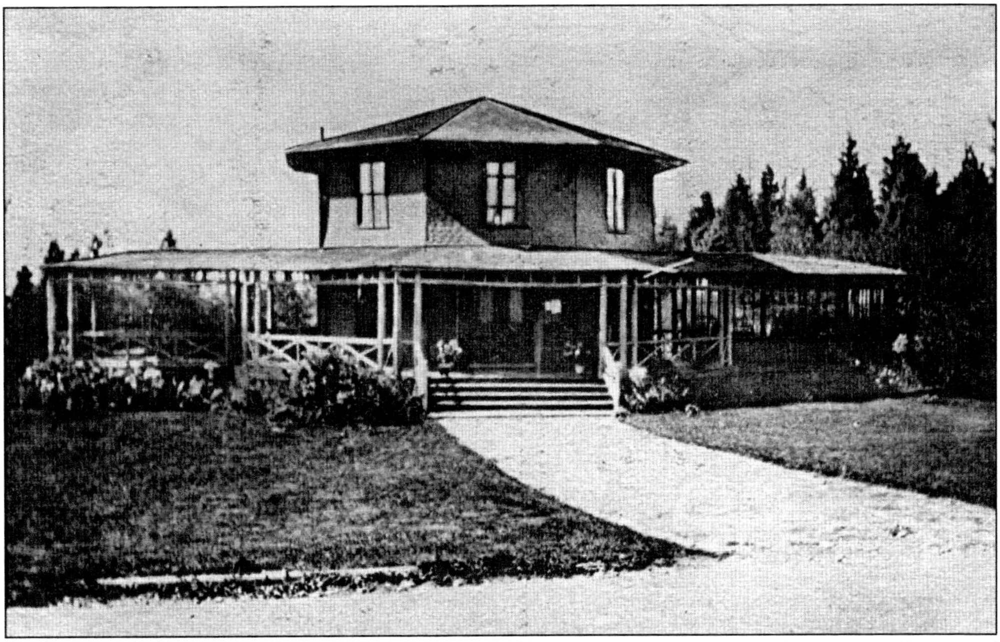

Hancock Point's century-old library was built in an octagonal design by Isaac Johnson of Bangor. Johnson was very familiar with eight-sided objects since he put up liniment oil in octagonal bottles. A lovely watercolor of the library by Carol Jessen appears on the back cover of the two-volume history, *The Sun Never Sets on Hancock Point.* (BPL.)

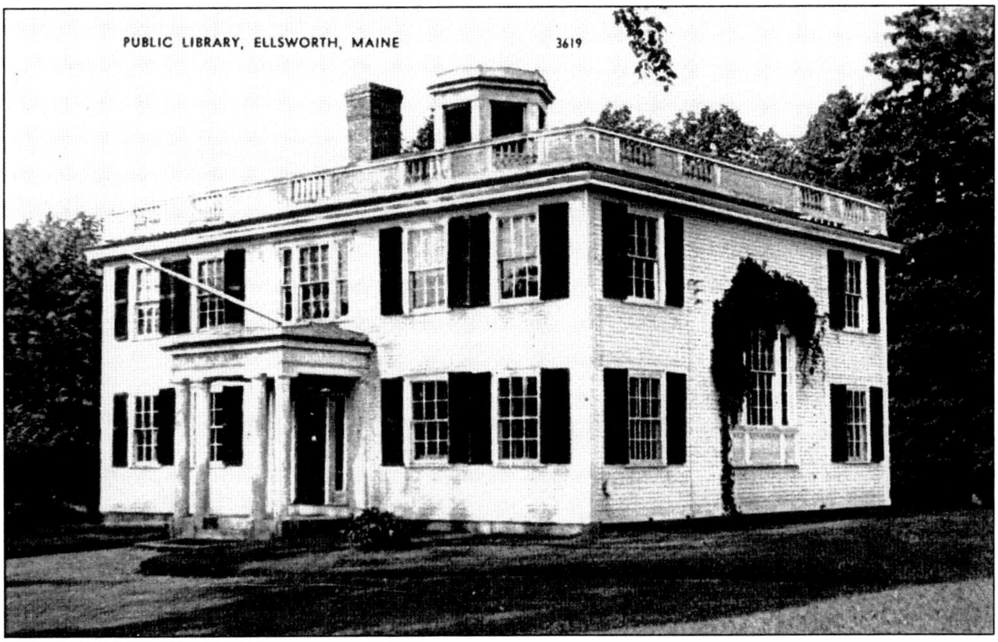

Walking into the Ellsworth Public Library is like entering someone's home. And in a way, library patrons are. In 1897, George Nixon Black Jr., grandson of Col. John Black, bought the 1817 Seth Tisdale house and had it remodeled as a public library. On December 24, 1897, the deed was turned over to the citizens of Ellsworth. Today a modern wing expands the library's space without losing its intimacy or charm. (Ellsworth Public Library.)

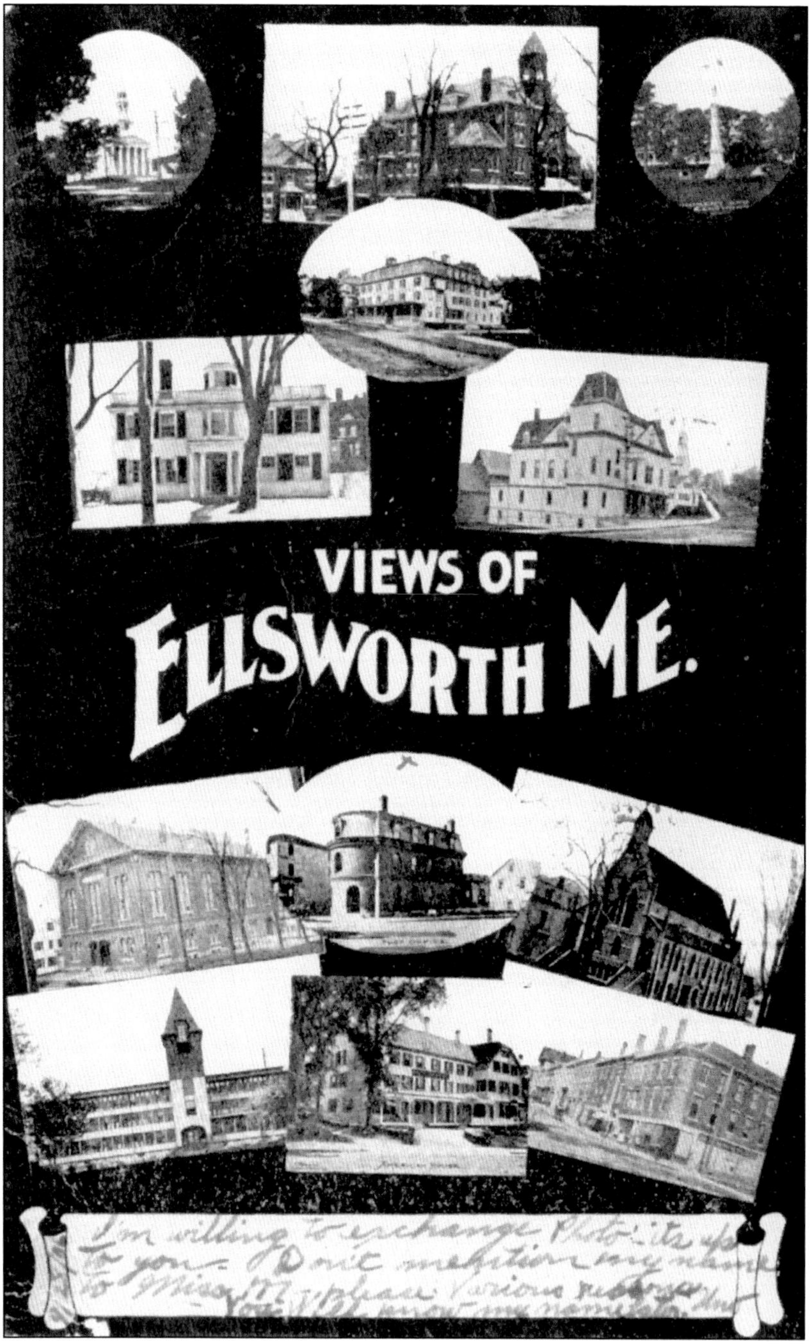

A multi-view 1906 postcard pictures a dozen landmarks. Separate fires destroyed the old Hancock County Courthouse (top, center), Hancock Hall (fourth row, left), and the Ellsworth Hardwood Company (bottom row, left). Demolished blocks include the Hancock House (second row), the old post office and customhouse (fourth row, center), and the Unitarian church (fourth row, right). Surviving landmarks shown are the First Congregational Church (top row, left), the Civil War monument (top row, right), the Ellsworth Public Library (third row, left), and 19th-century business blocks untouched by the 1933 fire (bottom, right). (RRS.)

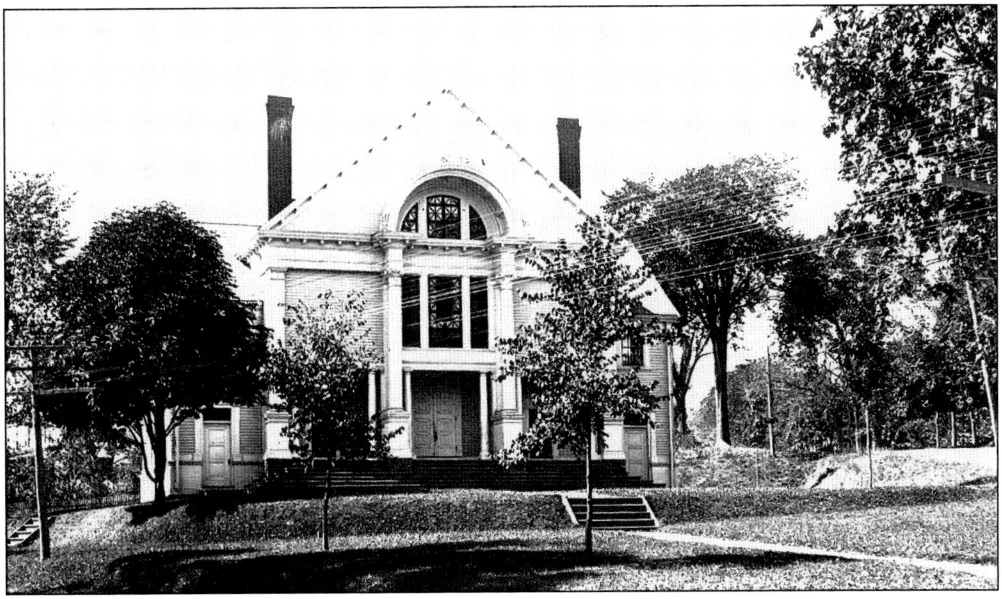

Blue Hill's landmarks stand in stark contrast to Ellsworth's. The smaller community is dotted with fewer brick blocks and more wooden landmarks like the town hall building, noted for its ornate wooden columns. Unlike Ellsworth, which has been ravaged by fire, Blue Hill has been spared this devastation, so most of its downtown treasures are intact. Cultural events such as New Surry Theatre productions are held in the old town hall, shown here. (RRS.)

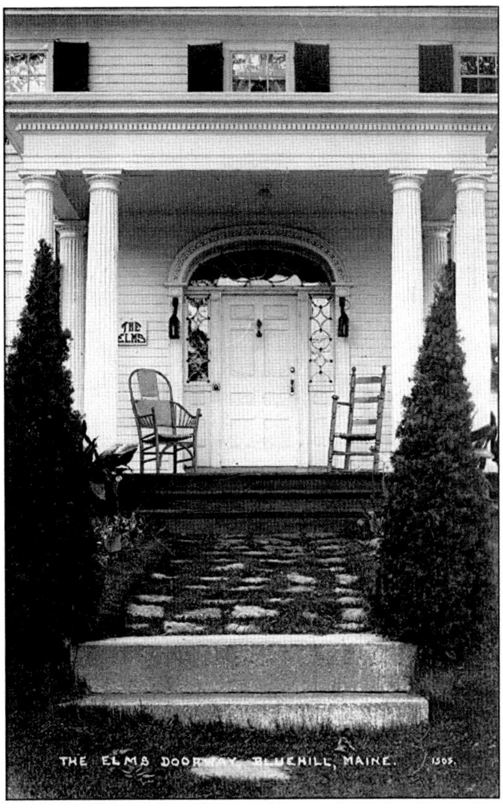

This could be Blue Hill's most photographed front door. The Elms, on Main Street and long known as the John Stevens House, was built in 1832 by Hosea Kittredge, a preceptor of Blue Hill Academy and the husband of Nancy Fisher (daughter of Parson Jonathan Fisher). In 1900, the Greek Revival–style front porch was added. (RRS.)

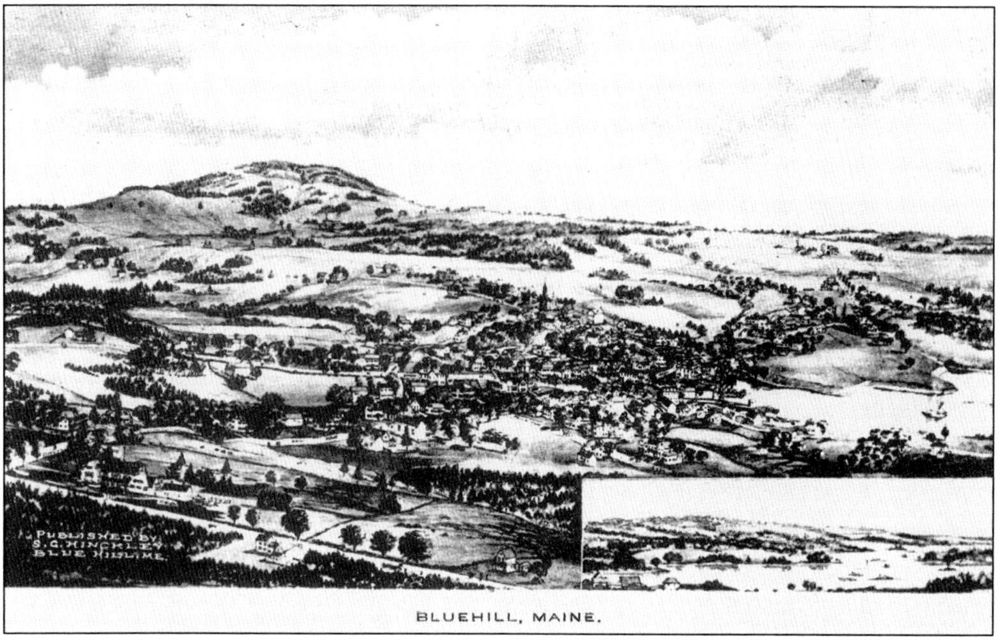

This postcard view depicts Blue Hill Mountain and the village below in a lithograph published by S. G. Hinckley. Many people assume the name derives from the blueberries that grow on the mountain. But hometown author Mary Ellen Chase, in her book *Jonathan Fisher, Maine Parson* quotes from one of Fisher's early descriptive sketches, "the fir, spruce and pine which cover this hill cause it to appear at a distance of a very dark color, hence its most natural name." (BPL.)

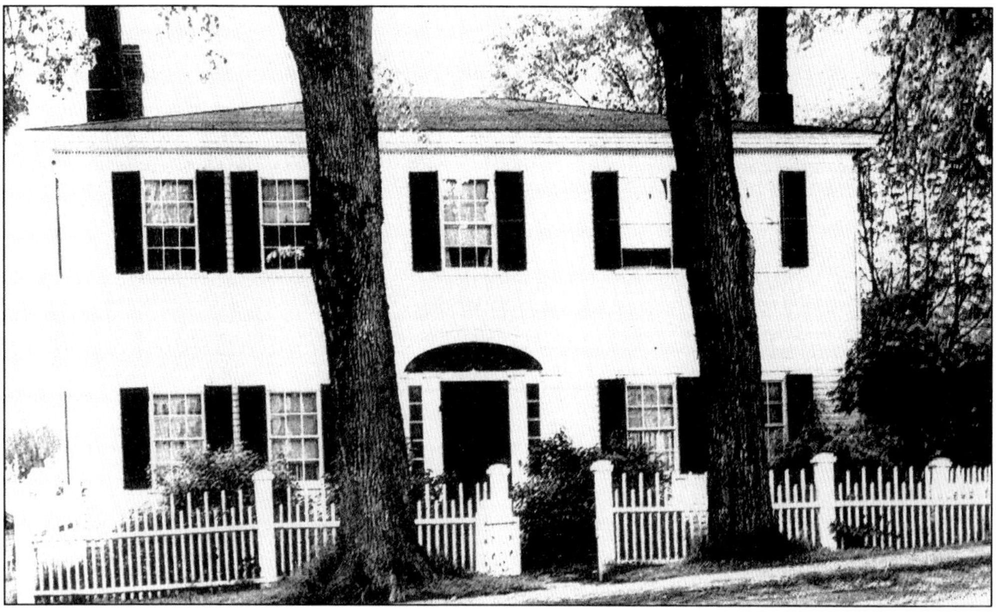

With its stenciled walls, rosette gate, and kitchen fireplace, the Holt House is an ideal home for the Blue Hill Historical Society. Located near downtown, on Water Street, the 1815 structure is open for tours in the summer. It was built by Jeremiah Thorndike Holt, the grandson of Nicholas Holt. Nicholas moved his family from Andover, Massachusetts, in 1765; they were the fifth family to arrive in town. (BHPL.)

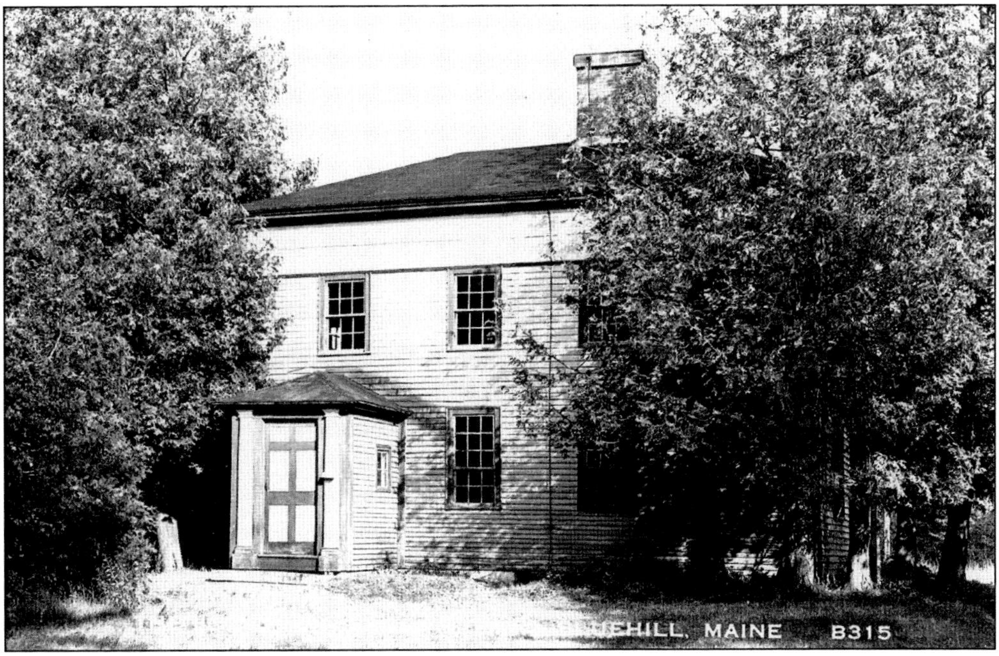

"Let every hour be filled to the brim," was a favorite saying of Parson Jonathan Fisher (1768–1847), Blue Hill's first renaissance man. With help from his Congregational church parishioners, Fisher built this house after moving to town in 1796. The Harvard-educated painter, poet, and farmer made the paint for his home from yellow ocher that he discovered nearby. The Jonathan Fisher Memorial is located at 44 Mines Road and is open for tours from July 1 to September 15. (RRS.)

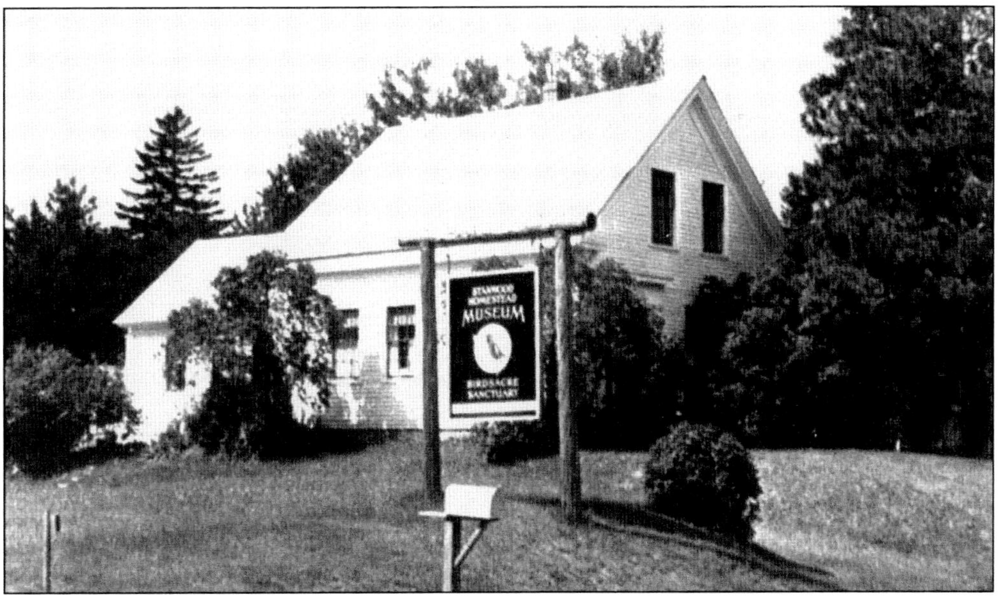

A natural Ellsworth attraction (pun intended) is Birdsacre, which encompasses the Richmond Nature Center at the Stanwood Wildlife Sanctuary. Located on Route 3, just beyond the junction of Route 1, the center is located in the house and surrounding acreage of Cordelia Stanwood (1865–1958), a wildlife photographer, naturalist, teacher, writer, and craftswoman. Its museum and hiking trails are open to the public year-round. (MHPC.)

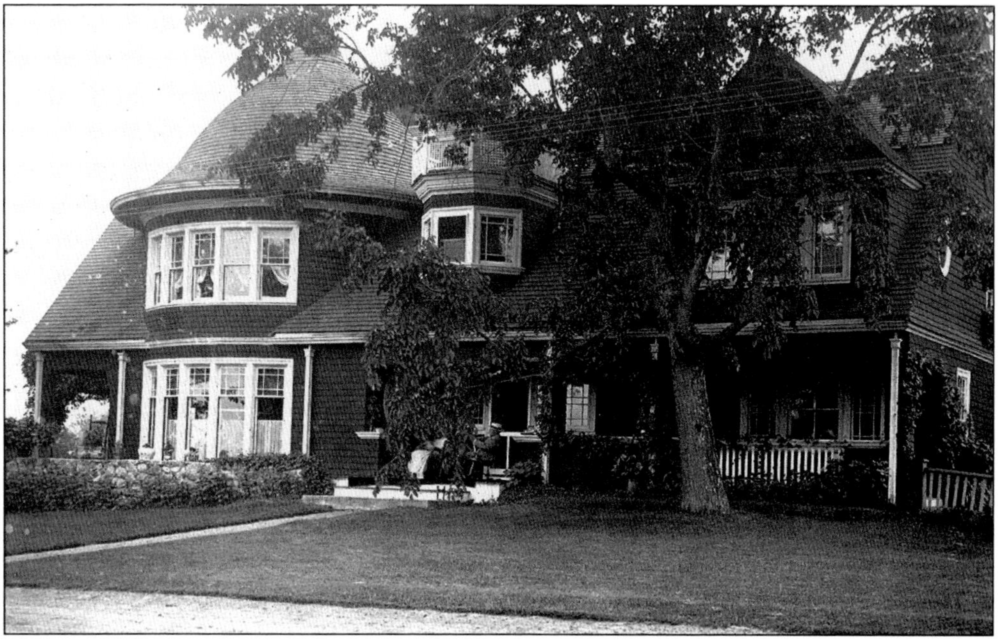

Effie Kline's large shingled cottage is still a landmark in Blue Hill. It is easily recognizable because of its massive design and its close proximity to the highway. Located not far from the Parker Ridge retirement community, it is one more surviving home from Blue Hill's storied past. (BHPL.)

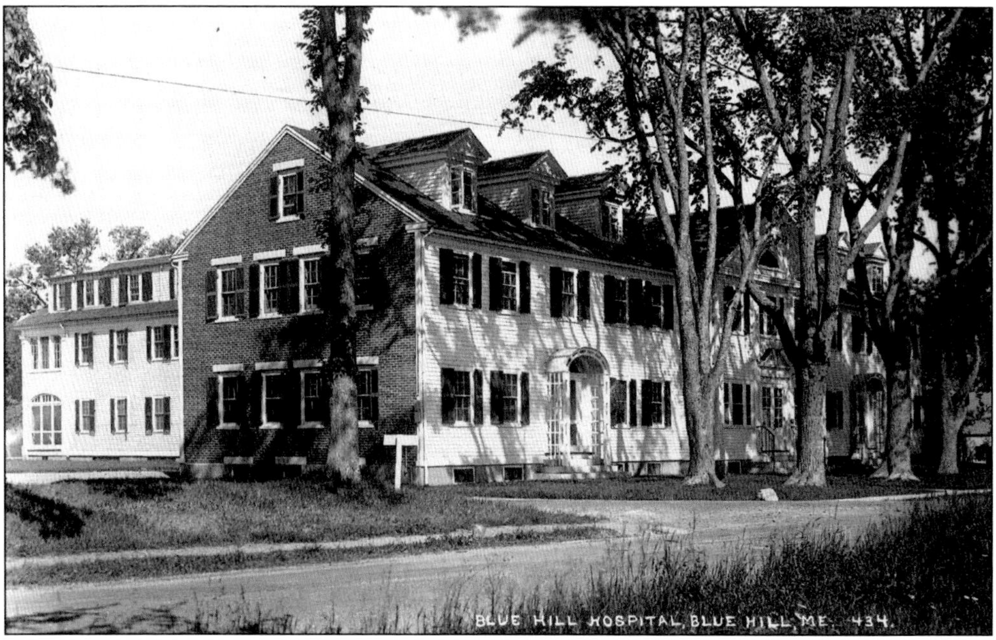

Originally a small facility, the Blue Hill Memorial Hospital on Water Street has grown to become a regional medical center, and further expansion is planned as it moves into the 21st century. The place was known as the Blue Hill Hospital when this view, dating to the early 1950s, was made. For years, townspeople referred to the hospital as the Bliss House, after Dr. R. N. V. Bliss, a long-time supervisor. (BPL.)

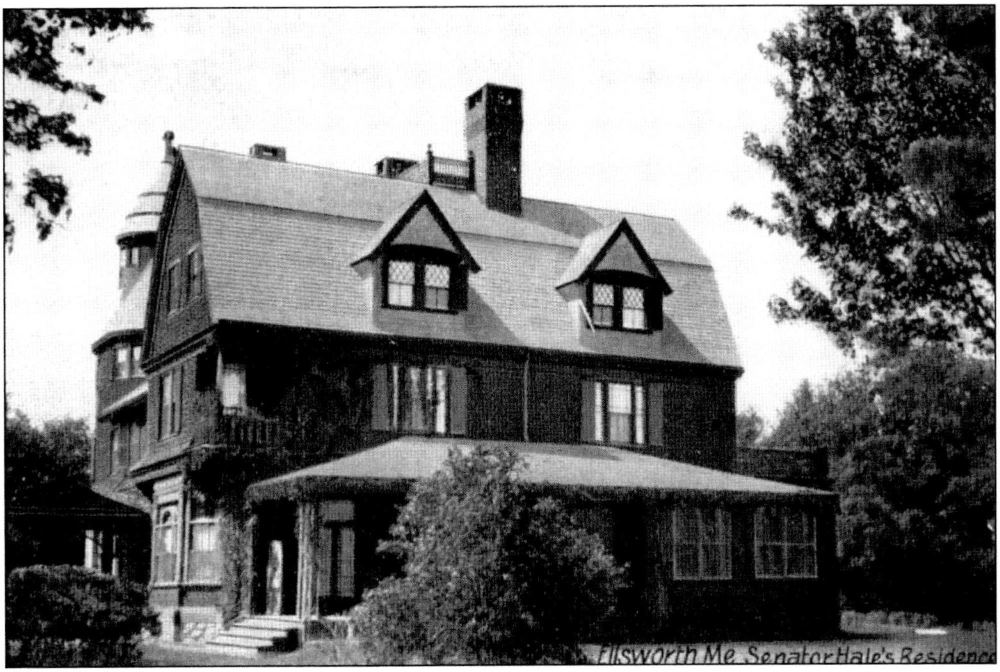

U.S. senator Eugene Hale (1836–1918) entertained many visitors at his home, once located near the present-day Maine Coast Memorial Hospital in Ellsworth. Hale's most famous guest may have been Pres. William Howard Taft, who stopped on a tour through Maine on July 23, 1910. The influential Republican senator's name lives on in the law firm of Hale and Hamlin. (RRS.)

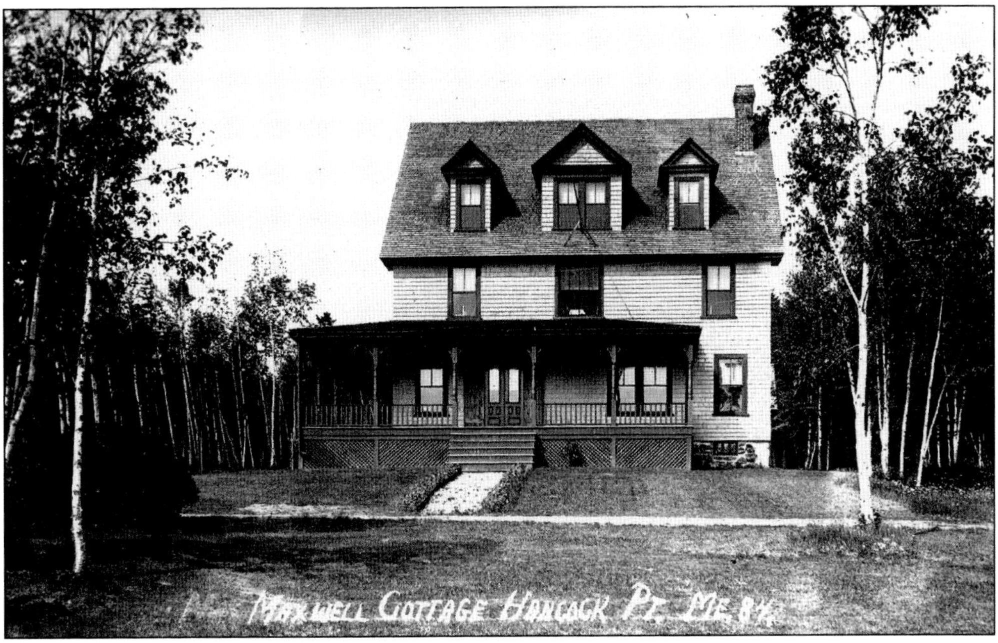

The Maxwell cottage at Hancock Point was razed around 1923. The Bellview Summer Tutoring School, sponsored by Princeton University, was built in its place. The Bellview property still stands but now is a private summer residence. (MHPC.)

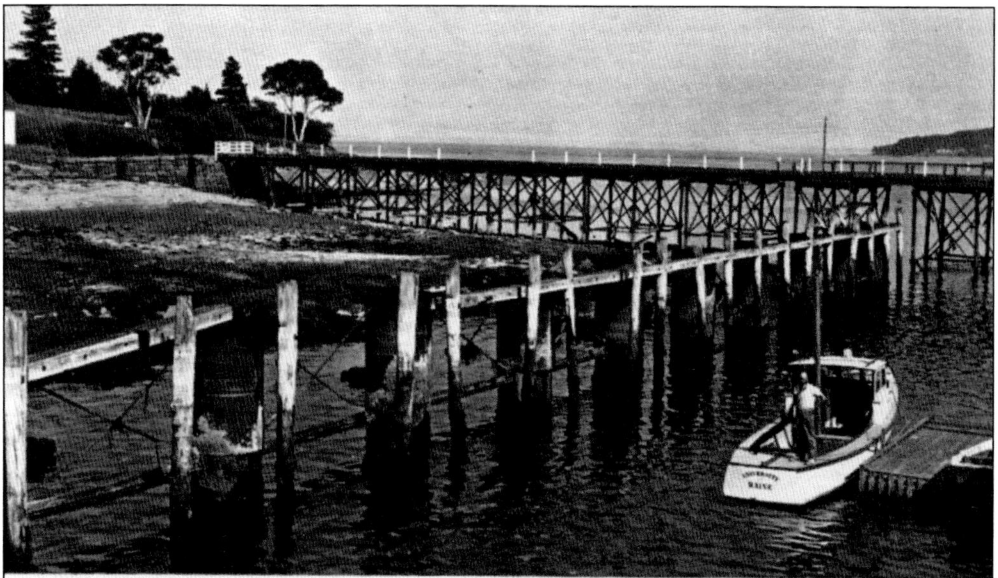

The Lamoine marine facility and the University of Maine navy in the mid-1930's. The location is now a state park.

Whoever wrote the caption on this postcard had his tongue firmly in his cheek while referring to the "University of Maine navy in the 1930s." That navy consists of only one man in his lobster boat. Maybe the writer remembered the failed U.S. Naval Coaling Station that was built on this spot at a cost of $200,000. Lamoine State Park now occupies this beautiful spot. (RRS.)

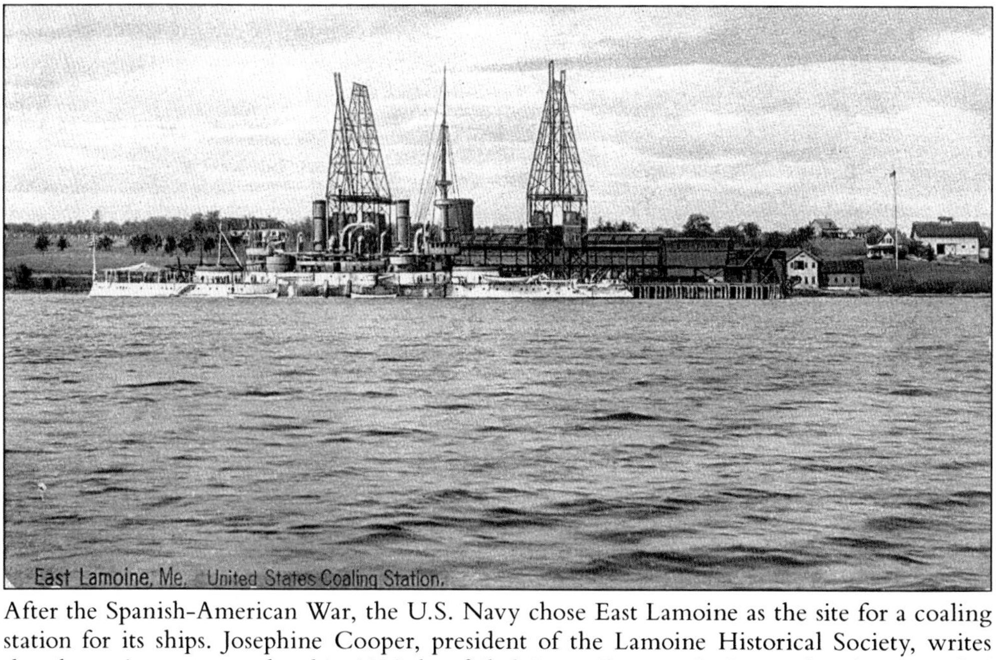

After the Spanish-American War, the U.S. Navy chose East Lamoine as the site for a coaling station for its ships. Josephine Cooper, president of the Lamoine Historical Society, writes that the station was completed in 1902, but failed since oil was replacing coal as the major fuel used by the navy. During World War I, the station was used for the storage of nitrates, used in making explosives, and then it was dismantled. (BPL.)

This curious old postcard pictures a tree, its variety unnamed, that was brought over by boat from France two centuries earlier by the Des Isle family. The tree was planted at what later was known as Lamoine Beach, which measures 2,740 yards long. The town was named after early resident Andre LeMoyne. (RRS.)

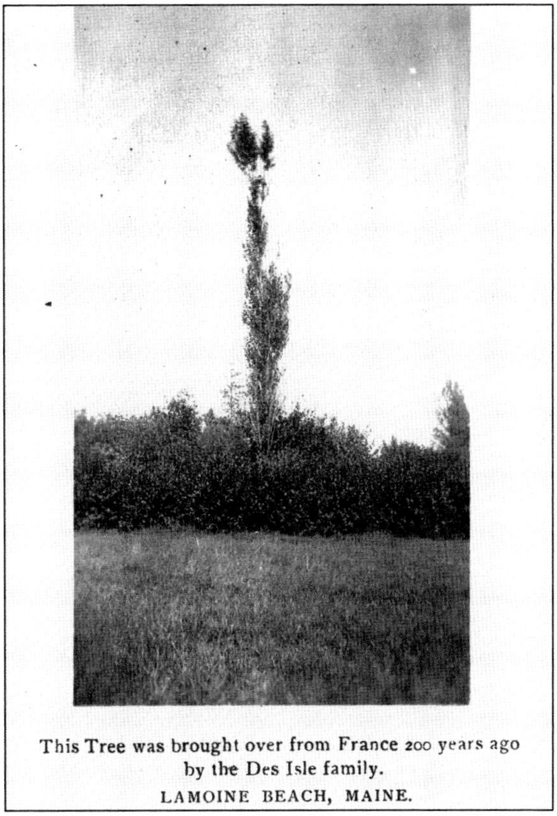

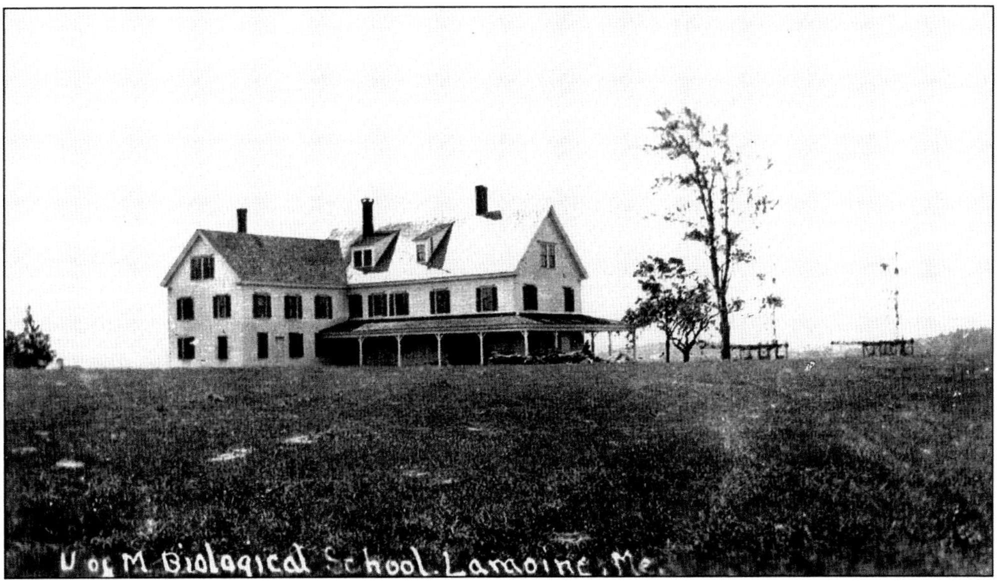

In the 1930s, the University of Maine acquired some of the buildings of the former U.S. Navy Coaling Station for a biological laboratory. This old postcard shows one of the huge buildings. Following that, the East Lamoine property became a state park in the 1950s. Often forgotten is that the university also started the Jackson Laboratory on nearby Mount Desert Island. (RRS.)

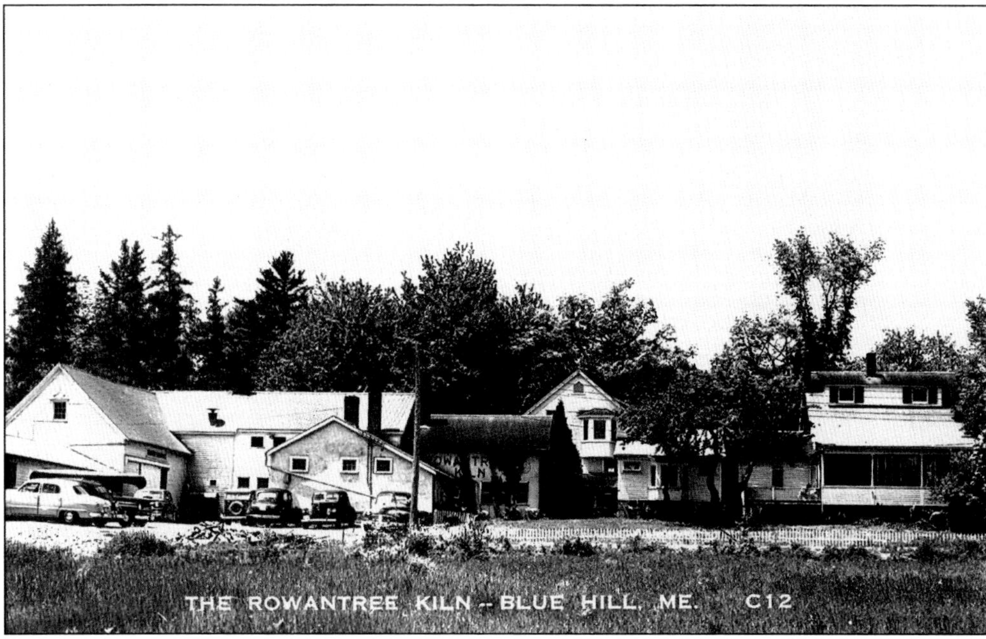

Rowantrees Pottery, a business inspired in 1934 by Adelaide Pearson through her friend Mahatma Gandhi, is still going strong on Union Street in Blue Hill. Sheila Varnum, who knew Pearson and her partner, Laura Paddock, purchased the pottery, famous for its unique glazes, in 1976. Rackliffe Pottery, an offshoot of Rowantrees Pottery, is located on Route 172 and sells fine kitchenware. (BPL.)

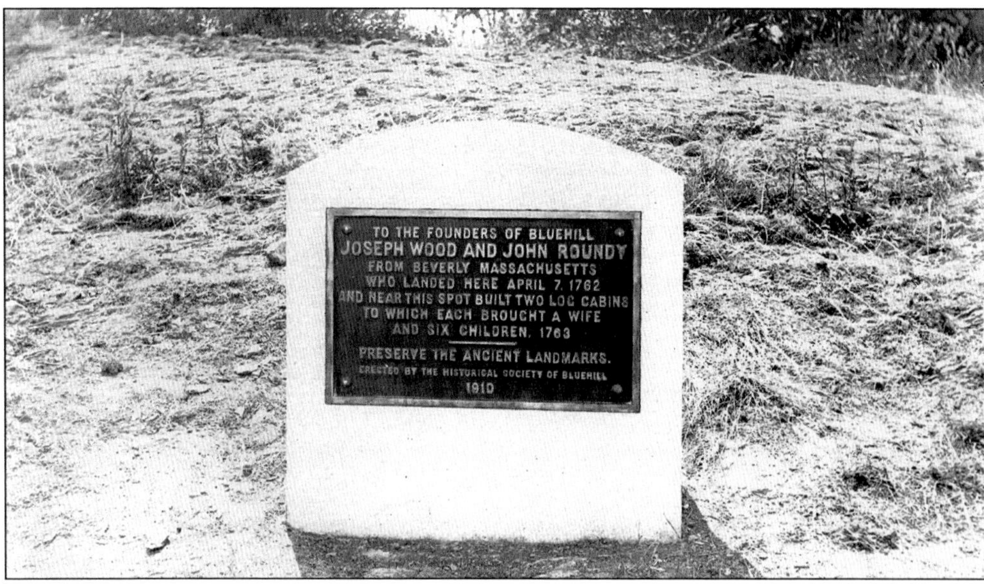

"The first comers to the area were Joseph Wood and John Roundy from [Beverly] Massachusetts, who built homes on Mill Island at the tidal falls [Blue Hill Falls]," writes author Esther E. Wood. "Other settlers joined them, and in this neighborhood were the first mill and schoolhouse. The area was first known as North Andover, then as New Port, and in 1789 the town charter established its name as Blue Hill." This marker at the Blue Hill Falls site was placed by the Blue Hill Historical Society in 1910. (BHPL.)

Eight

And All the Rest

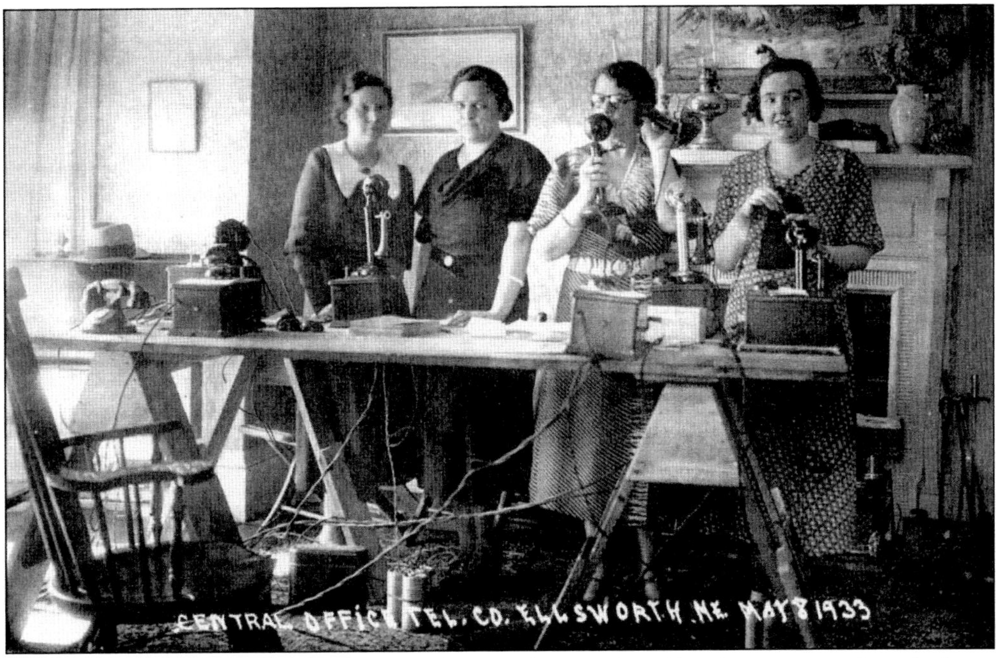

After the great Ellsworth fire of 1933 destroyed its main office downtown, the telephone exchange relocated to a house at Church and Oak Streets. Callers exercised patience as local operators made do with primitive equipment until service was restored. The operators are, from left to right, Margaret Davis, Phyllis Harrington, Ernestine Shea, and Catherine Morrison. (MHPC.)

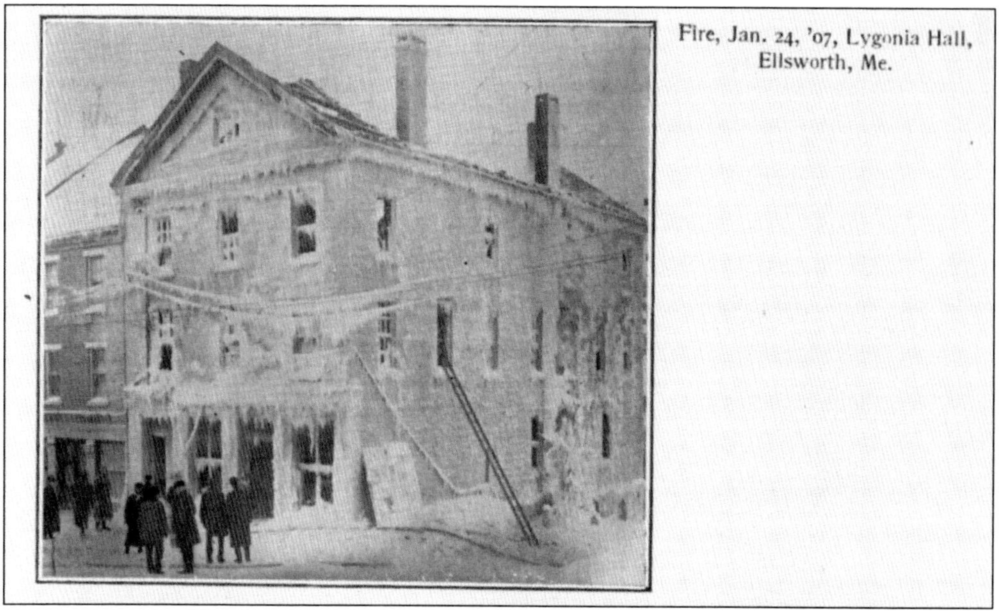

Icicles hang from the wreckage of a gutted brick building in 1907. Spectators congregated on State Street on January 24 to watch the burning of Lygonia Hall. The hall housed the Esoteric Lodge and was a total loss. As often happened after fires, Ellsworth residents and people from outside of town stopped by to survey the devastation. (MHPC.)

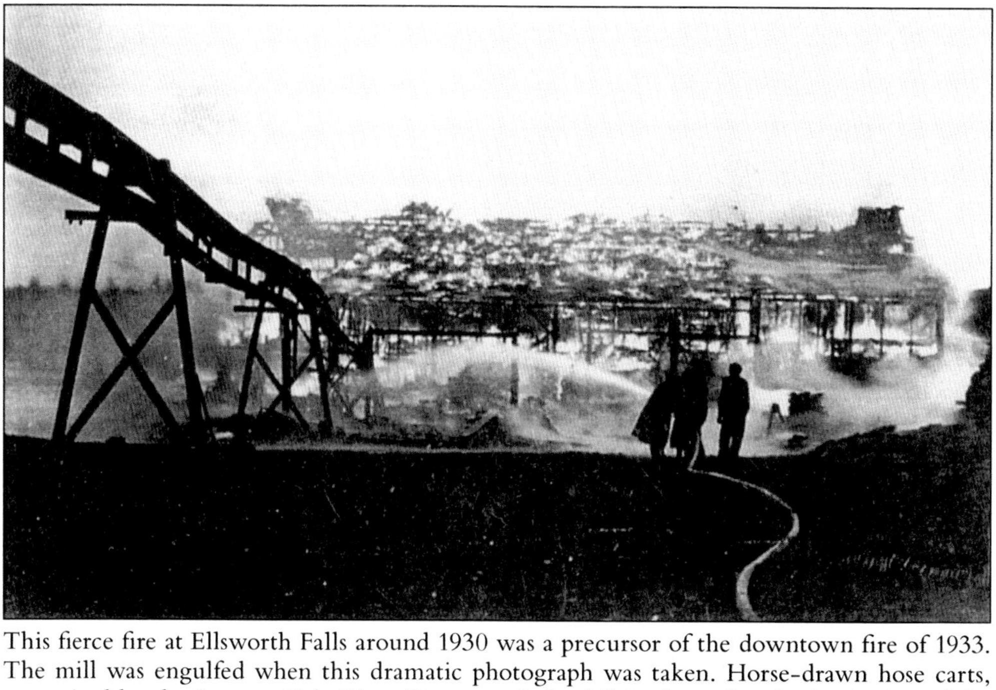

This fierce fire at Ellsworth Falls around 1930 was a precursor of the downtown fire of 1933. The mill was engulfed when this dramatic photograph was taken. Horse-drawn hose carts, supervised by the Senator Hale Hose Company, helped fight fires after the beginning of the 20th century. Before that, firefighters used hand-drawn pumpers. Motorized fire equipment was another innovation. (RRS.)

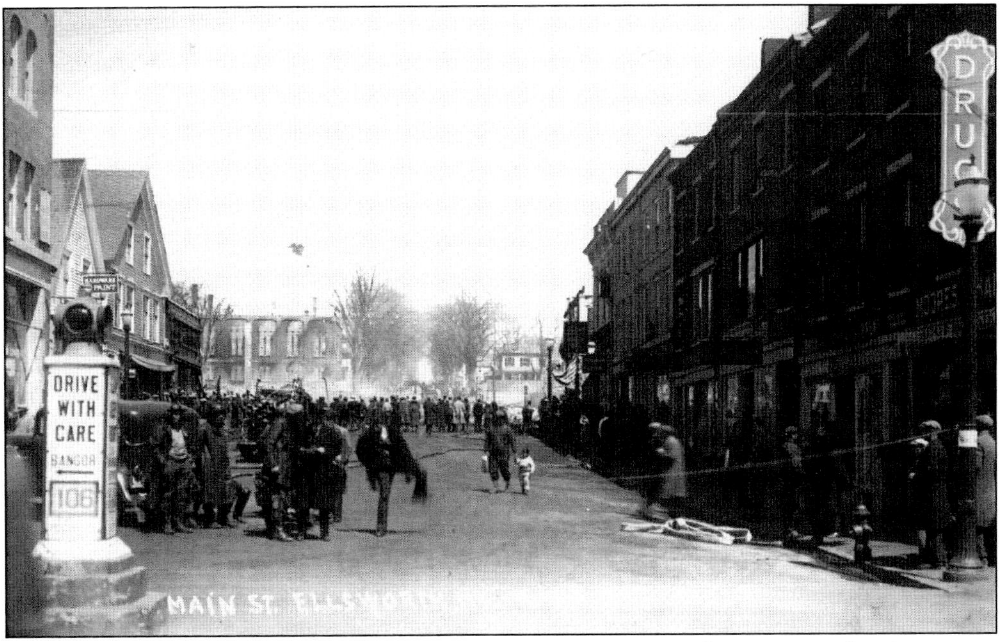

Ellsworth's great fire of May 7, 1933, was probably the city's single most transforming event. It started in an old theater building behind the north side of Main Street. A stiff wind carried the embers throughout downtown and burned three-quarters of the business district. Hordes of people showed up to help and watch the devastation. (MHPC.)

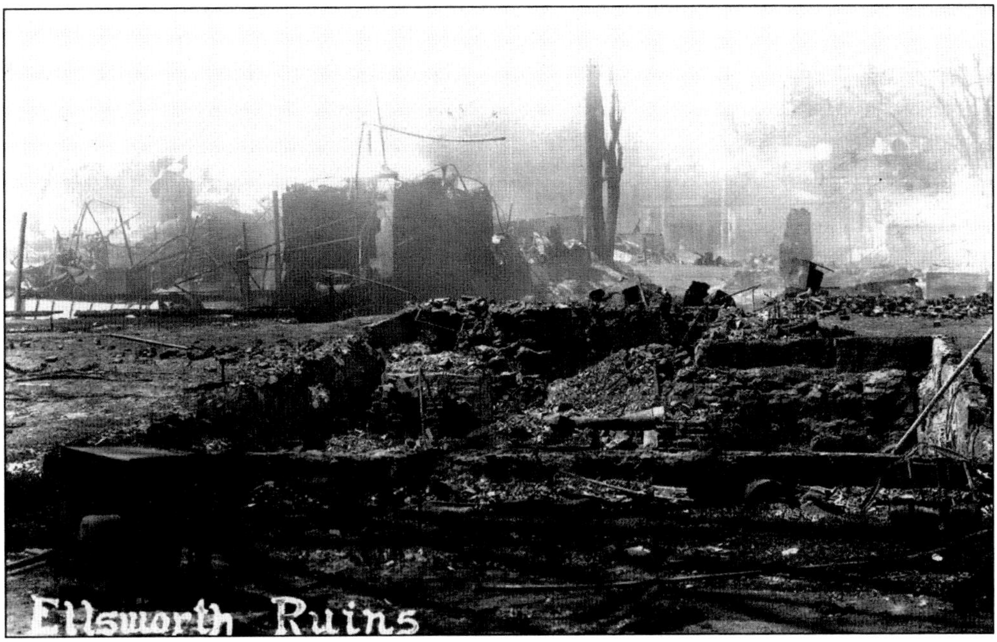

Property losses were staggering on the north and south sides of Main Street. Also damaged were buildings on State, Water, Hancock, Pine, Franklin, and School Streets. The *Ellsworth American* covered the disaster extensively. It reported that the city was placed under military rule because of the threat of looting and other lawless behavior. (MHPC.)

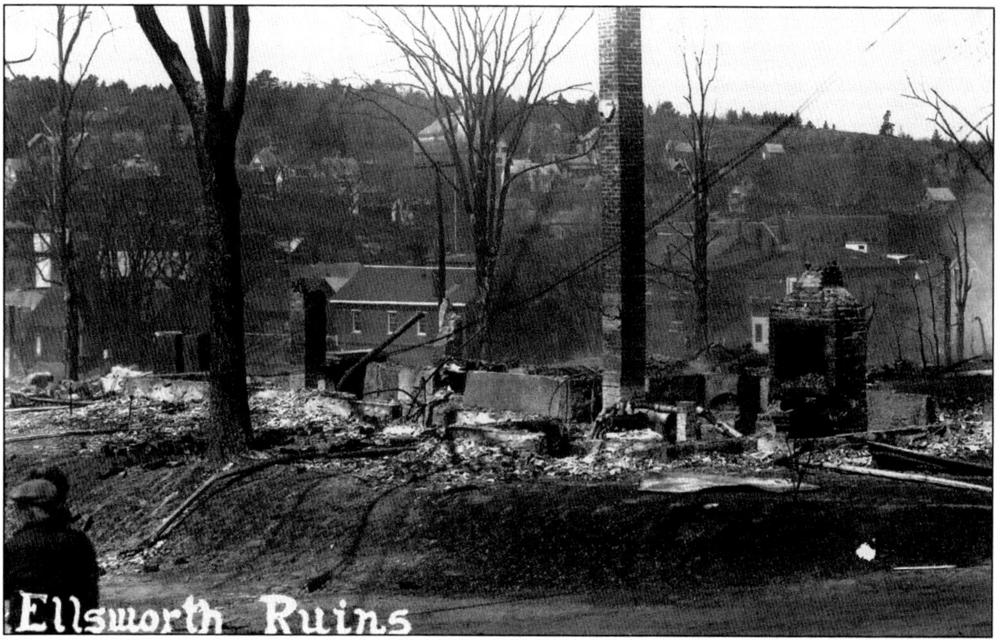

Just as the great Bangor fire had done in 1911, Ellsworth's big fire of 1933 transformed the downtown landscape. Once recognizable scenes resembled bombed European cities of World War I. Rebuilding began immediately, although many business owners had to borrow on good faith since Pres. Franklin Roosevelt had recently closed the banks to prevent collapse from over-withdrawals. (MHPC.)

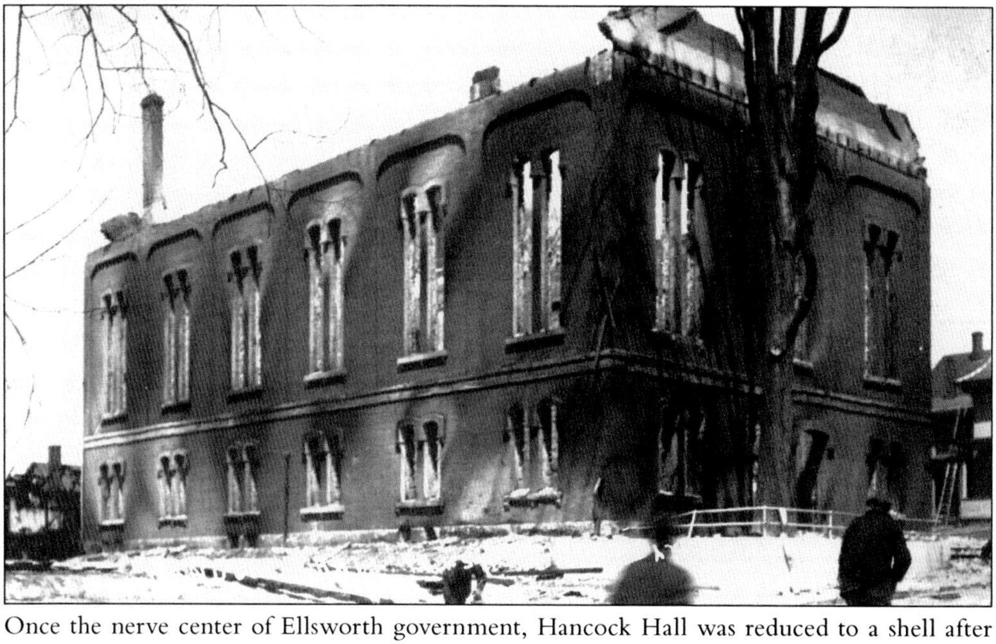

Once the nerve center of Ellsworth government, Hancock Hall was reduced to a shell after burning in the 1933 inferno. Attempting to save the massive Main Street building, firefighters dynamited a house next door, but they inadvertently set the hall on fire. (MHPC.)

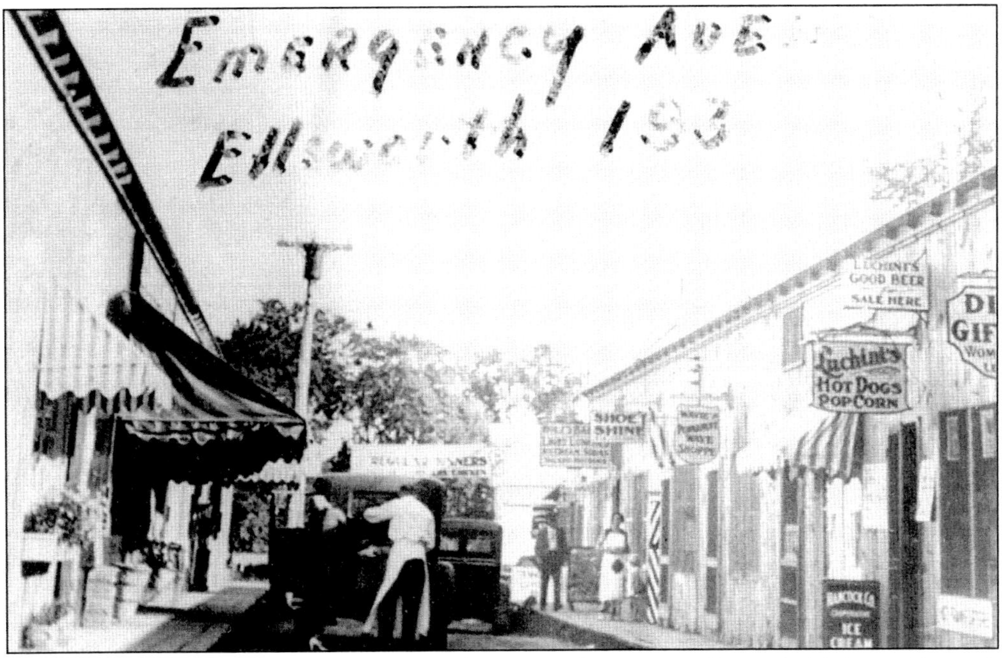

With the motto, "Necessity is the mother of invention," a group of forward-thinking Ellsworth businessmen set up Emergency Avenue following the 1933 fire. Stretching from Main Street to Spruce Street, near the current post office, the avenue included a temporary gift shop, shoeshine parlor, and Luchini's hot dogs, popcorn, and "good beer." Many established businesses had been burned out of their longtime locations by the inferno. (Connee Jellison.)

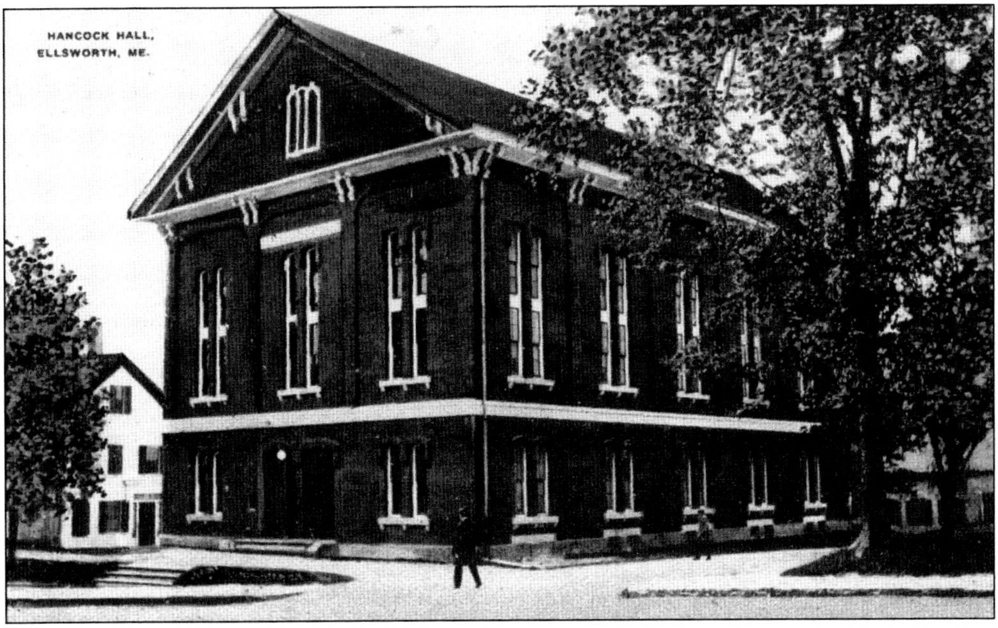

Shown here in better times, Hancock Hall housed the town offices on the first floor, and upstairs was a large hall where orchestras performed, politicians spoke, and Victorian-era couples danced the "Grand March" just like Scarlett O'Hara and Rhett Butler in *Gone with the Wind.* The site of the 1869 building is now the Masonic hall. (RRS.)

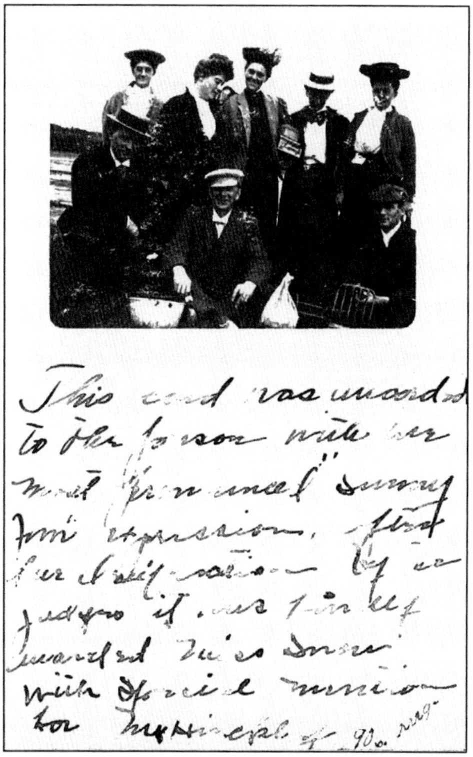

Somewhere in this group of eight Blue Hill picnickers is Josie Snow, who was awarded this 1906 postcard for having the sunniest expression. The fancy handwriting, from a time when messages could only be written on the card's front (picture) side, notes that the judges awarded an honorable mention to Mr. Hinckley. The whole matter seems like a good-natured joke. (BHPL.)

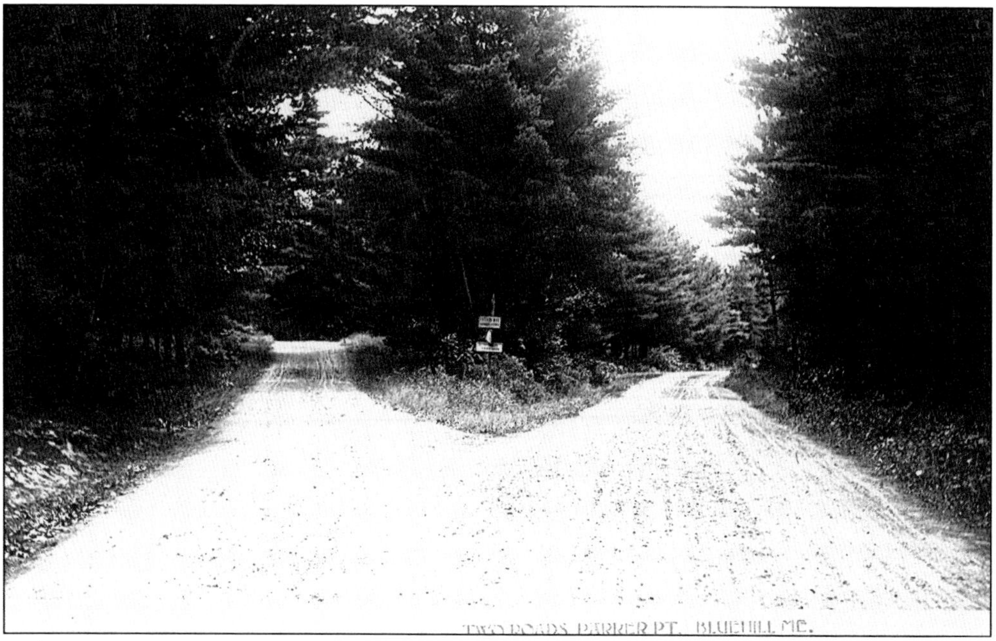

A favorite subject for photographers in the early 20th century was this bucolic scene, taken around 1910 at Blue Hill's exclusive Parker Point summer neighborhood. Titled "Two Roads," the view could have inspired a Robert Frost poem or a chapter in a novel by local author Mary Ellen Chase. Sharp eyes will discern the writing on the top sign, which unsurprisingly reads "Private Way." (BHPL.)

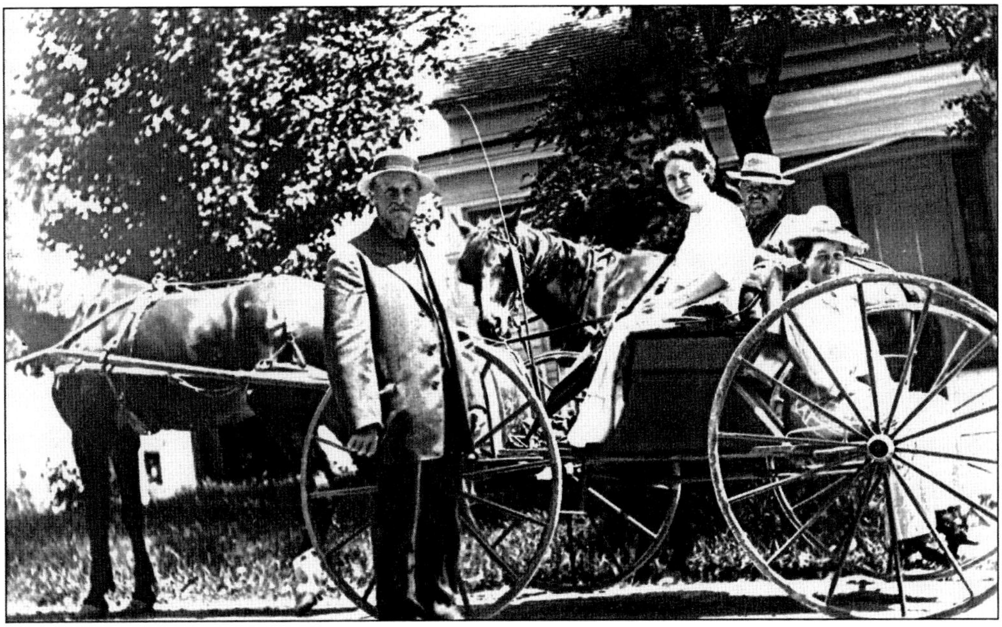

The four people in this early, undated postcard are not identified. Taken in front of the Snow house in Blue Hill, the view shows smiling people sitting on a wagon pulled by two horses. The woman in the rear is well dressed, down to her large white summer hat. All manner of wagons and carriages were common on Blue Hill's streets prior to, and even during, the introduction of the automobile. (BHPL.)

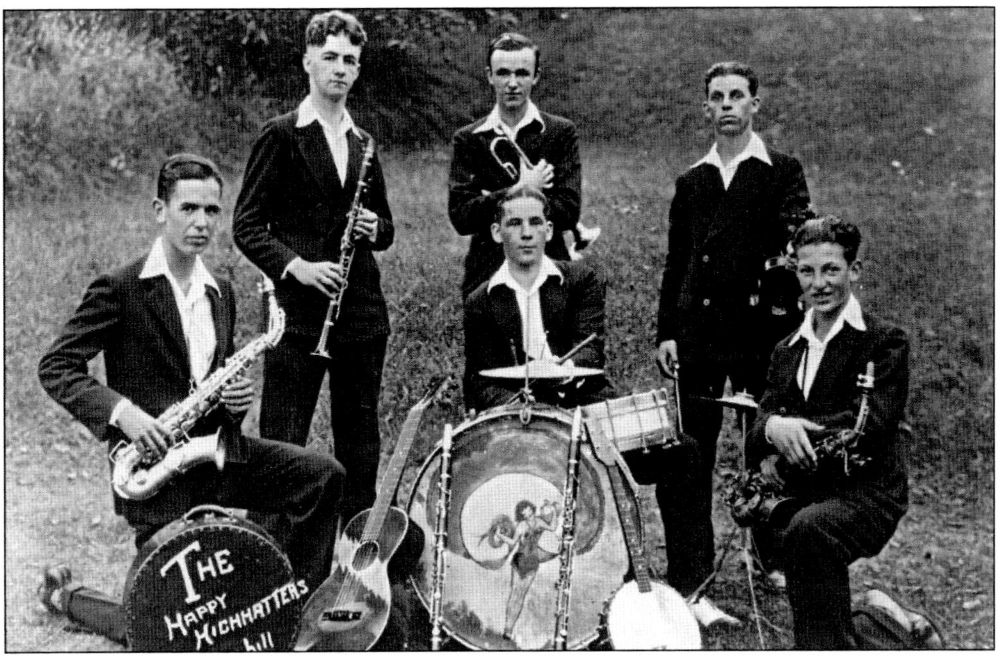

Blue Hill audiences enjoyed the Happy Highhatters, who played their music around 1930–1933. The young musicians are, from left to right: (first row) Austin Grindle, Philip O'Brien, and Edward Clark; (second row) Frederick Grindle, Paul Saunders, and Herbert Clark. Someone painted a dancing girl on O'Brien's bass drum. (BHPL.)

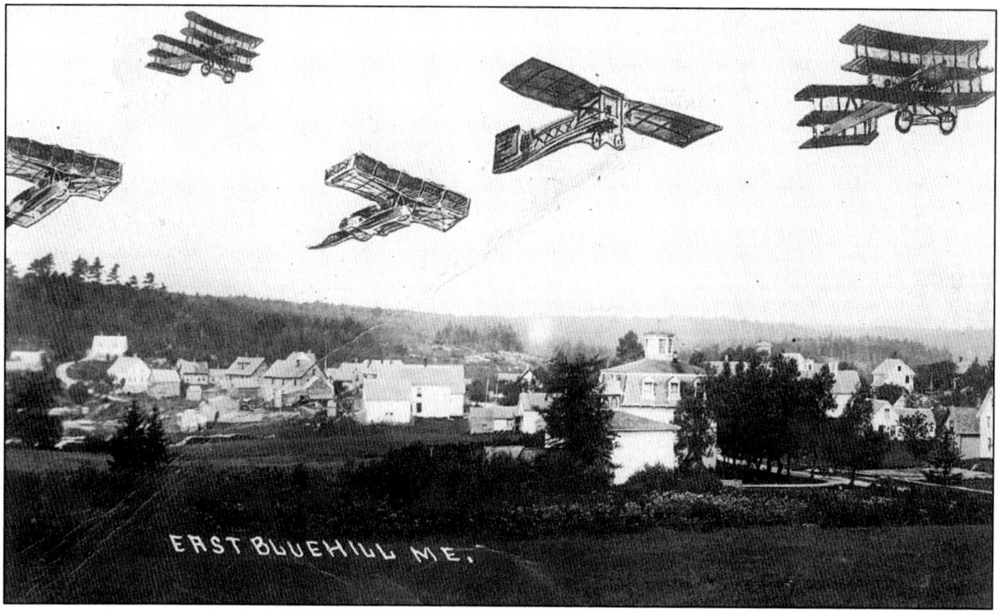

Movie audiences today are used to such computer-generated, or CGI, special effects as erupting volcanoes and towering infernos. But around 1912, when this postcard view was made, the flying planes were startling to residents and certainly a figment of the photographer's imagination. The people of East Blue Hill would have been thunderstruck to see such a variety of five aircraft zipping over their sedate little town. (BPL.)

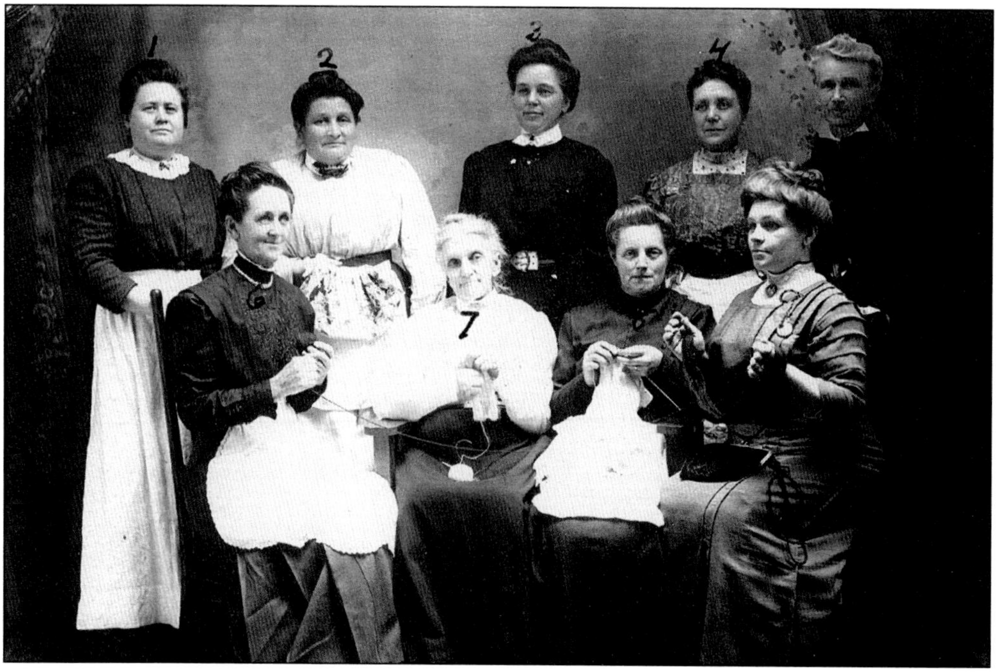

Blue Hill's nine-member knitting club looks as though they take their work seriously in this early 20th century view. Someone took the time to number each member: Lucy Hinckley (1), Clara Abrams (2), Edith D. Rowe (3), Christie Osgood (4), Frankie Curtis (5), Susan Abbott (6), Mrs. Dailey (Rowe's mother) (7), Ada Townsend (8), and Etta Stover (9). (BHPL.)

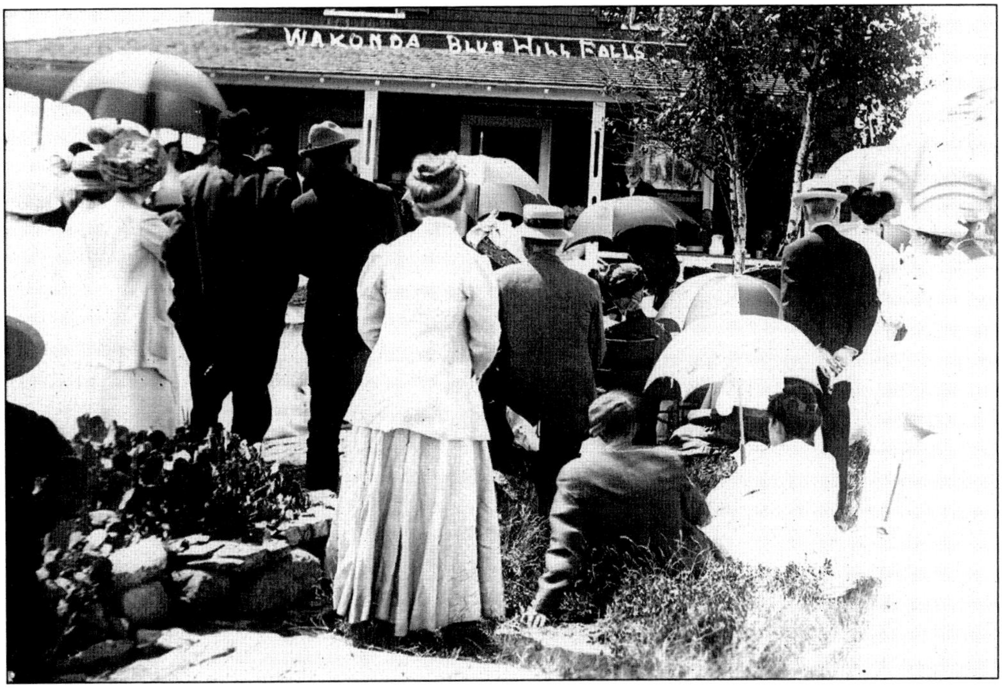

Wakonda, a cottage on Mill Island at Blue Hill Falls, was the scene of a ceremony in 1910 commemorating the arrival of the town's first settlers on April 7, 1762. A tablet (see page 108) in honor of Joseph Wood and John Roundy, of Beverly, Massachusetts, was unveiled during the ceremony. Umbrellas shielded the spectators from either broiling sun or driving rain. (BHPL.)

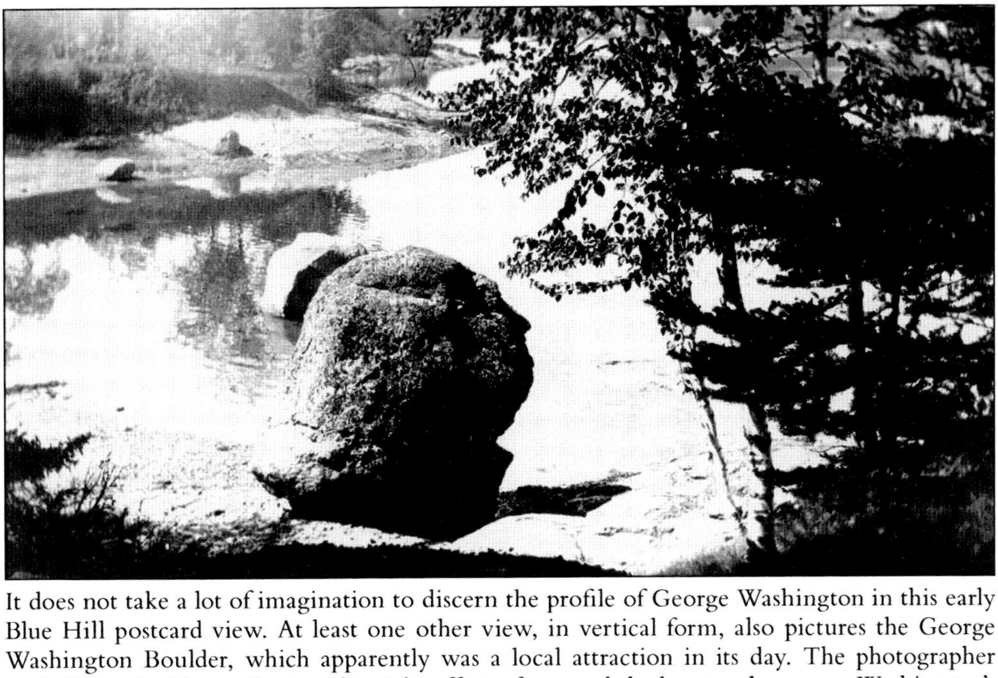

It does not take a lot of imagination to discern the profile of George Washington in this early Blue Hill postcard view. At least one other view, in vertical form, also pictures the George Washington Boulder, which apparently was a local attraction in its day. The photographer probably waited hours for just the right effect of sun and shadow to play across Washington's eyes and nose. (BHPL.)

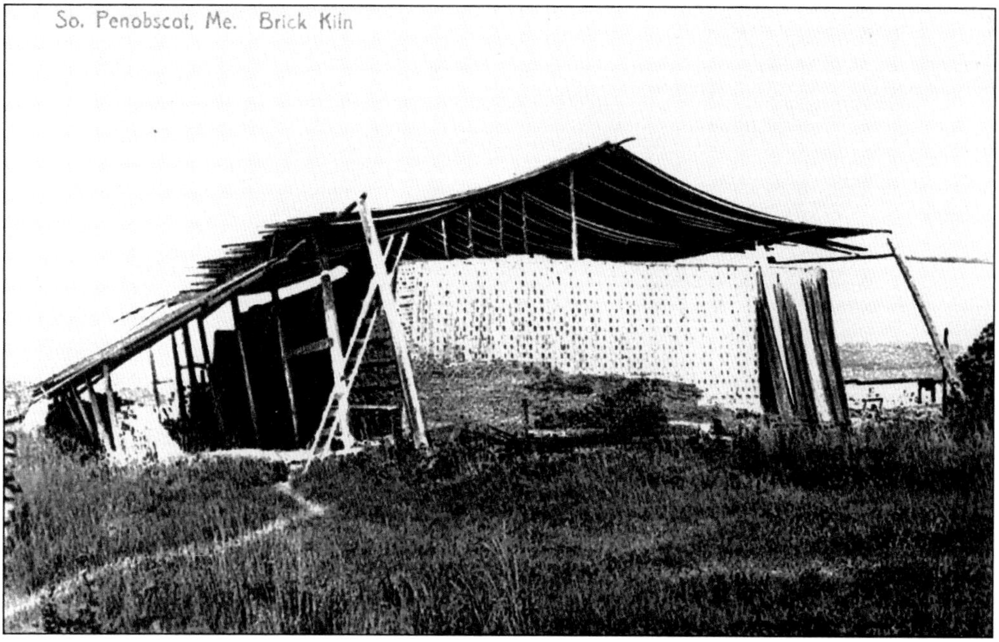

A brick kiln in South Penobscot was captured in a postcard photograph around 1920. This kiln appears to have been a crude affair, with large sticks holding up a rickety roof. Penobscot people also supported themselves by farming, harvesting ice, and building ships. The only kilns in the area today are used to make pottery. (BPL.)

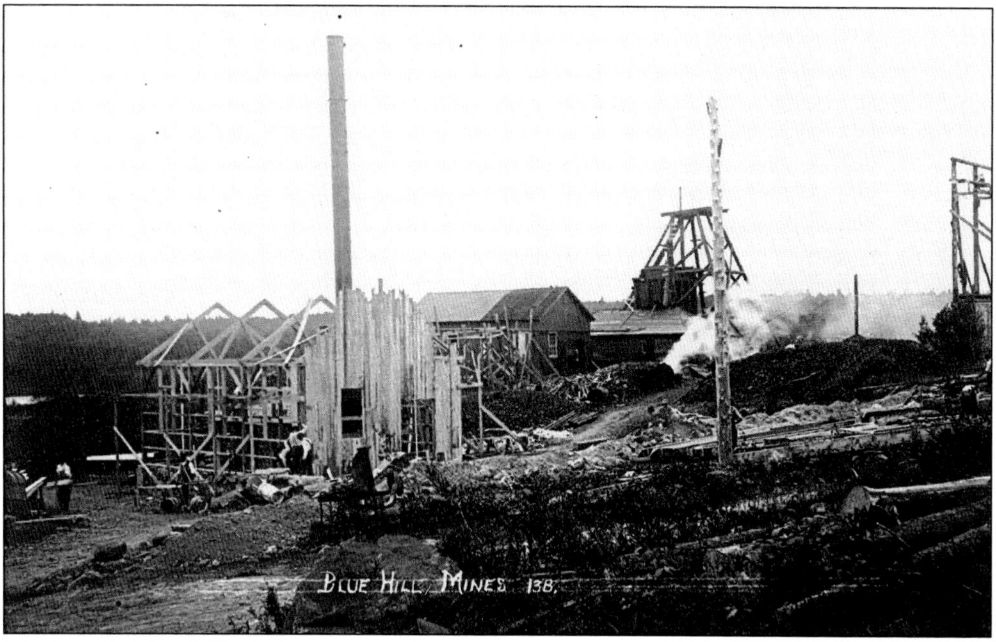

The first big Blue Hill mining rush was from 1879 to 1883. "William Stewart came to town and found William Darling mining copper in a small way and talking about silver in a big way," writes Esther E. Wood. By 1879, 600 people were digging, and by 1880, a $25 million value was put on stock that had been issued. But soon the mining bubble burst, and the mines closed. (BHPL.)

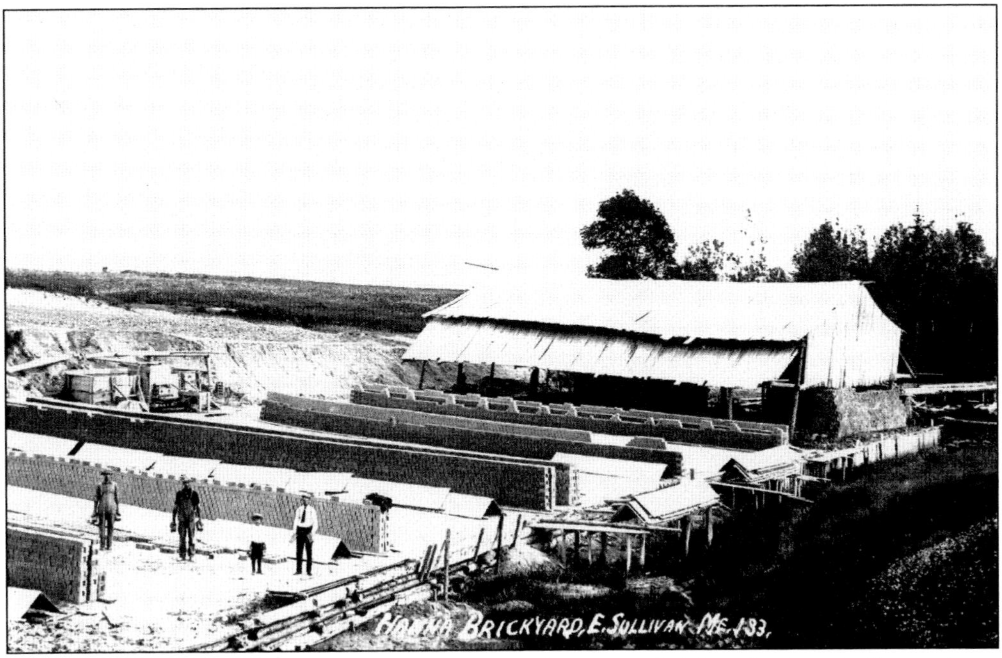

Bricks were made by the millions a century ago at the Hanna Brickyard in East Sullivan. Rows of bricks are stacked in this view, which shows a man in a white shirt and tie, two men in work clothes, and a child all holding a brick in each hand. Up the Penobscot River in Brewer, several companies manufactured bricks. Much of Boston's Beacon Hill neighborhood is said to have been rebuilt from Brewer bricks after the fire of 1872. (MHPC.)

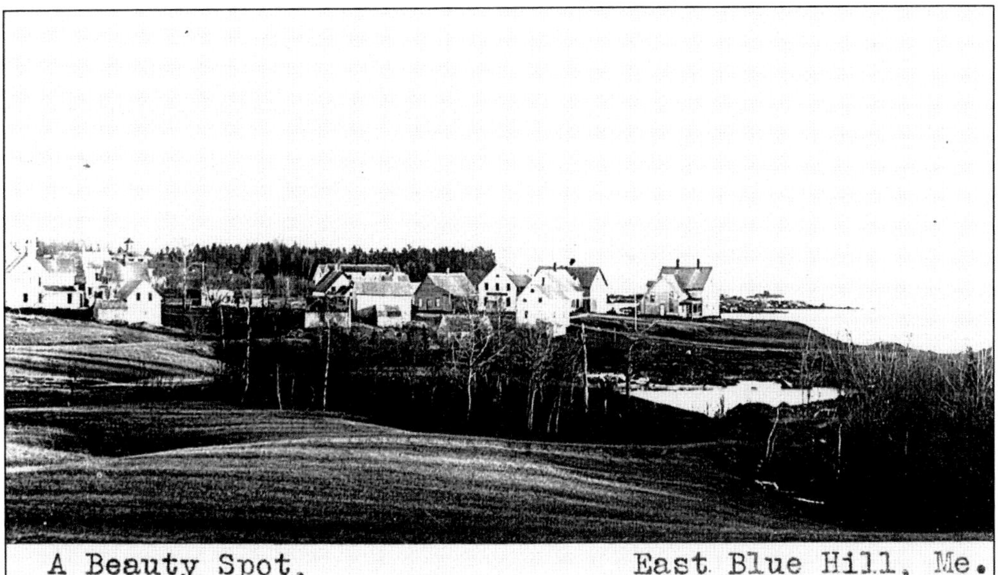

This homemade-looking postcard pictures the "beauty spot" of East Blue Hill when it was nothing more than a cluster of tidy white houses, a store, and a church. Although often overshadowed by Blue Hill village a few miles to the west, East Blue Hill was a thriving little community in the early 20th century. Granite was quarried there and shipyards turned out worthy vessels. (BPL.)

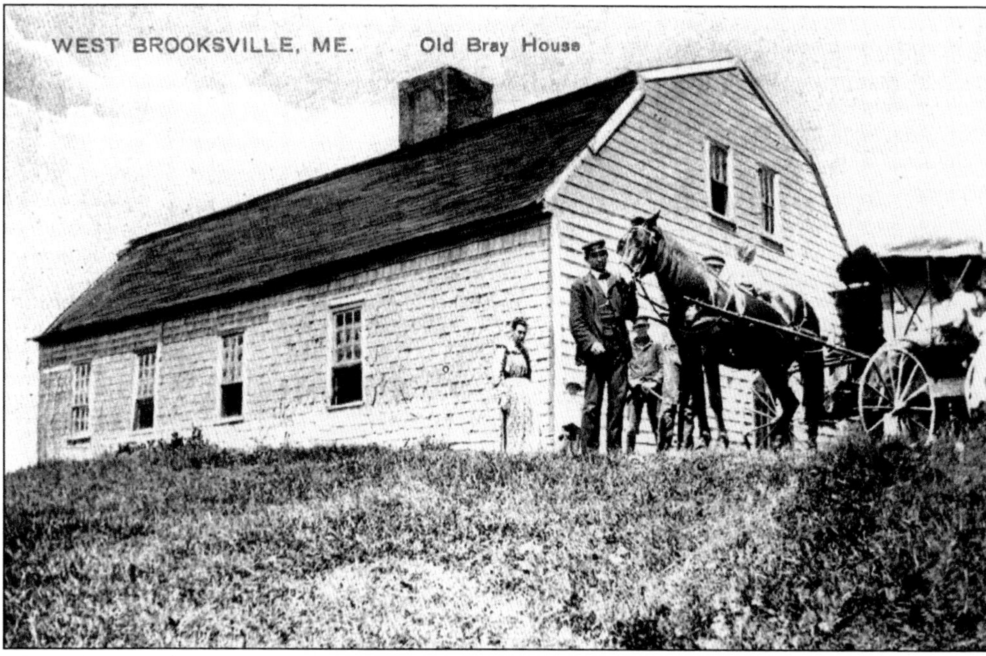

The John Bray house was well known in West Brooksville and reportedly was built during Revolutionary times. The Brooksvilles—North, South, and West—were named for John Brooks, the ninth governor of Massachusetts and a decorated Revolutionary War soldier. In 1777, he was appointed lieutenant colonel of the 8th Massachusetts Regiment. In 1818, he toured Maine and died in 1825. (MHPC.)

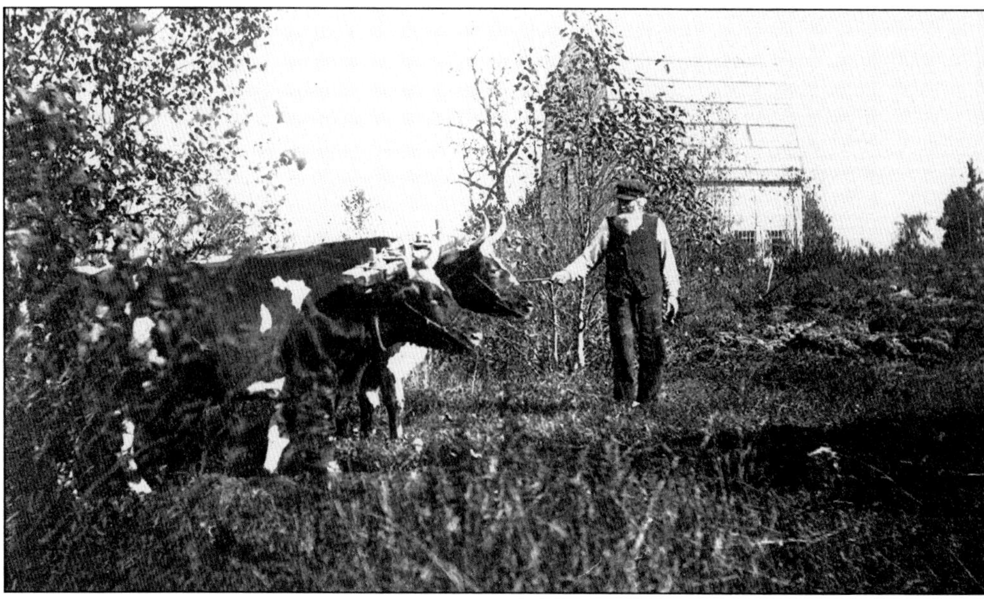

A bucolic early postcard scene shows a bearded man leading a team of oxen. A handwritten note on the back of the card identifies the man as "the elder Candage." The location is "Blanca Wills' studio at [Blue Hill] Falls." The date may have been around 1912. Oxen are still widely used on Maine farms and are displayed by farmers during summer fair week at the Blue Hill Fair. (BHPL.)

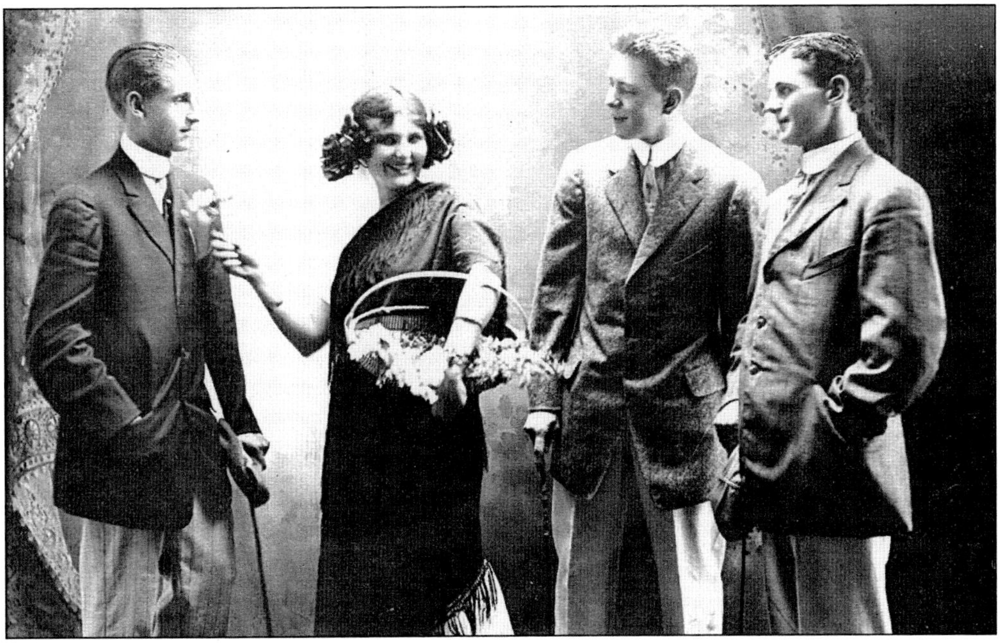

There is absolutely no identification on this postcard; no names, no date, no postmark. Selected from the vintage postcard collection of the Blue Hill Public Library, one can assume the scene dates to around 1915. It is also a fair assumption that the four well-dressed subjects were photographed in Blue Hill. At a school play? A social function of some sort? Whoever they are, the quartet certainly made handsome subjects for the photographer. (BHPL.)

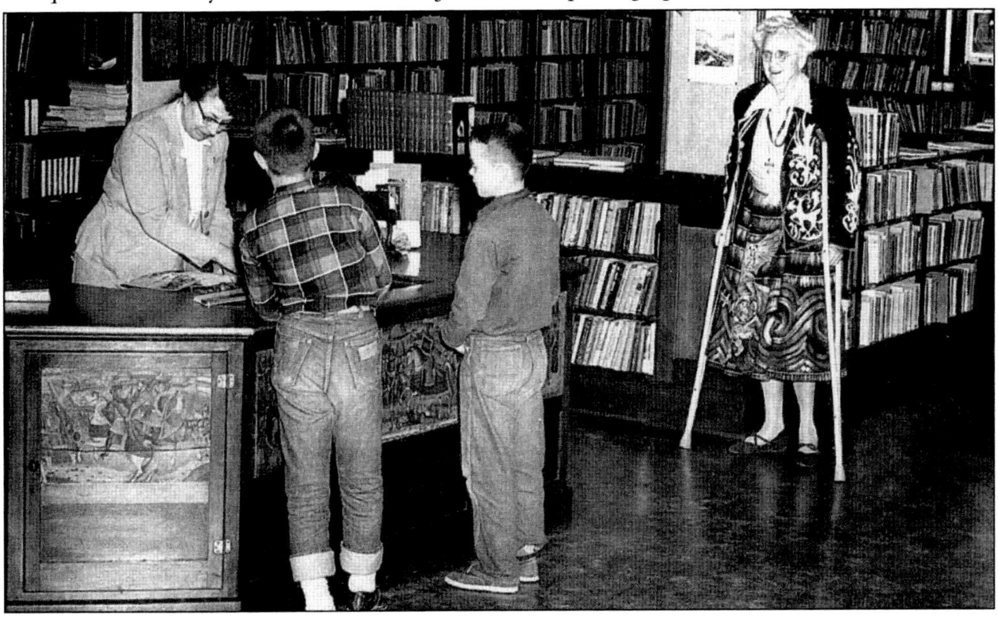

Blue Hill's well-respected public library was completed in 1940 and immediately began attracting locals and "summer people." Handicap accessibility is now a federal law, so the woman using crutches in this view would have no trouble accessing the building today. Modern elevators were installed when the library, located at 5 Parker Point Road, was renovated and enlarged a few years ago. (BHPL.)

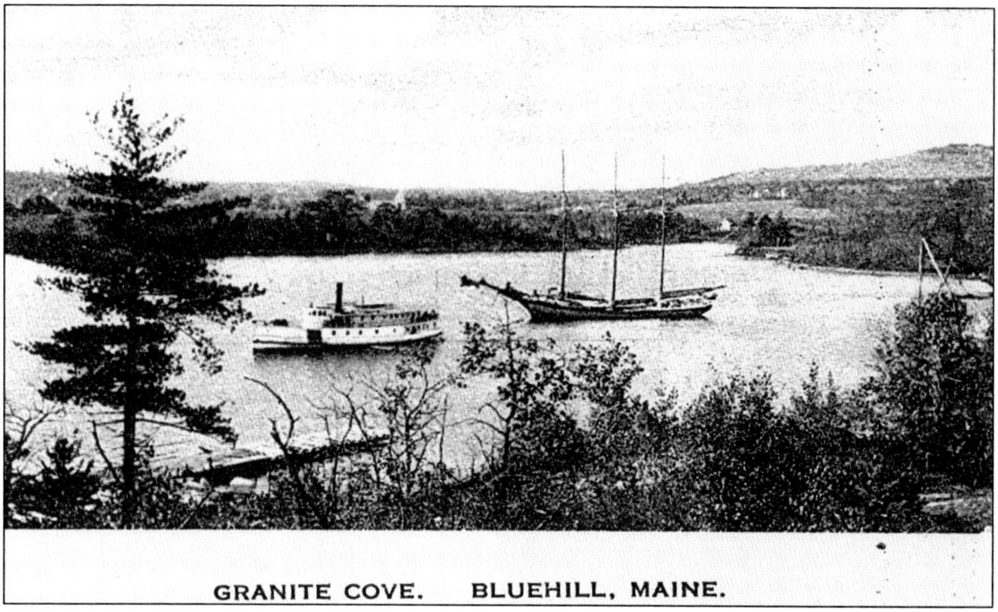

An excursion steamer appears to be towing a three-masted schooner in Blue Hill's Granite Cove, but it is probably only an optical illusion. The steamboat is probably moving, and the schooner, with its sails down, is probably at anchor. Granite was long a part of the area's history. A granite works, located off of the East Blue Hill Road, employed a large workforce in the last century and turned out quality stonework. (BHPL.)

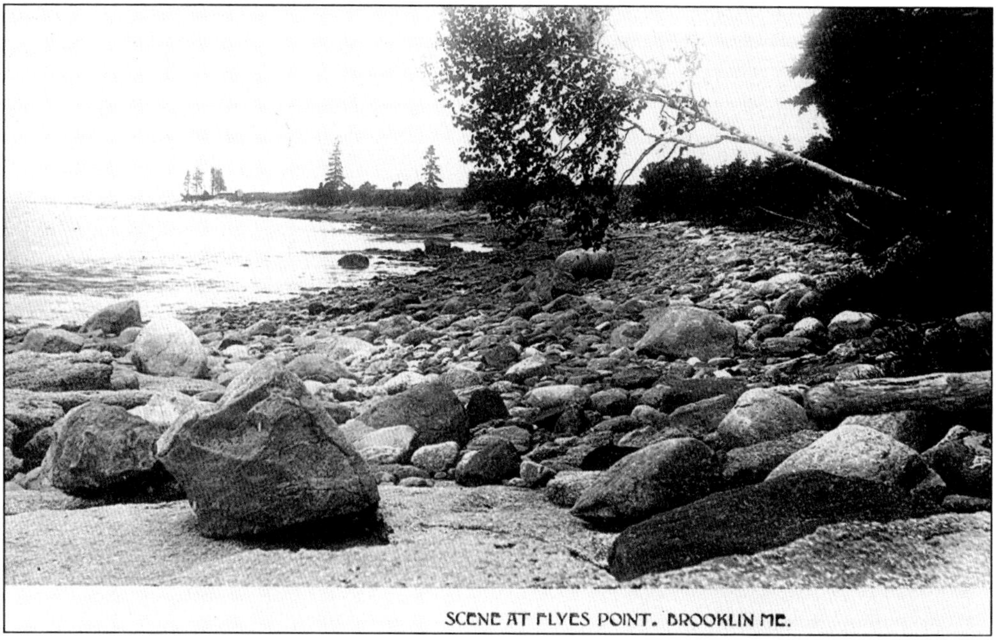

This scene of Flyes Point, taken sometime in the 1920s, shows a rocky coastline and a precipitously hanging birch tree. The area is now called Flye Point. Every year, thousands of art and music lovers converge on the back lawn of the Lookout Inn and Restaurant in Brooklin for the Flye Point Music and Arts Festival. Featured entertainers have included Judy Collins, Richie Havens, Odetta, and Noel Paul Stookey, who has a home in nearby South Blue Hill. (RRS.)

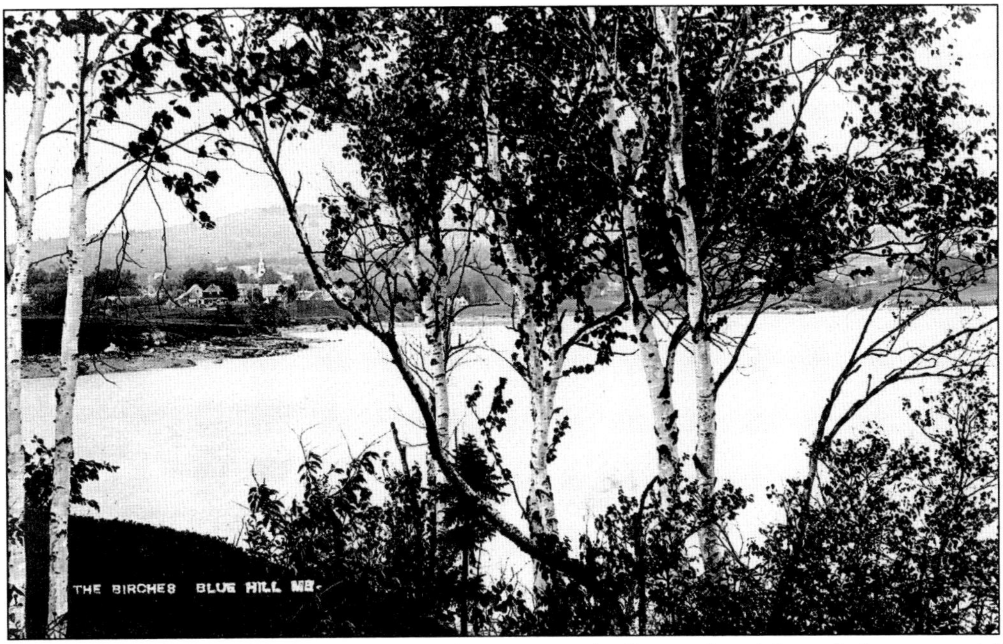

"When I see birches bend to left and right / Across the lines of straighter darker trees, / I like to think some boy's been swinging them. / But swinging doesn't bend them down to stay. / Ice-storms do that." Robert Frost wrote those lines in his oft-quoted poem, *Birches*. This view shows Blue Hill village through birch trees. One can hope an ice storm did not kill the trees, or some carefree boy swinging from their delicate limbs. (BHPL.)

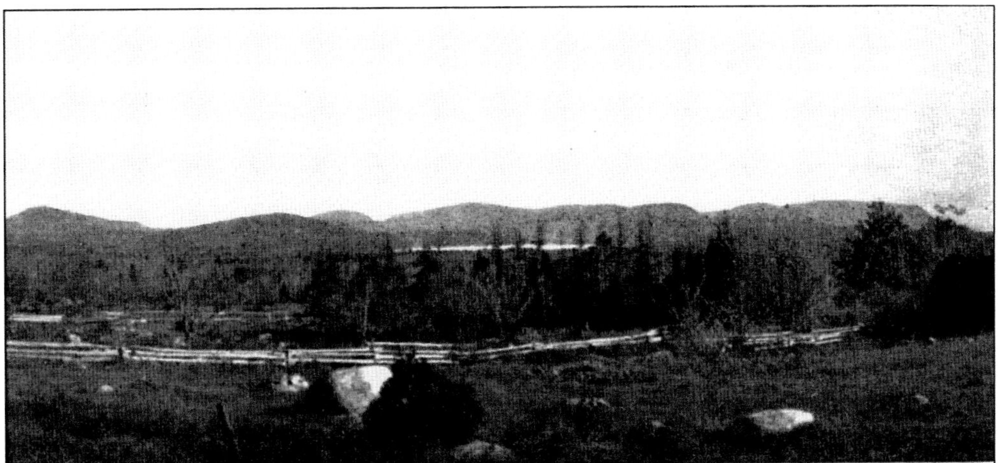

ENVIRONS OF SORRENTO, MAINE. THE BLACK HILLS FROM THE NORTH
PUBLISHED BY THE SORRENTO VILLAGE IMPROVEMENT ASSOCIATION

This old postcard shows the Black Hills from the north, in the vicinity of the eastern Hancock County village of Sorrento. The card was printed by the Sorrento Village Improvement Association, which still exists. This association sponsors many activities such as golf, tennis, sailing, swimming, and children's events. Sorrento's population swells in the summer as seasonal cottage owners return to live. (RRS.)

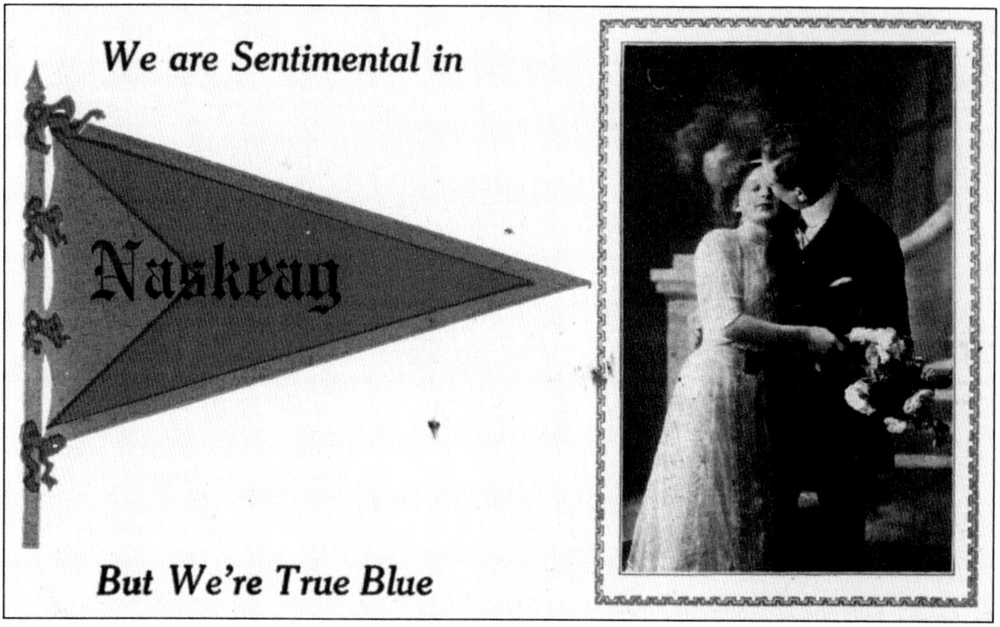

Pennant postcards gained favor with locals and tourists in the carefree years leading up to World War I. Shopkeepers near tiny Naskeag, a point of land located south of Blue Hill, probably sold this generic card for a penny. It was postmarked May 20, 1913, when the town, later annexed by Brooklin, had its own post office. "Dear Cousin Ruby," wrote a woman named Ruth, "I will send you this card so you will see I am in Naskeag." (RRS.)

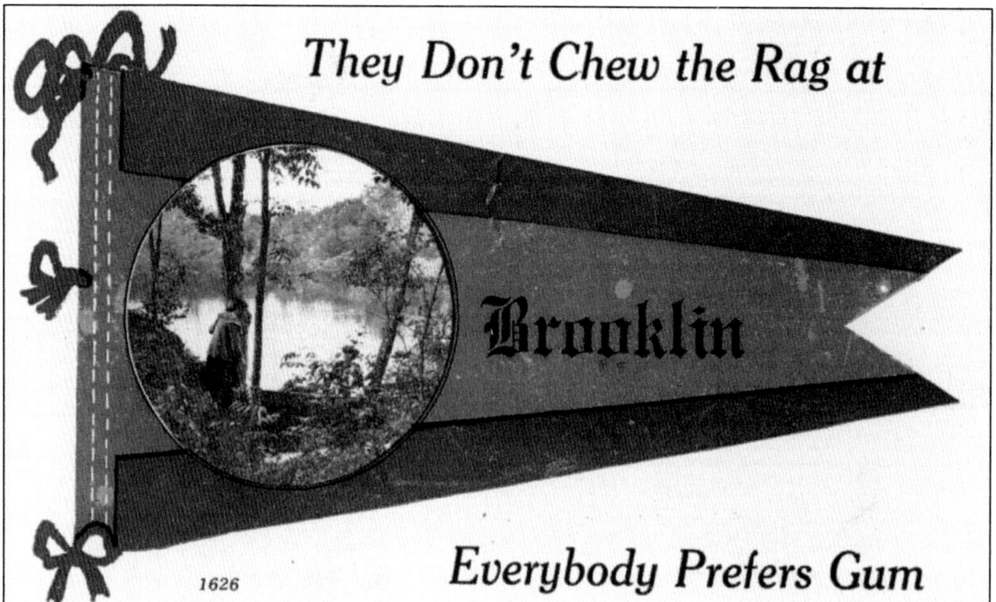

Maybe a historian or a folklorist could interpret the curious message on this pennant card, postmarked at Naskeag Point on August 1, 1913. "They don't chew the rag" may refer to the tight-lipped year-round residents and summer visitors of Brooklin, a rockbound community of stately white homes. They still keep to themselves, forgoing idle gossip for an afternoon sailboat ride or a stroll on the beach. (RRS.)

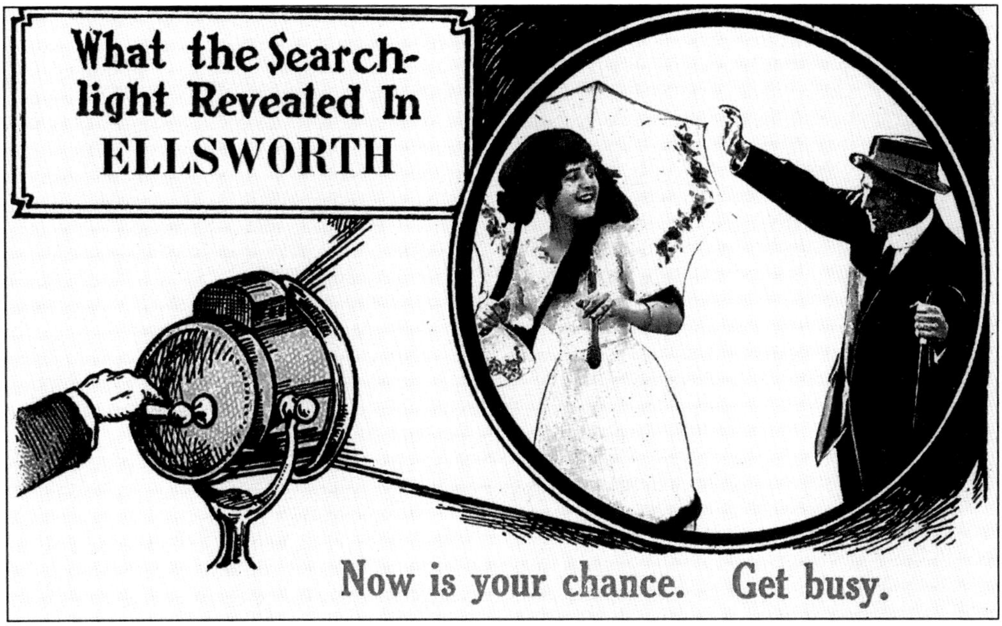

The hand-colored picture on this postcard was as risque as such souvenirs got in Ellsworth around World War I. Being Hancock County's shire town and its only city, Ellsworth boasted numerous shops and tourist stands along Main and High Streets that hawked inexpensive items to local residents and the burgeoning summer tourist traffic. The city's name was printed on a standardized card, which is a collector's item. (RRS.)

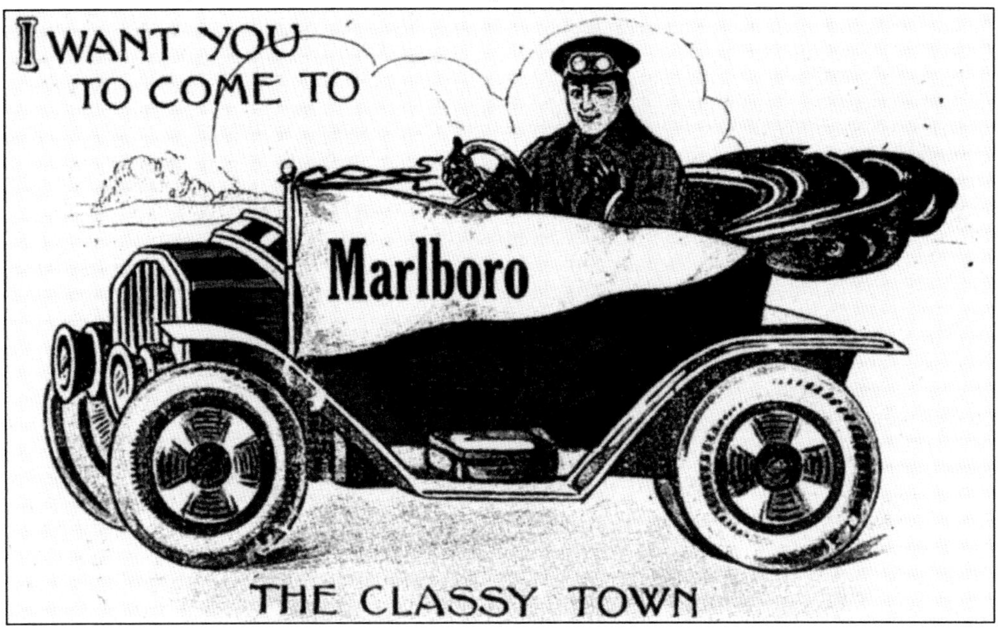

People still drove horse-drawn buggies in secluded Marlboro in 1913 when this postcard was mailed for a penny. So a dashing young man in an open roadster was quite a novelty back then in Marlboro, a small borough in the town of Lamoine, located southeast of Ellsworth and a 25-minute drive from Bar Harbor and Acadia National Park. Real estate developers now tout "Marlboro by the Sea," on Raccoon Cove, as a fine place to put down roots. (RRS.)

Bibliography

"An American Century." *Ellsworth American.* December 30, 1999.

Bonsey, Osmond C. *Surry, Maine: An Informal History.* Surry, ME: Town of Surry, 2003.

Brooklin Keeping Society. *Brooklin.* Charleston, SC: Arcadia Publishing, 2003.

Chadbourne, Ava Harriet. *Maine Place Names and the Peopling of Its Towns: Illustrated Hancock County Edition.* Freeport, ME: Bond Wheelwright Company, 1957.

Clough, Annie L. *Head of the Bay: Sketches and Pictures of Blue Hill, Maine, 1762–1952.* Blue Hill, ME: Shoreacre Press, 1953.

Davis, Albert H. *History of Ellsworth, Maine.* Lewiston, ME: Lewiston Journal Printshop, 1927.

Federal Writers' Project of the Works Progress Administration for the State of Maine. *Maine: A Guide "Down East."* Boston: Houghton Mifflin Company, 1937.

Hinckley, William. *Bits of Local History.* Blue Hill, ME: Blue Hill Historical Society, 1989.

Jellison, Connee. *Hancock County, a Rock-Bound Paradise: A Bicentennial Pictorial.* Virginia Beach, VA: Donning Company Publishers, 1990.

Lewis, Laurence. *Torna a. Sorrento, 1938–1973.* Worcester, MA: Commonwealth Press, 1973.

Obermann, Henry B. *Franklin, Maine: A History.* Rockland, ME: Maine Coast Printers, 1975.

Salisbury, Deale B. *Ellsworth, Crossroads of Downeast Maine: A Pictorial Review.* Virginia Beach, VA: Donning Company Publishers, 2005.

Sesquicentennial Committee of the Town of Hancock. *A History of the Town of Hancock, 1828–1978.* Hancock, ME: Town of Hancock, 1978.

Shaw, Richard R. *Around Ellsworth and Blue Hill.* Charleston, SC: Arcadia Publishing, 1995.

Phippen, Sanford, ed. *The Sun Never Sets on Hancock Point.* 2 vols. Hancock, ME: Historical Society of the Town of Hancock, Maine, 2000.

Index